GOVERNMENT
SECURITIES
MARKET

GOVERNMENT SECURITIES MARKET

Ira O. Scott, Jr.

Associate Professor of Finance
Graduate School of Business
Columbia University

McGRAW-HILL BOOK COMPANY
New York   St. Louis   San Francisco
Toronto   London   Sydney

To My Mother and Father

FOREWORD

Changes in the size, structure, and ownership of our public debt exert a pervasive influence in the economic life of the nation. The distribution of these securities and the terms upon which they are traded both affect and are affected by developments in all other financial markets, and are closely linked to the underlying flows of savings and investment that help shape both the over-all trend and the composition of business activity. The principal channel through which these influences are felt is the United States Government securities market—a market that, while relatively small in terms of men employed, has come to perform a critical function in our financial system. Professor Scott has recognized a genuine need in turning his efforts toward describing and analyzing this little-understood part of our financial mechanism.

Large as our public debt is—over $300 billion at the present time —public-debt instruments play a role more important than their magnitude alone suggests. Because of their liquidity, availability, and diversity of terms, these securities—with their common characteristic of uniform and unquestioned credit standing—have found a place in the assets of most business and investment enterprises in the United States. This widespread ownership, which is in part one of the legacies of World War II financing, is a major factor assuring the reasonably prompt and effective diffusion of the effects of monetary policy, as well as other financial impulses, throughout the financial markets and the economy as a whole.

Most thoughtful observers are aware in a general way of the key position now occupied by the Federal debt. Surprisingly little information is available, however, on the actual working of the intricate dealer market for Government securities in which this debt is actively traded and through which the influence of monetary and debt-management policies fan out into other financial markets. Still less is known of the manner in which the flow of transactions through this market both reflects and affects the trend of business activity.

One reason for the aura of mystery which has sometimes seemed to surround this market is the rapidity with which it has changed over recent years. It is only a little more than a decade since the prices of United States Government securities were freed from controls which kept them from being fully responsive to the forces of demand and supply in the market. In this short period, both market mechanisms and the techniques for implementing public-debt-management policies have been altered almost beyond recognition. But another reason is certainly the relative scarcity of readily available, reliable information on the operations of the market as they have developed over the postwar period. Understandably, most participants in these activities—on both the market and Government sides—have been too preoccupied with events to set down a comprehensive record of what they were doing and why they were doing it.

Professor Scott, who is able to combine economic scholarship with observations from day-to-day experience in a number of leading dealer firms, has happily broken out of this pattern. In the first of the chapters on the operations of dealer firms we are taken on a lively quickstep through a dealer's day, from commuter train in the morning through a hastily eaten desk lunch to a late-evening scanning of the next day's headlines. In the course of this day, Professor Scott not only presents to us the details of how a dealer firm operates; he also gives us a kaleidoscopic picture of the constant interplay between economic events and market decisions. These chapters not only give us a taste of market life but also provide a sample of the kind of imaginative use that can be made of source materials which have been largely inaccessible to, or neglected by, other scholars or interested observers up to the present time.

Professor Scott has also brought together in one place descriptions of the variety of United States Government securities and the mechanisms through which they are offered to the public. The information which he presents is seldom spelled out except in scattered Treasury offering circulars or in similar documents directed toward the immediate use of technicians. By providing straightforward explanations and illustrations of Treasury new-money offerings, redemptions, and re-fundings, Professor Scott has performed a service which will be most helpful to students of finance.

In his final chapter on the problems of public-debt management and monetary policy, Professor Scott puts forward some interesting views on a number of issues that have arisen in recent years. Whether or not there is agreement with his conclusions—and there will be many readers who disagree in whole or in part—Professor Scott's presentation of policy matters on which there is strong feeling and sharp divergence of opinion will prove of absorbing interest to both students and practitioners in the field.

Robert V. Roosa

PREFACE

This book is about United States Government securities. I was led naturally to this subject by my studies in monetary policy. Joseph H. Taggart was my first professor in money and banking, and I was later a student of Alvin H. Hansen and John H. Williams. In pursuing the present study, I was the beneficiary of a suggestion by Paul A. Samuelson.

The focus of the book is upon the so-called primary dealers in United States Government securities. Their operations are analyzed in Chapters 3, 4, and 5, and these three chapters comprise the heart of the study. Chapters 1 and 2 are of a background nature, and Chapter 6 contains some comments on related policy issues.

Chapter 1 is entitled "The Government Debt: Its Composition and Characteristics." In this introductory chapter I have provided certain background materials regarding the Federal debt and United States Government securities. The reader will be immediately aware that many of the topics dealt with here would require several volumes for a thoroughgoing treatment. I felt that the relevance of each topic to a study of Government securities warranted its inclusion, although space requirements compelled me to treat many in cursory fashion.

Dealers, by definition, make a market; but they do not operate in a vacuum. The markets which they make reflect, first, the forces of supply and demand as they converge upon the dealers, and, second, dealer expectations with regard to future conditions of supply and demand. Dominating the environment in which the dealers operate are the large institutional holders of United States securities. In Chapter 2, "Investment in Government Securities," the portfolio policies of the major investor groups are examined. The fundamental characteristics of Government securities described in Chapter 1 determine the role of these securities in the institutional investment strategies discussed in Chapter 2.

In Chapter 3, "Day-to-Day Operations of a Government Securities Dealer," attention is directed specifically to the day-to-day activities of a typical dealer firm. In this way, more intimate institutional background for the chapters to follow is provided.

Chapters 4 and 5 contain the analytic portions of the study. In Chapter 4, "A Theory of the Determination of Dealer Positions," an abstract model is constructed which is to serve as a theoretical foundation for the statistical investigation of dealer inventory policy.

Chapter 5 is entitled "An Empirical Evaluation of the Determination of Dealer Position Policy." In this chapter, an attempt is made to identify statistically some of the major determinants of dealer position policy. For years, without success, I tried to obtain aggregate figures for dealer positions. Where I had failed, the bond-market break of 1958 succeeded. Weekly data for the period surrounding this episode were eventually published, and these data form the empirical core of the study. The fact that only weekly data for a brief span of time were available must be emphasized, since this fact imposes severe limitations upon the potentialities of the data for statistical manipulation. I am under no illusions regarding the validity of the statistical relationships described in Chapter 5. The modest objective of this chapter is to provide an introductory contribution to a subject which will become susceptible to more thoroughgoing treatment as the present store of information concerning this market is gradually augmented.

The final chapter of the book, Chapter 6, is entitled "Some Public-policy Issues." Here, I have given my personal views regarding certain debt-management and other policies affecting the dealer market. The study is concluded with a bibliographic appendix dealing with selected related topics, which I hope will be of use to students of monetary policy and securities markets.

Numerous acknowledgments are necessary. First, a number of groups contributed to the financial support of the study. These were the Merrill Foundation for the Advancement of Financial Knowledge; the Commission on Money and Credit; the International Business Machines Corporation, Watson Scientific Computing Laboratory, Columbia University; and the Graduate School of Business, Columbia University.

It seems unnecessary to dwell upon the crucial role of the dealers themselves in this undertaking. Among the primary dealers, those who agreed to cooperate fully in the study were: Malon S. Andrus, Inc.; Bankers Trust Company; Blyth and Company, Inc.; C. F. Childs and Company; Continental Illinois National Bank and Trust Company; First National Bank of Chicago; First National City Bank; Morgan Guaranty Trust Company; Charles E. Quincey and Company; D. W. Rich and Company; Salomon Brothers and Hutzler; and Second District Securities Company, Inc. Without the assistance of these firms, this book could not have been written.

Finally, I wish to express my appreciation to Marshall Kolin, who supervised the statistical programming, to Do Quang Nang, who prepared the index, and to each of the following, who criticized a part or all of the manuscript: Gary S. Becker, Karl Brunner, Albert L. Ehinger, Jr., William C. Freund, Thomas Mayer, Allan H. Meltzer, Jacob Mincer, Peter S. Nagan, Almarin Phillips, R. S. Sayers, Peter D. Sternlight, and Paul A. Volcker. Of course, the usual caveat regarding responsibility applies, since none of these critics would agree with everything, and many would disagree with much, in the final draft.

Ira O. Scott, Jr.

CONTENTS

chapter 1

THE GOVERNMENT DEBT:
ITS COMPOSITION
AND CHARACTERISTICS

The Government debt is a product of war and depression—the heritage left by a nation incapable of taxing itself to the full measure of war and by an economic system unequal to the scourge of poverty. Despite its unsavory origins, the Government debt has come to play a crucial role in the transmission and dispersion—in the mobility, as it were— of capital-market pressures and vacuums. Consequently, it not only imparts fluidity to the capital market but provides the key channel of communication between the central bank and the private economy.

An investigation of the dealer firms which form the nucleus of the Government securities market is the principal objective of this study. This chapter and the next are introductory in content. This chapter lays the groundwork by providing an account of the debt structure and the terms and methods of debt issue. These descriptive materials are accompanied by brief forays into the economics of the debt and the theory of the interest-rate structure, which serve to assess the economic impact of the debt and to identify some of the economic characteristics of Government securities.

AUTHORITY TO CONTRACT DEBT OF THE UNITED STATES

Authority to issue direct obligations of the United States Treasury now outstanding was conferred upon the Secretary of the Treasury by Congress through the enactment of the Second Liberty Bond Act, of September 24, 1917, as amended.[1] The authority of the Secretary of the Treasury to incur indebtedness, however, has always been limited. Prior to World War I, Congress usually conferred specific borrowing authority whenever the need for funds arose. Sometimes the terms as well as the amount of the issue were designated. With the advent of World War I, Congress introduced the practice of setting limits to the issuance of particular types of securities. The Second Liberty Bond Act placed a ceiling of $7,538,945,460 on the amount of bonds to be issued and $4 billion on the amount of certificates of indebtedness outstanding. In 1929, greater latitude was given the Treasury by making a single ceiling applicable to certificates and bills together. Finally, in 1939, the debt limit was made to apply to the total amount outstanding irrespective of the type of security.[2] (See Table 1-1.)

The statutory limitation on the authority to issue securities has, of course, grown with the size of the debt. But the use of the debt ceiling as a device for fiscal control has developed only recently, with the shrinking of the differential between the ceiling and the outstanding debt. In 1957 and 1958, for example, the excess of the ceiling over the outstanding debt fell to $0.8 billion and to $1.8 billion, respectively. (See Table 1-2.) This was seriously below the $3 billion margin considered to be necessary for efficient Treasury operations. A sufficient margin is required to provide an adequate cash balance. The cash balance fluctuated in the neighborhood of $4 billion during fiscal 1957, 1958, and 1959. This amounted to less than 60 percent of average monthly budget expenditures during fiscal 1959. If the cash balance

---

[1] For a full description of this authority, see United States Code, title 31, "Money and Finance," chap. 12, "The Public Debt." For a review of the development of the authority to issue obligations of the United States, see testimony by John W. Snyder in *Monetary Policy and the Management of the Public Debt, Their Role in Achieving Price Stability and High-level Employment,* replies to questions and other material for the use of the Subcommittee on General Credit Control and Debt Management, Joint Committee on the Economic Report, 82d Congress, 2d Session, Washington, D.C.: Government Printing Office, 1952, part 1, pp. 41–50. Also see Gilman G. Udell (comp.), *Liberty Loan Acts,* Washington, D.C.: Government Printing Office, 1959.

For a brief history of the Treasury Department, see *The United States Treasury,* Washington, D.C.: Treasury Department, October, 1961.

[2] The legal reference to the debt ceiling is 31 U.S.C. § 757b. Not all obligations of the United States are subject to the debt limitation. See below in this chapter for details.

TABLE 1-1   History of statutory debt limitation beginning with the Second Liberty Bond Act[1]

Date of enactment	Securities to which limitation applies	Amount of limitation[2]
Sept. 24, 1917	Bonds	$ 7,538,945,460[3]
	Certificates	4,000,000,000
Apr. 4, 1918	Bonds	12,000,000,000[3]
	Certificates	8,000,000,000
July 9, 1918	Bonds	20,000,000,000[3]
Mar. 3, 1919	Certificates	10,000,000,000
	Notes	7,000,000,000[3]
Nov. 23, 1921	Notes	7,500,000,000
June 17, 1929	Bills and certificates	10,000,000,000
Mar. 3, 1931	Bonds	28,000,000,000[3]
Jan. 30, 1934	Notes	10,000,000,000
Feb. 4, 1935	Bonds	25,000,000,000
	Bills, certificates, and notes	20,000,000,000
May 26, 1938	Bills, certificates, notes, and bonds	45,000,000,000
	Bonds	30,000,000,000
June 20, 1939	Total	45,000,000,000
June 25, 1940	National Defense Series[4]	4,000,000,000[5]
Feb. 19, 1941	Total	65,000,000,000
Mar. 28, 1942	Total	125,000,000,000
Apr. 11, 1943	Total	210,000,000,000
June 9, 1944	Total	260,000,000,000
Apr. 3, 1945	Total	300,000,000,000
June 26, 1946	Total	275,000,000,000
Aug. 28, 1954	Total	281,000,000,000
July 9, 1956	Total	278,000,000,000
June 26, 1946[6]	Total	275,000,000,000
Feb. 26, 1958	Total	280,000,000,000
Sept. 2, 1958	Total	288,000,000,000
June 30, 1959	Total	295,000,000,000
June 30, 1960	Total	293,000,000,000

[1]SOURCE: Annual Report of the Secretary of the Treasury on the State of the Finances for the Fiscal Year Ended June 30, 1960, Washington, D.C.: Government Printing Office, 1961, table 31, pp. 513–515.

[2] Limitation on the amount of the security or securities outstanding unless otherwise indicated.

[3] Limitation on the amount of the particular security to be issued.

[4] This was a series of notes issued to finance defense expenditures.

[5] Limitation on the amount issued less retirements. This presumably represents a limitation on outstanding also. Apparently the different wording simply represents legal usage at the time of enactment.

[6] Effective July 1, 1957, the limitation reverted to that provided by the act of June 26, 1946.

TABLE 1-2   The debt ceiling and the outstanding debt[1]

Date of enactment	Debt limitation			Temporary increase included in total	Outstanding debt subject to limitation at end of month before next change in limit		Excess of debt ceiling over outstanding debt subject to ceiling
	Effective date	Expiration date	Amount		Date	Amount	
Feb. 19, 1941	Mar. 1, 1941	Mar. 27, 1942	65		Feb. 28, 1942	63.6	1.4
Mar. 28, 1942	Mar. 28, 1942	Apr. 9, 1943	125		Mar. 31, 1943	118.5	6.5
Apr. 10, 1943	Apr. 10, 1943	June 8, 1944	210		May 31, 1944	193.0	17.0
June 9, 1944	June 9, 1944	Apr. 2, 1945	260		Mar. 31, 1945	242.7	17.3
Apr. 3, 1945	Apr. 3, 1945	June 25, 1946	300[2]		May 31, 1946	282.7	17.3
June 26, 1946	June 26, 1946	Aug. 27, 1954	275[3]		July 31, 1954	270.5	4.5
Aug. 28, 1954	Aug. 28, 1954	June 30, 1955	281	6	June 30, 1955	273.9	7.1
June 30, 1955	July 1, 1955	June 30, 1956	281	6	June 30, 1956	272.4	8.6
July 9, 1956	July 1, 1956	June 30, 1957	278	3	June 30, 1957	270.2	7.8
June 26, 1946	July 1, 1957	Feb. 25, 1958	275		Jan. 31, 1958	274.2	0.8
Feb. 26, 1958	Feb. 26, 1958	June 30, 1959	280	5	Aug. 31, 1958	278.2	1.8
Sept. 2, 1958	Sept. 2, 1958	June 30, 1959[4]	288	5	June 30, 1959	284.4	3.6
June 30, 1959	July 1, 1959	June 30, 1960	295	10	June 30, 1960	286.1	8.9
June 30, 1960	July 1, 1960	June 30, 1961	293	8			

[1] SOURCE: Annual Report of the Secretary of the Treasury on the State of the Finances for the Fiscal Year Ended June 30, 1958, Washington, D.C.: Government Printing Office, 1959, table 28, p. 495; Annual Report of the Secretary of the Treasury on the State of the Finances for the Fiscal Year Ended June 30, 1960, Washington, D.C.: Government Printing Office, 1961, table 31, p. 515, and table 30, p. 512. Amounts are in billions of dollars.

[2] Guaranteed securities held outside the Treasury were not included in the statutory debt limitation until Apr. 3, 1945.

[3] Since June 26, 1946, United States savings bonds have been included in the public debt at their current redemption value. Before that date they were carried at maturity value for purposes of the limitation.

[4] Applies only to the temporary increase of $5 billion. The act of Sept. 2, 1958, increased the limitation to $283 billion.

is driven too low, the Treasury cannot vary the timing of its financing operations in order to exploit more advantageous market conditions. Moreover, some leeway is needed to take care of unforeseen contingencies and seasonal fluctuations in budget receipts.

Resort may be had to various devices in the event of an emergency. Federal agencies may be required to sell their own obligations or securities holdings instead of drawing funds from the Treasury. A slow-up in the payment of Government bills may be ordered. Free gold may be monetized. But these measures are at best temporary and at worst exceedingly costly to the taxpayer. Recurrent conflict between the legislative and executive branches over the debt ceiling, however, appears to be a permanent feature of the political scene.[3]

THE GOVERNMENT DEBT IN PERSPECTIVE

Many of the economic effects which are often attributed to the Government debt are in reality the result of either fiscal or debt-management policy. Fiscal, or budget, policy encompasses both tax policy, which concerns the level and structure of tax rates and receipts, and expenditure policy, which involves the level and structure of Government outlays. The economic effects of fiscal policy thus depend upon the level of taxes, the distribution of the tax burden, the level of expenditures, and their distribution. This is the traditional conception of fiscal policy.[4] Additional effects can be ignored, however, only if the aggregative objectives of fiscal policy are achieved through changes in the level of tax-financed expenditures. Traditional models leave out of account the economic effects of accompanying changes in the debt or money supply.[5] Strictly, the effects of fiscal policy consist of the com-

---

[3] See appendix for a bibliography on the debt and interest-rate ceilings.

[4] For definitions of various policy instruments, see *Staff Report on Employment, Growth, and Price Levels,* prepared for consideration by the Joint Economic Committee, 86th Congress, 1st Session, Dec. 24, 1959, Washington, D.C.: Government Printing Office, 1959; and Warren L. Smith, *Debt Management in the United States,* Study Paper no. 19, materials prepared in connection with the study of employment, growth, and price levels, Joint Economic Committee, 86th Congress, 2d Session, Jan. 28, 1960, Washington, D.C.: Government Printing Office, 1960.

[5] For recognition of the interaction of various policy instruments see, e.g., Lawrence S. Ritter, "Functional Finance and the Banking System," *American Journal of Economics and Sociology,* vol. 15, no. 4, July, 1956, pp. 395–404;

bined effects of tax and expenditure policies and of accompanying changes in the money supply and in the size and composition of the publicly held debt.[6]

Debt-management policy, as traditionally defined, consists of the

---

Earl R. Rolph, "The Incidence of Public Operations," *National Tax Journal,* vol. 9, no. 4, December, 1956, pp. 339–353; testimony by James Tobin in *Fiscal Policy Implications of the Economic Outlook and Budget Developments, Hearings before the Subcommittee on Fiscal Policy of the Joint Economic Committee,* 85th Congress, 1st Session, June 3, 4, 5, 6, 7, 13, 14, 1957, Washington, D.C.: Government Printing Office, 1957, p. 67; and Emile Benoit, "The Propensity to Reduce the National Debt Out of Defense Savings," *American Economic Review,* vol. 21, no. 2, May, 1961, pp. 455–459.

A mistaken view of the interaction of fiscal and debt effects sometimes appears in money-market letters and the financial press. Commentaries may refer to the "easing" effect of a budget surplus and debt retirement. Such would be the case if the surplus resulted from *active* fiscal policy, that is, from a decrease in expenditures or an increase in tax rates. But a surplus may be the result of a rise in income that is generated by an increase in economic activity in the private sector. Such an increase in income produces an increase in tax receipts. The resulting surplus is *passive,* and it will be accompanied by a hardening, not an easing, of money rates. In other words, the acceleration of private spending causes a budget surplus and a hardening of money rates at the same time. For an exception among such commentaries, see Robert Van Cleave, *C. F. Childs and Company Review,* no. 328, Jan. 18, 1960.

[6] The economic effects of an increase in the Government debt are not unambiguous. Suppose that publicly held assets consist of money, subject to price-level risks, Governments, subject to market and price-level risk, and equities, subject to market and credit risk. An increase in Governments, given the quantity of money and equities, results in an increase in wealth which in turn results in an increase in the demand for money and equities. With the increase in wealth and in Governments the investor is less liquid in that he holds proportionately less money. Therefore the demand for money increases, and the yield of Governments in terms of money increases also. At the same time, the investor is more liquid than before in the sense that he holds proportionately fewer equities. Thus, the demand for equities increases, and the yield of Governments in terms of equities rises also. But does the yield of equities fall in terms of money? Whether it does depends upon the utility of "expending" the increased wealth in a reduction of market risk or in a reduction of price-level risk.

The question becomes even more complex if increased taxes to service the debt are taken into account. See Robert A. Mundell, "The Public Debt, Corporate Income Taxes, and the Rate of Interest," *Journal of Political Economy,* vol. 63, no. 6, December, 1960, pp. 622–626.

determination of the structure of a debt of given size.[7] Changes in the structure consist of changes in various dimensions of the loan contract. The most important of these is, of course, maturity, which may vary all the way from a demand obligation, such as a nonmarketable United States savings bond, to a perpetuity, such as a British consol. Given changes in the size of the debt, that is, fiscal policy, debt management involves the financing required by budget deficits plus additional drains outside the budget process, the disposition of budget surpluses, and the refinancing of maturing issues which the Treasury is unable or does not wish to retire. Within certain constraints imposed by Congress, the Treasury may set the terms of these financing operations. Debt-management policy consists of the determination of those terms.

If maturing securities must be refinanced, the Treasury must first decide whether to offer an exchange issue or combine a cash offering with a cash redemption of the maturing securities. If it is to be a cash offering, either for new cash or to retire a maturing issue, the Treasury must next decide whether to sell the issue to the Federal Reserve System or to private investors, institutional or individual. There is a legal limit on direct sales to the Federal Reserve System,[8] and they are sel-

[7] Broadly conceived, debt policy includes the budget effects of changing interest costs as the given debt is refinanced.

Some would treat monetary and debt-management policy as one. Thus certain kinds of money may be treated as a non-interest-bearing form of Government debt; and the execution of monetary policy may entail changes in the public's holdings of Governments. See, for example, Earl R. Rolph, "Principles of Debt Management," *American Economic Review*, vol. 47, no. 3, June, 1957, pp. 302–320; and James Tobin, "An Essay on Principles of Debt Management," in *Fiscal and Debt Management Policies*, Commission on Money and Credit, Englewood Cliffs, N.J.: Prentice-Hall, Inc., 1963, pp. 143–218.

Narrowly conceived, monetary policy would consist solely of changes in the quantity of money. Such a pure form would occur as a result of changes in discount policy or changes in reserve requirements. Open-market operations, in addition to affecting the money supply, would involve debt-management policy, since they would result in changes in the size and composition of the publicly held debt. In addition to the central bank, the Treasury would be engaging in monetary policy when it conducted open-market operations and varied the size of its cash balance, thus affecting the quantity of money as well as the size and composition of the publicly held debt.

[8] See 31 U.S.C. § 355; Federal Reserve Act, sec. 14, par. 3; Mabel B. Wallich and Irving M. Auerbach, "Direct Purchases of Special Treasury Certificates of Indebtedness by Federal Reserve Banks," in *The Treasury and the*

dom made because of the traditional reluctance of the central bank to accommodate the Treasury in this manner. This reluctance is due in part to the fact that expenditures so financed entail a corresponding increase in the reserves of the banking system, which may provide the basis for a multiple expansion of the money supply. When deficits are financed through the commercial banking system, there may be a corresponding increase in the money supply.[9] Only in the case of sales of the new securities to savings banks, nonbanking institutions, or individuals can one be assured that a deficit will not entail such an in-

---

Money Market, Federal Reserve Bank of New York, May, 1954, pp. 40–42; and *Amend Section 14(b) of the Federal Reserve Act, Hearing before the Committee on Banking and Currency,* on *H.R. 11499,* 88th Congress, 2d Session, June 11, 1964, Washington, D.C.: Government Printing Office, 1964.

[9] This bit of textbook dogma has been learned too well by some. See, e.g., W. Randolph Burgess, "Federal Debt and Budget in the Past Four and One-half Years," *Commercial and Financial Chronicle,* June 21, 1957; and Michael E. Levy, "Inflationary Impact of Changes in Federal Debt," *Conference Board Business Record,* vol. 16, no. 10, October, 1959, pp. 458–460. In fact, restrictive availability effects of monetary and debt-management policy would be achieved precisely by means of inducing the banks to take on Governments as a substitute for loans, in which case the money supply would not be affected. See Ira O. Scott, Jr., "The Implications of the Changing Ownership of Federal Securities," *Proceedings of the Business and Economic Statistics Section,* American Statistical Association, 1957, pp. 154–158; "Some Overripe Problems in Federal Debt Management," *Commercial and Financial Chronicle,* Dec. 31, 1959; "The Availability Doctrine: Development and Implications," *Canadian Journal of Economics and Political Science,* vol. 23, no. 4, November, 1957, pp. 532–539; and "The Availability Doctrine: Theoretical Underpinnings," *Review of Economic Studies,* vol. 25, no. 1, pp. 41–48. Critics of the availability doctrine have supported their argument by citing postwar institutional shifts out of Governments. These shifts, of course, prove nothing. Indeed, neither the debt-management nor the monetary authorities have ever really put the availability doctrine to a test—presumably because of constraints on interest-rate movements—though there was a glimpse of possible availability effects when the "Magic 5s" were offered. See Robert Van Cleave, "Resolution Pays Off," *C. F. Childs and Company Review,* no. 322, Oct. 12, 1959; " 'Magic Fives,' " *Business Week,* Oct. 17, 1959; Charls E. Walker, "Problems of Treasury Debt Management," address before annual convention of the U.S. Savings and Loan League, Dallas, Tex., Nov. 11, 1959; "Government Issues Attract Personal Savings," *Federal Reserve Bank of Chicago Business Conditions,* January, 1960; and D. A. Alhadeff, "Credit Controls and Financial Intermediaries," *American Economic Review,* vol. 2, no. 4, September, 1960, p. 670.

crease. The retirement of outstanding and maturing securities will have opposite and symmetrical effects upon the quantity of money.

In planning cash sales to private investors or an exchange offering where a substantial portion of the maturing issue is held outside the Federal Reserve System, the Treasury must decide upon the maturity of the new issue, the amount it hopes to sell, and, unless the issue is to be sold at auction, the interest rate which it is necessary to pay in order to sell the issue. By adjusting other dimensions of the loan contract, the Treasury may affect to some extent the interest rate which it must pay.

Finally, an important facet of debt-management policy consists of the Treasury's determination of portfolio policy for the Treasury-managed trust funds and the determination of open-market policy by the Federal Open Market Committee.

It is clear, therefore, that the size and composition of the publicly held debt may be a function of a wide range of economic policies effected by a variety of policy instruments. Specifically, changes in the size and composition of the debt depend upon the policy mix.[10] However, the economic impact of the debt, per se, should be evaluated in isolation from the policies that determined its existing size and composition, in so far as such an evaluation is possible.[11]

From 1790 to 1960, a period which spans almost a century and three-quarters, the Government debt rose from $75 million to more than $280 billion.[12] From 1853 to 1960, the per capita debt increased from $2.32 to $1,584.77. (See Table 1-3.) There are a number of ways in which these figures may be put in perspective.[13] One method is to

[10] See appendix for a bibliography on the policy mix.

[11] See appendix for a bibliography on the economics of the debt.

[12] The Federal Government has obligations in excess of this total, of course. It guarantees debt issued by Government corporations and credit agencies. It is involved indirectly in the insurance of private mortgage debt. And there are spending authorizations approved by Congress, which may or may not be covered by future tax receipts. See Maurice H. Stans, "The Responsibilities of a Free People," an address before the Conference of Bank Correspondents, First National Bank of Chicago, Nov. 30, 1959; and "The Government's Contingent Obligations," *Morgan Guaranty Survey*, May, 1960, pp. 3–5.

[13] See, e.g., Marshall A. Robinson, *The National Debt Ceiling*, Washington, D.C.: The Brookings Institution, 1959; and Walter W. Heller, "Why a Federal Debt Limit?" *Proceedings of the Fifty-first Annual Conference on Taxation*, 1958, pp. 246–256.

On the role of debt generally in the economy, see Paul W. McCracken,

relate the debt to the economy's capacity to bear it as measured by the gross national product (GNP). In 1929, the ratio of the debt to the GNP was 0.16. At the close of World War II, in 1946, this ratio had risen to 1.28. But by 1960, it had declined to 0.57. (See Table 1-4.)

Even more relevant, perhaps, are figures showing the interest cost of the debt. Interest costs grew from $22,900,000 in 1913 to $4,747,500,-000 in 1946 and to $9,179,600,000 in 1960. (See Table 1-5.) Thus, as a percentage of the GNP, these charges declined in the postwar period from 2.3 percent to 1.8 percent.

A further vantage point from which the Federal debt may be viewed is in its relationship to the total debt of the economy, including Federal agency, state and local, corporate, and individual and noncorporate debt. (See Table 1-6.) During the postwar period, the Federal Government debt declined from 57 percent to 28 percent of the economy's total public and private indebtedness.

An even more realistic picture of the size of the debt may be obtained by taking it on a net rather than a gross basis. (See Table 1-7.) A strong case can be made for subtracting from the outstanding debt those securities held by Federal agencies and trust funds and by the Federal Reserve banks. To the extent that these holdings will continue to grow or at least maintain their present size, the securities involved may, in effect, be considered to have been retired. As noted above, the 1960 ratio of the gross debt to the GNP was 0.57. On a net basis this ratio was 0.41.

Similarly, the estimated distribution of interest on the debt may be used to compute the net interest burden. (See Table 1-8.) Subtracting interest on securities held by the Federal Reserve banks and the Government investment accounts reduces the annual interest cost of the debt by 28 percent. It has been shown that on a gross basis, an-

---

"The Debt Problem and Economic Growth," *Michigan Business Review*, vol. 8, no. 5, November, 1956, pp. 11–15; Marshall A. Robinson, "Debt in the American Economy," *Proceedings of the Fifty-first Annual Conference on Taxation*, 1958, pp. 205–215; John G. Gurley and Edward S. Shaw, *Money in a Theory of Finance*, Washington, D.C.: The Brookings Institution, 1960; Marcus Nadler, "Debt and Economic Growth," *Hanover Bank Letter*, November, 1960; Chamber of Commerce of the United States, *Debt: Public and Private*, Washington, D.C.: 1961; and Dorothy M. Nichols and Charlotte H. Scott, *The Two Faces of Debt*, Federal Reserve Bank of Chicago, October, 1963.

TABLE 1-3   Gross debt of the Federal Government, 1790-1960[1]

Date	Total gross debt[2]	Date	Total gross debt[2]	Date	Total gross debt[2]
Dec. 31—		Dec. 31—		Dec. 31—	
1790	$75,463,477	1812	$ 55,962,828	1833	$ 4,760,082
1791	77,227,925	1813	81,487,846	1834	37,733
1792	80,358,634	1814	99,833,660	1835	37,513
1793	78,427,405	1815	127,334,934	1836	336,958
1794	80,747,587	1816	123,491,965	1837	3,308,124
1795	83,762,172	1817	103,466,634	1838	10,434,221
1796	82,064,479	1818	95,529,648	1839	3,573,344
1797	79,228,529	1819	91,015,566	1840	5,250,876
1798	78,408,670	1820	89,987,428	1841	13,594,481
1799	82,976,294	1821	93,546,677	1842	20,201,226
1800	83,038,051	1822	90,875,877	June 30—	
1801	80,712,632	1823	90,269,778	1843	32,742,922
1802	77,054,686	1824	83,788,433	1844	23,461,653
1803	86,427,121	1825	81,054,060	1845	15,925,303
1804	82,312,151	1826	73,987,357	1846	15,550,203
1805	75,723,271	1827	67,475,044	1847	38,826,535
1806	69,218,399	1828	58,421,414	1848	47,044,862
1807	65,196,318	1829	48,565,407	1849	63,061,859
1808	57,023,192	1830	39,123,192	1850	63,452,774
1809	53,173,218	1831	24,322,235	1851	68,304,796
1810	48,005,588	1832	7,011,699	1852	66,199,342
1811	45,209,737				

Date	Interest-bearing[3]	Matured debt on which interest has ceased	Debt bearing no interest	Total gross debt[2]	Gross debt per capita[4]
June 30—					
1853	$ 59,642,412	$ 162,249		$ 59,804,661	$ 2.32
1854	42,044,517	199,248		42,243,765	1.59
1855	35,418,001	170,498		35,588,499	1.30
1856	31,805,180	168,901		31,974,081	1.13
1857	28,503,377	197,998		28,701,375	.99
1858	44,743,256	170,168		44,913,424	1.50
1859	58,333,156	165,225		58,498,381	1.91
1860	64,683,256	160,575		64,843,831	2.06
1861	90,423,292	159,125		90,582,417	2.80
1862	365,356,045	230,520	$158,591,390	524,117,955	15.79
1863	707,834,255	171,970	411,767,456	1,119,773,681	32.91
1864	1,360,026,914	366,629	455,437,271	1,815,830,814	52.08
1865	2,217,709,407	2,129,425	458,090,180	2,677,929,012	75.01
1866	2,322,116,330	4,435,865	429,211,734	2,755,763,929	75.42
1867	2,238,954,794	1,739,108	409,474,321	2,650,168,223	70.91
1868	2,191,326,130	1,246,334	390,873,992	2,583,446,456	67.61
1869	2,151,495,065	5,112,034	388,503,491	2,545,110,590	65.17
1870	2,035,881,095	3,569,664	397,002,510	2,436,453,269	61.06
1871	1,920,696,750	1,948,902	399,406,489	2,322,052,141	56.72
1872	1,800,794,100	7,926,547	401,270,191	2,209,990,838	52.65
1873	1,696,483,950	51,929,460	402,796,935	2,151,210,345	50.02
1874	1,724,930,750	3,216,340	431,785,640	2,159,932,730	49.05
1875	1,708,676,300	11,425,570	436,174,779	2,156,276,649	47.84

TABLE 1-3   Gross debt of the Federal Government, 1790–1960 (continued)

Date	Interest-bearing[3]	Matured debt on which interest has ceased	Debt bearing no interest	Total gross debt[2]	Gross debt per capita[4]
June 30—					
1876	$ 1,696,685,450	$ 3,902,170	$430,258,158	$ 2,130,845,778	$ 46.22
1877	1,697,888,500	16,648,610	393,222,793	2,107,759,903	44.71
1878	1,780,735,650	5,594,070	373,088,595	2,159,418,315	44.82
1879	1,887,716,110	37,015,380	374,181,153	2,298,912,643	46.72
1880	1,709,993,100	7,621,205	373,294,567	2,090,908,872	41.60
1881	1,625,567,750	6,723,615	386,994,363	2,019,285,728	39.18
1882	1,449,810,400	16,260,555	390,844,689	1,856,915,644	35.16
1883	1,324,229,150	7,831,165	389,898,603	1,721,958,918	31.83
1884	1,212,563,850	19,655,955	393,087,639	1,625,307,444	29.35
1885	1,182,150,950	4,100,745	392,299,474	1,578,551,169	27.86
1886	1,132,014,100	9,704,195	413,941,255	1,555,659,550	26.85
1887	1,007,692,350	6,114,915	451,678,029	1,465,485,294	24.75
1888	936,522,500	2,495,845	445,613,311	1,384,631,656	22.89
1889	815,853,990	1,911,235	431,705,286	1,249,470,511	20.23
1890	711,313,110	1,815,555	409,267,919	1,122,396,584	17.80
1891	610,529,120	1,614,705	393,662,736	1,005,806,561	15.63
1892	585,029,330	2,785,875	380,403,636	968,218,841	14.74
1893	585,037,100	2,094,060	374,300,606	961,431,766	14.36
1894	635,041,890	1,851,240	380,004,687	1,016,897,817	14.89
1895	716,202,060	1,721,590	378,989,470	1,096,913,120	15.76
1896	847,363,890	1,636,890	373,728,570	1,222,729,350	17.25
1897	847,365,130	1,346,880	378,081,703	1,226,793,713	16.99
1898	847,367,470	1,262,680	384,112,913	1,232,743,063	16.77
1899	1,046,048,750	1,218,300	389,433,654	1,436,700,704	19.21
1900	1,023,478,860	1,176,320	238,761,733	1,263,416,913	16.60
1901	987,141,040	1,415,620	233,015,585	1,221,572,245	15.74
1902	931,070,340	1,280,860	245,680,157	1,178,031,357	14.88
1903	914,541,410	1,205,090	243,659,413	1,159,405,913	14.38
1904	895,157,440	1,970,920	239,130,656	1,136,259,016	13.83
1905	895,158,340	1,370,245	235,828,510	1,132,357,095	13.51
1906	895,159,140	1,128,135	246,235,695	1,142,522,970	13.37
1907	894,834,280	1,086,815	251,257,098	1,147,178,193	13.19
1908	897,503,990	4,130,015	276,056,398	1,177,690,403	13.28
1909	913,317,490	2,883,855	232,114,027	1,148,315,372	12.69
1910	913,317,490	2,124,895	231,497,584	1,146,939,969	12.41
1911	915,353,190	1,879,830	236,751,917	1,153,984,937	12.29
1912	963,776,770	1,760,450	228,301,285	1,193,838,505	12.52
1913	965,706,610	1,659,550	225,681,585	1,193,047,745	12.27
1914	967,953,310	1,552,560	218,729,530	1,188,235,400	11.99
1915	969,759,090	1,507,260	219,997,718	1,191,264,068	11.85
1916	971,562,590	1,473,100	252,109,877	1,225,145,568	12.02
1917	2,712,549,477	14,232,230	248,836,878	2,975,618,585	28.77
1918	12,197,507,642	20,242,550	237,475,173	12,455,225,365	119.13
1919	25,236,947,172	11,176,250	236,382,738	25,484,506,160	242.56
1920	24,062,500,285	6,745,237	230,075,945	24,299,321,467	228.23
1921	23,738,900,085	10,688,160	227,862,308	23,977,450,553	220.91
1922	22,710,338,105	25,250,880	227,792,723	22,963,381,708	208.65
1923	22,007,043,612	98,738,910	243,924,844	22,349,707,365	199.64
1924	20,981,242,042	30,278,200	239,292,747	21,250,812,989	186.23
1925	20,210,906,915	30,258,980	275,027,993	20,516,193,888	177.12
1926	19,383,770,860	13,359,900	246,085,555	19,643,216,315	167.32
1927	18,252,664,666	14,718,585	244,523,681	18,511,906,932	155.51
1928	17,317,694,182	45,335,060	241,263,959	17,604,293,201	146.09
1929	16,638,941,379	50,749,199	241,397,905	16,931,088,484	139.04
1930	15,921,892,350	31,716,870	231,700,611	16,185,309,831	131.51

TABLE 1-3   Gross debt of the Federal Government, 1790-1960 (continued)

Date	Interest-bearing[3]	Matured debt on which interest has ceased	Debt bearing no interest	Total gross debt[2]	Gross debt per capita[4]
June 30—					
1931	$ 16,519,588,640	$ 51,819,095	$ 229,873,756	$ 16,801,281,492	$ 135.45
1932	19,161,273,540	60,079,385	265,649,519	19,487,002,444	156.10
1933	22,157,643,120	65,911,170	315,118,270	22,538,672,560	179.48
1934	26,480,487,870	54,266,830	518,386,714	27,053,141,414	214.07
1935	27,645,241,089	230,663,155	824,989,381	28,700,892,625	225.55
1936	32,988,790,135	169,363,395	620,389,964	33,778,543,494	263.79
1937	35,800,109,418	118,529,815	505,974,499	36,424,613,732	282.75
1938	36,575,925,880	141,362,460	447,451,975	37,164,740,315	286.27
1939	39,885,969,732	142,283,140	411,279,539	40,439,532,411	308.98
1940	42,376,495,928	204,591,190	386,443,919	42,967,531,038	325.23
1941	48,387,399,539	204,999,860	369,044,137	48,961,443,536	367.09
1942	71,968,418,098	98,299,730	355,727,288	72,422,445,116	537.13
1943	135,380,305,795	140,500,090	1,175,284,445	136,696,090,330	999.83
1944	199,543,355,301	200,851,160	1,259,180,760	210,003,387,221	1,452.44
1945	256,356,615,818	268,667,135	2,056,904,457	258,682,187,410	1,848.60
1946	268,110,872,218	376,406,860	934,820,095	269,422,099,173	1,905.42
1947	255,113,412,039	230,913,536	2,942,057,534	258,286,383,109	1,792.05
1948	250,063,348,379	279,751,730	1,949,146,403	252,292,246,513	1,720.71
1949	250,761,636,723	244,757,458	1,763,965,680	252,770,359,860	1,694.75
1950	255,209,353,372	264,770,705	1,883,228,274	257,357,352,351	1,696.61
1951	252,851,765,497	512,046,600	1,858,164,718	255,221,976,815	1,654.25
1952	256,862,861,128	418,692,165	1,823,625,492	259,105,178,785	1,650.91
1953	263,946,017,740	298,420,570	1,826,623,328	266,071,061,639	1,667.54
1954	268,909,766,654	437,184,655	1,912,647,799	271,259,599,108	1,670.44
1955	271,741,267,507	588,601,480	2,044,353,816	274,374,222,803	1,660.10
1956	269,883,068,041	666,051,697	2,201,693,911	272,750,813,649	1,621.35
1957	268,485,562,677	529,241,585	1,512,367,635	270,527,171,896	1,579.46
1958	274,697,560,009	597,324,889	1,048,332,847	276,343,217,746	1,586.78
1959	281,833,362,429	476,455,003	2,396,089,647	284,705,907,078	1,606.10
1960	283,241,182,755	444,608,630	2,644,969,463	286,330,760,848	1,584.77

[1] SOURCE: Annual Report of the Secretary of the Treasury on the State of the Finances for the Fiscal Year Ended June 30, 1960, Washington, D.C.: Government Printing Office, 1961, table 21, pp. 480-481.

From 1789 to 1843, the fiscal year ended on Dec. 31; from 1843, on June 30. Detailed figures for 1790-1852 are not available on a basis comparable with those of later years. The amounts for 1790-1852, except for 1835, are from the 1900 Annual Report of the Secretary of the Treasury; for 1835, from the 1834-1835 Annual Reports, pp. 504, 629; for 1853-1885, from the "Statement of Receipts and Expenditures of the Government from 1855 to 1885 and Principal of Public Debt from 1791 to 1885" compiled from the Register's official records; for 1886-1915, from the monthly debt statements and revised figures in the Secretary's Annual Reports; and for 1916 to date, from the Statement of the Public Debt in the daily Treasury statements.

[2] Includes certain obligations not subject to statutory limitation. See Table 1-9.

[3] Exclusive of bonds issued to the Pacific railroads (acts of 1862, 1864, and 1878), since statutory provision was made to secure the Treasury against both principal and interest, and the Navy pension fund, which was not a debt because principal and interest were the property of the United States. The Statement of the Public Debt included the railroad bonds from issuance and the Navy fund from Sept. 1, 1866, until the Statement of June 30, 1890.

[4] Based on the Bureau of the Census estimated population for continental United States.

TABLE 1-4   Gross national product and the Government debt,
1929-1960[1]

Year	Gross national product[2]	Total gross debt[2,3]	Ratio of debt to gross national product
1929	104.4	16.9	0.162
1930	91.1	16.2	0.178
1931	76.3	16.8	0.220
1932	58.5	19.5	0.333
1933	56.0	22.5	0.402
1934	65.0	27.1	0.417
1935	72.5	28.7	0.396
1936	82.7	33.8	0.409
1937	90.8	36.4	0.401
1938	85.2	37.2	0.437
1939	91.1	40.4	0.443
1940	100.6	43.0	0.427
1941	125.8	49.0	0.390
1942	159.1	72.4	0.455
1943	192.5	136.7	0.710
1944	211.4	201.0	0.951
1945	213.6	258.7	1.211
1946	210.7	269.4	1.279
1947	234.3	258.3	1.102
1948	259.4	252.3	0.973
1949	258.1	252.8	0.979
1950	284.6	257.4	0.904
1951	329.0	255.2	0.776
1952	347.0	259.1	0.747
1953	365.4	266.1	0.728
1954	363.1	271.3	0.747
1955	397.5	274.4	0.690
1956	419.2	272.8	0.651
1957	442.8	270.5	0.611
1958	444.5	276.3	0.622
1959	482.7	284.7	0.590
1960	502.6	286.3	0.570

[1] SOURCE: Survey of Current Business, July, 1959; July, 1961.
[2] Amounts are in billions of dollars. Those for the GNP are on a calendar-year basis; those for the debt are on a fiscal-year basis.
[3] See Table 1-3.

nual interest charges were 1.8 percent of the GNP in 1960. Putting the cost on a net basis reduces this figure to 1.3 percent.[14] Thus, what-

[14] Since the income of some of the trust funds really accrues to certain sectors of the public, an argument can be made for omitting trust fund holdings from the netting process. See Thomas Mayer, "Interest Minimization as a Criterion of Federal Debt Management Policy" (Unpublished ms.) .

The case for subtracting interest paid on securities held by the Federal

TABLE 1-5   Interest on the Federal debt,
1913-1960[1]

Year	Amount	Year	Amount
1913	22.9	1937	866.8
1914	22.9	1938	926.2
1915	22.9	1939	941.0
1916	22.9	1940	1,041.4
1917	24.7	1941	1,110.2
1918	197.5	1942	1,260.1
1919	615.9	1943	1,813.0
1920	1,024.0	1944	2,610.1
1921	996.7	1945	3,621.9
1922	989.5	1946	4,747.5
1923	1,055.1	1947	4,958.0
1924	938.7	1948	5,187.8
1925	882.0	1949	5,352.3
1926	831.5	1950	5,496.3
1927	787.8	1951	5,615.1
1928	731.9	1952	5,853.0
1929	679.0	1953	6,503.6
1930	658.6	1954	6,382.5
1931	610.8	1955	6,370.4
1932	599.7	1956	6,786.6
1933	689.2	1957	7,244.2
1934	757.2	1958	7,606.8
1935	821.5	1959	7,592.8
1936	747.9	1960	9,179.6

[1] SOURCE: Annual Report of the Secretary of the Treasury on the State of the Finances for the Fiscal Year Ended June 30, 1948, Washington, D.C.: Government Printing Office, 1949, p. 539; 1952, p. 645; 1960, p. 589. Amounts are in millions of dollars and according to fiscal year. Amount of interest paid includes increase in redemption value of United States savings bonds and discount on unmatured issues of Treasury bills. Figures for 1940 to 1949, inclusive, represent actual interest payments; figures for 1950 to 1954, inclusive, represent interest which became due and payable during those years without regard to actual payments; figures for 1955 to 1960, inclusive, are shown on an accrual basis. Guaranteed debt is not included.

Reserve banks is strengthened by the fact that these banks turn over to the Treasury each year 90 percent or more of their earnings after expenses and dividends. See Federal Reserve Act, sec. 16, par. 4; *Thirty-fourth Annual Report of the Board of Governors of the Federal Reserve System Covering Operations for the Year 1947,* p. 49; and *Investigation of the Financial Condition of the United States, Hearings before the Committee on Finance,* Senate, 85th Congress, 1st Session, Aug. 13, 14, 15, 16, 19, 1957, Washington, D.C.: Government Printing Office, 1957, pp. 1580, 1582–1585.

TABLE 1-6   Gross public and private debt, 1929-1960[1]

End of calendar year	Total	Federal Government[2]	Federal agency	State and local[3]	Corporate	Individual and noncorporate[4]
1929	214.0	16.3	1.2	17.2	107.0	72.3
1930	214.3	16.0	1.3	18.5	107.4	71.1
1931	203.3	17.8	1.2	19.5	100.3	64.4
1932	195.2	20.8	2.0	19.6	96.1	56.7
1933	190.5	23.8	3.9	19.8	92.4	50.6
1934	197.3	28.5	9.4	19.2	90.6	49.6
1935	200.2	30.6	11.1	19.3	89.8	49.4
1936	205.9	34.4	10.7	19.6	90.9	50.3
1937	208.5	37.3	10.6	19.6	90.2	50.9
1938	203.6	39.4	8.0	19.6	86.8	49.8
1939	207.7	42.0	8.2	20.0	86.8	50.8
1940	215.8	45.0	8.5	20.2	89.0	53.0
1941	242.3	58.0	11.0	20.2	97.5	55.6
1942	299.1	108.2	15.0	19.7	106.3	49.9
1943	364.5	165.9	20.8	18.7	110.3	48.8
1944	430.9	230.6	23.1	17.5	109.0	50.7
1945	463.3	278.1	14.5	16.6	99.5	54.7
1946	457.9	259.1	13.0	15.9	109.3	60.6
1947	485.6	256.9	12.9	16.8	128.2	70.8
1948	498.6	252.8	5.2	18.7	138.8	83.1
1949	520.3	257.1	8.9	20.9	139.6	93.7
1950	566.4	256.7	9.7	24.2	167.0	108.8
1951	607.5	259.4	10.8	27.0	190.6	119.7
1952	646.0	267.4	11.9	29.6	201.6	135.5
1953	683.9	275.2	14.1	32.7	211.5	150.5
1954	714.1	278.8	15.6	37.9	216.3	165.5
1955	786.4	280.8	21.0	43.2	251.0	190.3
1956	831.1	276.6	23.9	48.0	274.9	207.7
1957	867.3	274.9	26.8	52.5	292.1	221.1
1958	916.8	282.9	27.7	57.2	309.5	239.5
1959	986.1	290.8	31.1	62.4	337.7	264.1
1960	1,036.1	290.2	31.8	67.1	360.3	286.6

[1] SOURCE: Survey of Current Business, October, 1950; September, 1953; May, 1958; July, 1960; July, 1961. Amounts are in billions of dollars. They may not add to totals because of rounding.
[2] Includes categories of debt not subject to the statutory debt limit. See Table 1-9.
[3] Data are for June 30 of each year. State loans to local units are included.
[4] Includes mortgage debt.

ever its economic impact, the relative importance of the debt appears to have declined since World War II.

The problems posed by a debt of given size are by and large of an internal nature. That is, we do owe it for the most part to ourselves. If a substantial portion of the debt were held by residents of foreign

TABLE 1-7   Gross and net Federal Government debt, 1929-1960[1]

Year	Gross debt[2]	Held by Federal agencies and trust funds	Held by Federal Reserve banks	Held by Federal agencies and trust funds and Federal Reserve banks	Net debt[3]
1929	16.3	0.9	0.5	1.4	14.9
1930	16.0	0.7	0.7	1.4	14.6
1931	17.8	0.5	0.8	1.3	16.5
1932	20.8	0.6	1.9	2.5	18.3
1933	23.8	1.0	2.4	3.4	20.4
1934	28.5	2.8	2.4	5.2	23.3
1935	30.6	1.7	2.4	4.1	26.5
1936	34.4	2.5	2.4	4.9	29.5
1937	37.3	3.8	2.6	6.4	30.9
1938	39.4	5.0	2.6	7.6	31.8
1939	42.0	6.2	2.5	8.7	33.3
1940	45.0	7.3	2.2	9.5	35.5
1941	58.0	9.2	2.3	11.5	46.5
1942	108.2	11.9	6.2	18.1	90.1
1943	165.9	16.5	11.5	28.0	137.9
1944	230.6	21.7	18.8	40.5	190.1
1945	278.1	27.0	24.3	51.3	226.8
1946	259.1	30.9	23.3	54.2	204.8
1947	256.9	34.4	22.6	57.0	199.9
1948	252.8	37.3	23.3	60.6	192.2
1949	257.1	39.3	18.9	58.2	198.9
1950	256.7	39.2	20.8	60.0	196.7
1951	259.4	42.3	23.8	66.1	193.3
1952	267.4	45.9	24.7	70.6	196.8
1953	275.2	48.3	25.9	74.2	201.0
1954	278.8	49.6	24.9	74.5	204.3
1955	280.8	51.7	24.8	76.5	204.3
1956	276.6	54.0	24.9	78.9	197.7
1957	274.9	55.2	24.2	79.4	195.5
1958	282.9	54.3	26.3	80.6	202.3
1959	290.8	53.7	26.6	80.3	210.6
1960	290.2	55.0	27.4	82.4	208.3

[1] SOURCE: Table 1-6 and Federal Reserve Bulletin. Amounts are in billions of dollars and refer to the calendar year.
[2] Includes categories of the debt not subject to the statutory debt limit but does not include guaranteed debt. See Table 1-9.
[3] Gross debt less Government securities held by Federal agencies and trust funds and by the Federal Reserve banks.

lands, servicing the debt would involve a transfer of resources to foreign use. This is not the same as saying that external borrowing cannot make a net contribution to a country's welfare. However, international borrowing does involve external transfers of resources.

TABLE 1-8 Estimated distribution of the interest on the public debt, calendar years 1941–1960[1]

Calendar years	Individuals — Savings bonds Amt.	%	Individuals — Other securities Amt.	%	Individuals — Total Amt.	%	Commercial banks Amt.	%	Mutual savings banks Amt.	%	Insurance companies Amt.	%	Non-financial corporations Amt.	%	State and local governments Amt.	%	Miscellaneous investors Amt.	%	Federal Reserve banks Amt.	%	Government investment accounts Amt.	%	Total budget expenditures Amt.	%
1941	0.1	9	0.1	9	0.2	18	0.4	36	0.1	9	0.2	18	[2]		[2]		[2]		[2]		0.2	18	1.1	100
1946	0.8	16	0.5	10	1.3	26	1.4	28	0.3	6	0.6	12	0.2	4	0.2	4	0.2	4	0.1	2	0.7	14	5.0	100
1947	0.9	18	0.5	10	1.4	28	1.3	26	0.3	6	0.6	12	0.2	4	0.1	2	0.2	4	0.2	4	0.8	16	5.0	100
1948	1.1	20	0.4	7	1.5	28	1.2	22	0.3	6	0.5	9	0.2	4	0.2	4	0.2	4	0.3	6	1.0	19	5.4	100
1949	1.2	23	0.4	8	1.6	30	1.2	23	0.3	5	0.5	9	0.2	4	0.2	4	0.2	4	0.3	6	0.8	15	5.3[3]	100
1950	1.4	25	0.3	5	1.7	30	1.2	21	0.3	5	0.5	9	0.3	5	0.2	4	0.2	3	0.3	5	1.0	18	5.6	100
1951	1.4	23	0.3	5	1.8	30	1.3	22	0.2	3	0.4	7	0.3	5	0.2	3	0.2	3	0.4	7	1.2	20	6.0	100
1952	1.5	25	0.3	5	1.8	30	1.3	21	0.2	3	0.4	7	0.3	5	0.2	3	0.2	3	0.4	7	1.2	20	6.1	100
1953	1.5	23	0.3	5	1.8	28	1.3	20	0.2	3	0.4	6	0.4	7	0.8	12	0.2	3	0.5	8	1.3	20	6.4	100
1954	1.5	23	0.4	6	1.9	29	1.3	20	0.2	3	0.4	6	0.5	8	0.4	6	0.4	6	0.4	6	1.3	20	6.6	100
1955	1.5	23	0.3	5	1.8	28	1.4	22	0.2	3	0.4	6	0.3	5	0.3	5	0.3	5	0.4	6	1.3	20	6.5[4]	100
1956	1.4	20	0.4	6	1.8	26	1.4	20	0.2	3	0.3	4	0.4	6	0.4	6	0.4	6	0.6	9	1.4	20	7.0	100
1957	1.4	18	0.5	7	1.9	25	1.5	20	0.2	3	0.3	4	0.5	7	0.5	7	0.4	5	0.7	9	1.5	20	7.6	100
1958	1.4	19	0.4	5	1.8	24	1.6	22	0.2	2	0.3	4	0.4	5	0.5	7	0.4	5	0.7	9	1.5	20	7.4	100
1959	1.4	17	0.6	7	2.0	24	1.8	21	0.2	2	0.3	4	0.6	7	0.6	7	0.6	7	0.9	11	1.5	18	8.4	100
1960	1.5	16	0.8	9	2.3	25	1.8	19	0.2	2	0.3	3	0.7	8	0.6	6	0.7	8	1.1	12	1.5	16	9.3	100

[1] SOURCE: Office of the Secretary of the Treasury, Debt Analysis Staff. Amounts are in billions of dollars. Percentages are percentages of total budget expenditures on interest. Figures may not add to totals because of rounding.

[2] Less than $50 million.

[3] Excludes $225 million of outstanding unpaid interest resulting from a change from an interest-paid to a due-and-payable accounting basis.

[4] Excludes $279 million in July–December, 1955, resulting from a change from a due-and-payable to an accrual accounting basis on July 1, 1955.

18

Moreover, an internally held debt does not give rise to the potential threat to national solvency which may be posed by an externally held debt. A country which borrows abroad and lacks the resources to service and repay its debt may be forced to default. In this respect, the borrowing nation is like an individual, a business corporation, a state government, or one of its political subdivisions. In each of these cases, the debtor's capacity to meet obligations depends upon the debtor's income and wealth and willingness to curtail expenditures. Our public debt is not subject to this risk, since virtually all of it is held internally. The Federal Government would default in meeting its obligations only if it so willed. It can always pay interest and redeem maturing securities when due by exercising its constitutional prerogatives either to tax or to create money. It is, of course, true that taxes may be burdensome and new money may have an inflationary impact upon the price level. But these are matters of fiscal and monetary policy; and it is inaccurate to lay the blame for onerous taxes and inflation upon the debt per se. So long as these policies are conducted in a manner which preserves economic stability, the debt can be serviced and, if it is so desired, reduced in size without undue stress and strain. Meeting interest payments when they come due and refunding maturing issues present certain problems; but in an environment of economic stability, they do not erect unsurmountable obstacles.

The fact that the debt is held largely by residents of this country does not mean, however, that there are no social costs involved in the internal transfers due the debt service. On the contrary, the impact of these tax charges and interest payments is precisely the focal point of whatever burden the debt may impose. The expenditure of almost a tenth of the Federal budget for interest is not the same as an equal expenditure on arms, roads, or schools. It does not draw an equivalent amount of resources away from private use. Most of the expenditures on interest are transfer payments—they shift income about, but they do not represent an increase in the Government's command over resources. In other words, the private economy does not, as a result of the tax-interest transfer, lose any of its capacity to spend for its own use. On the other hand, while it is true that we owe the national debt to ourselves, the "we" is not throughout the same as the "ourselves." Normally, interest charges are met from tax receipts and hence are borne by taxpayers. But interest is received by investors in the public debt. In so far as each taxpayer does not own that portion of the public debt which is precisely equal to his share of the Federal tax bill, the tax-interest transfer involves a redistribution of income as well as other subsidiary effects.

It is difficult to evaluate the effects of the tax and interest payments, but the available evidence tends to minimize their importance.[15] To begin with, the Federal tax structure is fairly broad in coverage, and at the same time it is progressive. Thus the burden of paying interest on the debt is borne by a large number of individuals, families, and businesses. Also, the burden tends to rise more than proportionately with a taxpayer's income. Ownership of the debt, on the other hand, is also widely distributed throughout the economy. Consequently, interest payments are widely distributed too. This combination of the distribution of tax payments and interest receipts implies that the tax-interest transfer does not have a marked effect upon the pattern of income distribution and spending.

It is also argued that the tax-interest transfer will tend to restrict the output of the economy through its effect on incentives. On the one hand, interest receipts may dull the work incentives of the bondholders. On the other hand, higher tax rates may have a dampening effect on the work incentives of taxpayers. The outcome of these effects is uncertain, however, for it is possible that higher tax rates will provide even stronger incentives for the expenditure of effort.

This evaluation of the tax-interest transfer is necessarily tentative because of a serious methodological difficulty. Suppose that an attempt has been made to ascertain the effect upon the distribution of income of the process of servicing a debt of given size. Even if it could be concluded categorically that the effect of this process is, say, to worsen the distribution of income, this would not be to say that the mere *existence* of the debt leads to a worsening of the distribution of income. In order to make the latter statement, it would be necessary to compare the distribution of income in an economic system which has a public debt with one in which alternative policies are followed, such as financing the expenditures with taxes, forgoing the expenditures entirely, and so on. The necessity of making such a comparison makes it impossible, in practice, to identify the net economic impact of the public debt.

[15] See Oswald Brownlee and Alfred Conrad, "Macro-economic Theories of Income Distribution," *American Economic Review, Papers and Proceedings*, vol. 51, no. 2, May, 1961, pp. 74–85; and Thomas Mayer, "Interest Minimization as a Criterion of Federal Debt Management Policy" (Unpublished ms.).

Three technical aspects of the existence of the public debt merit consideration. First, the debt provides a great pool of liquidity which is potentially a force for stability or instability, depending upon the state of the private economy. In periods of strong inflationary pressures, this source of liquidity may be mobilized to accentuate the upward movement of prices. During a recession, on the other hand, the debt provides its owners with a means of sustaining purchasing power in the face of declining income. Thus in one environment, the debt may require offsetting policies, while in the other case, the debt may lighten the need for compensatory action.

Second, the public debt must regularly be refinanced. If the Treasury's visits to the market are too frequent, it is possible that the efficient execution of monetary policy will be hindered.

Finally, a large and widely held debt improves the contact which the central bank has with various sectors of the capital market. The direct effects of open-market operations in Government securities are thus communicated more rapidly.

The last factor appears favorable, the first neutral, and the second may be ameliorated by improved debt management. Thus the technical aspects of the existence of the debt do not indicate a pressing need for debt reduction. Moreover, it must be pointed out that whatever advantages might conceivably accrue to the economy as a result of debt reduction must be weighed in the balance against the "costs" involved in generating the required surplus, through reduced expenditures or increased taxes or both.

INVESTMENT CHARACTERISTICS OF GOVERNMENT SECURITIES:
THEIR RELATIVE LIQUIDITY AND THE RISK STRUCTURE
OF ASSET YIELDS

Government securities are unique among investment media because they are not subject to default risk. This unique characteristic conveys to United States obligations a superior liquidity status. That is, *ceteris paribus,* a reduction in default, or credit, risk will lead to a reduction in market risk, which implies an increase in liquidity.[16] In other words,

---

[16] Cf. Ira O. Scott, Jr., "The Availability Doctrine: Theoretical Underpinnings," *Review of Economic Studies,* vol. 25, no. 1, pp. 41–48; and O. H. Brownlee and Ira O. Scott, "Utility, Liquidity, and Debt Management," *Econometrica,* vol. 31, no. 3, July, 1963, pp. 349–362.

an asset which has a relatively low default risk will have a relatively narrow dispersion of expected prices precisely because of its superior quality. This market characteristic may serve as the basis for an operational definition of liquidity. Thus the liquidity of an asset can be measured in terms of the slope of its demand curve at the relevant point, given the joint distribution of expected prices for this and other assets. Hence if two assets have identical differences between current and future prices, the asset which has the lower variance of expected future prices will face a demand curve of greater slope than the other asset, and by definition its liquidity may be said to be greater.

Slope, rather than elasticity, is the crucial parameter, for the absolute amount of cash into which a block of securities can be converted is the matter of concern to a portfolio manager. Moreover, all securities being compared would be measured in the same units.

The comparative risk position of Government securities, therefore, accounts for their role in investment portfolios as an instrument of diversification not only to provide certainty of capital value at maturity but also to reduce the uncertainty of capital value prior to maturity. The demand for such an investment outlet, in turn, explains the relatively low yield which may be gotten from this sector of the capital market.

Among income-producing assets generally, Government securities, of course, share those characteristics which distinguish debt or fixed-income obligations from equities. Prominent among these characteristics is price-level risk. As a consequence, the money rate of interest tends to be equal to the real rate plus the rate of change in prices. It is for this reason that yields of equities may actually fall below those of high-grade debt instruments.

Hence the place of Government securities in the risk structure of yields is determined by two characteristics: first, their relative liquidity, and second, their susceptibility to changes in real value.[17]

INVESTMENT CHARACTERISTICS OF GOVERNMENT SECURITIES: THE TERM STRUCTURE OF INTEREST RATES

Over the business cycle, the Treasury yield pattern shifts in a manner which, by and large, appears to be consistent with the so-called expecta-

[17] See appendix for a bibliography on the risk structure of asset yields.

tions theory of the term structure.[18] Institutional constraints which inhibit the free movement of investors over the maturity scale prevent the full applicability of the expectational model.[19] But to the extent that funds do move freely, there will tend to be an adjustment in the yield pattern bringing equality between the expected returns of all possible maturity combinations throughout the currency of the longest-outstanding security. Such a condition of equality then implies that expectations of declining interest rates during the period of time represented by the yield pattern will result in a negatively sloped pattern.

Suppose, for example, that the yield curve is fairly horizontal. Then suppose that lower short-term rates are expected. Investors having these changed expectations will lengthen their portfolios until the yield pattern has become sufficiently negative to satisfy the aforementioned equilibrium condition.[20] Alternatively, an expected rise in short rates will lead to a positively sloped pattern.

Expectations of, say, lower rates on long securities not yet issued are also said to lead to a negatively sloped yield curve. Such expectations would produce this result because in these circumstances investors would tend to lengthen their portfolios, while borrowers would tend to shorten their commitments. This explanation of the relationship between the yield pattern and expectations regarding long-term interest rates cannot be inferred from the equilibrium condition stated above, for that condition applies strictly only to maturities within the span of the current yield pattern. The explanation becomes plausible if there is a persistent tendency toward cyclical periodicity, with the slope of the yield pattern shifting with its level and the tempo of economic activity. The absence of such periodicity would assure a learning process and the revision of expectations. To explain a persisting slope of one kind or the other, reliance must be placed upon the element of uncertainty.

With uncertain expectations, the term structure will be determined not only by the pattern of those expectations but by the balance of investor preferences for capital-value and income certainty relative to

---

[18] See appendix for a bibliography on the term structure of interest rates.

[19] Such constraints are also a necessary condition for the operation of debt-management policy, given lender expectations. If the debt managers can affect these expectations, however, institutional constraints are not required.

[20] At this point the bears in the securities market will once again equal the bulls. If all investors are satisfied, trading will cease altogether.

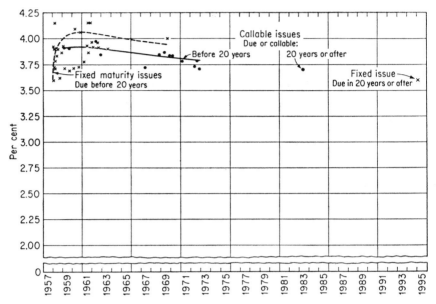

Chart 1-1. Term structure of yields of Government securities, October 31, 1957. Source: *Treasury Bulletin*, December, 1957, p. 45. Yields are based on closing bid quotations for taxable Treasury obligations. Points on the chart represent yields to call when prices are above par and to maturity when prices are at par or below. Curves are fitted by hand. Issues for which an exchange offer has been made or which are due or callable in less than three months are excluded.

the supply of short- and long-term securities. Suppose an investor is concerned with the preservation of capital value. Assume, also, diminishing marginal utility of wealth and an equal probability of a rise and fall in long-term bond prices. Then the loss in utility due to a fall in bond prices will exceed the gain in utility due to a rise.[21] Given the characteristic behavior of the capital market, wherein long-term securities prices fluctuate over a wider range than the prices of short-term securities, the lender will invest in short-term securities.

On the other hand, if the investor emphasizes the preservation of income, he will prefer to invest in long-term obligations. For interest rates on long-term securities tend to fluctuate over a more narrow range than those on short-term obligations, and the utility of a pos-

[21] Cf. the model used in Chap. 6 in connection with the discussion of the bills-only policy.

sible rise in interest rates will be less than the utility of a possible decline.[22] It follows that the preponderance of investor preferences with respect to capital and income certainty will add its weight to expectations and noneconomic portfolio constraints in the determination of the term structure of interest rates.

Examples of Treasury yield patterns are depicted in Charts 1-1 and 1-2. These patterns represent the structure of yields near cyclical turning points. The balance of investor preferences with regard to capital and income certainty is therefore overlaid in each instance by expectations of interest-rate changes. The force of these expectations,

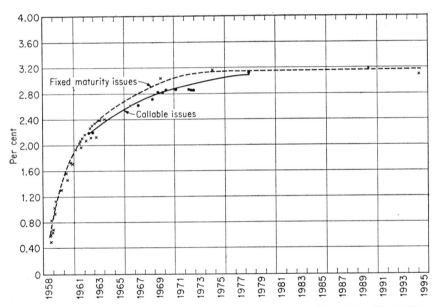

Chart 1-2. Term structure of yields of Government securities, May 29, 1958. Source: *Treasury Bulletin*, July, 1958, p. 47. Yields are based on closing bid quotations for taxable Treasury obligations. Points on the chart represent yields to call when prices are above par and to maturity when prices are at par or below. Curves are fitted by hand. Issues for which an exchange offer has been made or which are due or callable in less than three months are excluded.

[22] Cash has uncertain income in terms of convenience because of the uncertain need for liquidity. But its capital value is certain. Hence, it is preferred by those who emphasize this aspect. However, no one would hold cash if the cost of investing in one-day, risk-free bills were less than the return on such obligations.

however, is apparently not sufficiently strong to offset investor concern for liquidity; hence the hump-shaped curve near the cyclical peak.[23]

COMPOSITION OF THE DEBT

On June 30, 1960, total outstanding direct and guaranteed obligations of the United States amounted to $286,471,000,000. Of this total, $286,065,000,000 worth of securities was subject to the statutory debt limitation. (See Table 1-9.)

That portion of the debt not subject to statutory limitation includes Panama Canal bonds, certain matured debt on which interest has ceased, and certain debt bearing no interest. Of the total subject to the debt ceiling, $140,000,000 consists of guaranteed obligations. These securities are chiefly debentures issued by the Federal Farm Mortgage Corporation, the Federal Housing Administration, and the Home Owners' Loan Corporation.

The remaining $285,925,000,000 of debt subject to limitation consists of direct obligations. These include $2,292,000,000 in securities bearing no interest, chiefly special demand notes issued to the International Monetary Fund under the terms of United States participation in the Bretton Woods Agreement. Also included is $442,000,000 in matured debt on which interest has ceased, consisting of various savings bonds and practically every type of marketable issue.

Of the $283,241,000,000 in interest-bearing securities, $238,342,-000,000 is public issues, and $44,899,000,000 is special issues. Special issues are sold to various Government trust funds and agencies, including the Civil Service Retirement Fund, the Federal Deposit Insurance Corporation, the Federal Housing Administration, the Federal Old-age and Survivors Insurance Trust Fund, the National Service Life Insurance Fund, and the Unemployment Trust Fund.[24] The public issues are composed of $54,497,000,000 in nonmarketable obligations and $183,845,000,000 in marketable obligations. Thus 35 percent of the

---

[23] The reliability of published yield patterns may be questioned on the ground that underlying quotations may not represent firm bids for comparable blocks of securities. See Chap. 3.

[24] The resources of these various funds may also be invested in marketable issues. This occurs, e.g., when the Treasury prepares the market for a new issue or refunding operation. Cf. Deane Carson, "Treasury Open Market Operations," *Review of Economics and Statistics,* vol. 41, no. 4, November, 1959, pp. 438–442.

TABLE 1-9   Direct and guaranteed debt of the United States, June 30, 1960[1]

Class of security	Subject to statutory debt limitation	Not subject to statutory limitation	Total out-standing
Public debt			
Interest-bearing securities			
Marketable:			
Treasury bills	33,415		33,415
Certificates of indebtedness	17,650		17,650
Treasury notes	51,483		51,483
Treasury bonds	81,247		81,247
Panama Canal bonds		50	50
Total marketable	183,795	50	183,845
Nonmarketable:			
U.S. savings bonds (current redemption value)	47,544		47,544
Depository bonds	170		170
Treasury bonds, investment series	6,783		6,783
Total nonmarketable	54,497		54,497
Special issues to Government agencies and trust funds	44,899		44,899
Total interest-bearing securities	283,191	50	283,241
Matured debt on which interest has ceased	442	3	445
Debt bearing no interest:			
U.S. savings stamps	53		53
Excess-profits tax refund bonds	1		1
Special notes of the U.S., International Monetary Fund Series	2,238		2,238
U.S. notes (less gold reserve)		191	191
Deposits for retirement of national bank and Federal Reserve bank notes		157	157
Other debt bearing no interest		6	6
Total debt bearing no interest	2,292	353	2,645
Total public debt[2]	285,925	406	286,331
Guaranteed obligations held outside Treasury:			
Interest-bearing	139		139
Matured	1		1
Total guaranteed obligations	140		140
Total public debt and guaranteed obligations	286,065	406	286,471

[1] SOURCE: Annual Report of the Secretary of the Treasury on the Finances for the Fiscal Year Ended June 30, 1960, Washington, D.C.: Government Printing Office, 1961, table 30, part 2, p. 512. Amounts are in millions of dollars.

[2] Includes public debt incurred to finance expenditures of certain wholly owned Government corporations and other business-type activities in exchange for which obligations of the corporations and activities were issued to the Treasury. For detailed breakdown of this and other items, see ibid., pp. 490–511.

direct, interest-bearing debt is in the form of nonmarketable public or special issues. The Treasury, in effect, pegs the prices of nonmarketable public issues since they are payable on demand. Special issues in the portfolios of various agencies and trust funds and the non-interest-bearing notes issued to the International Monetary Fund are potentially of the same nature, depending, of course, upon the needs of the various investors.

The nonmarketable portion of the public issues is largely composed of savings bonds.[25] There are six issues outstanding, Series E, F, G, H, J, and K. All issues are registered, noncallable, and nontransferable. They mature over a period of seven years and nine months to twelve years, and they may be redeemed on demand after a preliminary waiting period. Series E, F, and J have been sold on a discount basis, with the effective interest rate increasing over time. Series G, H, and K were issued at par, with interest paid semiannually. Purchase of savings bonds by an individual or institutional investor is subject to a maximum limitation. At the present time, the Treasury offers only Series E and H bonds, which are made available on a tap basis.[26] Series E bonds are issued at a discount with the effective interest rate increasing over time, while Series H bonds carry coupons which may be cashed semiannually.

Included in the nonmarketable portion of the public issues are the depositary bonds. These 2 percent bonds were allotted to banks designated as depositary and financial agents of the Federal Government in order to provide an income which would offset the costs of handling the Treasury's business.[27]

Two investment series of Treasury bonds complete the nonmarketable public issues. Series A bonds of 1965, dated October 1, 1947, maturing October 1, 1965, were made available in limited quantities to the major thrift institutions.[28]

Investment Series B bonds of 1980/75 were dated April 1, 1951, and mature April 1, 1980. These $2\frac{3}{4}$ percent bonds are the better known of the two investment series, since their issue was provided for in the terms of the famous Treasury–Federal Reserve Accord of March 4, 1951. The $2\frac{3}{4}$s were offered in exchange for $2\frac{1}{2}$s of 1972/67, dated June

[25] See appendix for a bibliography on savings bonds.
[26] I.e., they are always available upon the subscriber's request.
[27] See Treasury Department Circular no. 660 (1941) as amended.
[28] See Treasury Department Circular no. 814, Sept. 22, 1947.

1, 1945, or November 15, 1945. They represented, in effect, acceptance by the Treasury of Federal Reserve demands for a more realistic long-term coupon; and it was hoped that the exchange would reduce the pressure on the bond market caused by sales of the $2\frac{1}{2}$s. Although non-marketable, the $2\frac{3}{4}$s are exchangeable into marketable $1\frac{1}{2}$ percent five-year notes, dated April 1 and October 1 next preceding the date of the exchange. Thus holders of the $2\frac{3}{4}$s who seek cash are subject to market pressures.[29]

Since this study is focused upon the Government securities dealers, primary interest lies in the $183,845,000,000 of marketable debt. Sixty-five percent of the direct, interest-bearing debt is marketable. There are four major types of marketable issues, which are differentiated chiefly according to maturity.[30] These are bills, certificates of indebtedness, notes, and bonds. Treasury bills have an original maturity of three months to one year. Certificates generally mature in one year, notes in one to five years, and bonds in more than five years. At the end of fiscal 1960, there were $33,415,000,000 in bills, $17,650,000,000 in certificates, $51,483,000,000 in notes, and $81,297,000,000 in bonds.

During much of the postwar period, the average length of the marketable debt has exhibited a downward trend.[31] At the end of calendar 1945, the average length of the marketable debt was 107.1 months. The corresponding figure for the end of 1960 was 54.8. (See Table 1-10.)

Moreover, the record of debt-management policy from the point of view of economic stability has left much to be desired. (See Table 1-11.) During the immediate postwar period, favorable shifts in the maturity structure were largely vitiated by the effect of the pegged-market policy

[29] See Treasury Department Circular no. 883, Mar. 26, 1951.

[30] See Helen J. Cooke, "Marketable Issues of the United States Treasury," in *The Treasury and the Money Market,* Federal Reserve Bank of New York, May, 1954, pp. 24–32; and Jules I. Bogen (ed.), *Financial Handbook,* New York: The Ronald Press Company, 1957, pp. 173–185. Also see the historical summaries of Treasury financings published by C. F. Childs and Company.

[31] This experience led one financial commentator to quip, "Alice explains to the Red Queen, 'We're deciding when it's a good time, a poor time, and no time, to float a long-term Treasury bond issue. As you see, most time is no time.'" This quotation is from Burton C. Hallowell and Kossuth M. Williamson, "Study of the Economic Effects of Federal Debt Management Policies" (Unpublished ms.). Recently, the Treasury has been able to achieve a significant increase in the maturity of the debt through advance refunding. See appendix for a bibliography on advance refunding.

TABLE 1-10   Average length of marketable United States Government securities outstanding[1]

Month	1945	1946	1947	1948	1949	1950	1951	1952	1953	1954	1955	1956	1957	1958	1959	1960
January		106.8		110.7	107.8	101.0	98.5	72.1	62.4	59.3	65.0	64.6	58.0	53.6	56.4	50.4
February				111.2	107.0	100.4	97.6	71.2	52.5	65.0	71.3	63.8	58.0	59.2	56.9	51.3
March			113.4	111.8	107.1	100.7	96.7	72.2	62.7	66.5	72.5	65.3	57.9	59.9	57.1	51.6
April				111.3	106.4	101.1	80.0	71.3	61.8	65.2	70.2	64.3	57.0	59.4	55.9	51.1
May				110.3	105.3	99.2	79.1	70.0	63.7	65.6	69.1	63.5	56.5	58.2	55.3	51.3
June		109.0	113.4	110.1	104.9	98.5	78.8	68.4	63.8	66.0	69.6	64.5	57.3	62.9	55.3	52.3
July				110.2	104.6	98.1	77.6	68.0	60.6	65.1	69.7	64.5	55.5	62.0	53.2	50.9
August				109.5	102.9	97.2	76.8	67.3	60.0	65.0	69.4	62.8	56.0	61.2	53.9	51.1
September			111.9	109.6	102.0	97.6	75.8	66.6	60.7	64.1	68.3	62.3	55.4	60.9	53.5	50.4
October				109.5	101.8	97.8	75.3	65.7	59.8	62.4	66.4	60.9	55.0	58.8	52.2	55.2
November				108.7	100.6	96.9	73.8	64.0	59.4	61.5	65.5	59.4	54.2	57.0	52.4	55.6
December	107.1	112.8	110.9	107.9	101.3	97.1	73.0	63.3	60.2	65.9	65.5	58.8	54.6	57.2	51.5	54.8

[1] SOURCE: Treasury Department. Lengths are in months. Maturity of partially tax-exempt bonds is computed to the earliest call date, callable bonds to maturity date.

TABLE 1-11   The cyclical pattern of the term structure
of the marketable debt[1]

Month	Total marketable debt	Marketable debt due or callable within one year	Percentage of total in one-year category
January, 1946	199.7	70.5	35
November, 1948[2]	157.7	45.0	29
October, 1949[3]	155.4	58.6	38
July, 1953[2]	153.8	82.4	54
August, 1954[3]	154.0	63.1	41
July, 1957[2]	158.8	79.7	50
April, 1958[3]	166.0	75.5	46
January, 1960[2]	189.9	90.2	

[1] SOURCE: Treasury Department. Amounts are in billions of dollars. For the maturity distribution of the marketable debt in various call and maturity classes for fiscal years 1946–1960, see the Annual Report of the Secretary of the Treasury on the State of the Finances for the Fiscal Year Ended June 30, 1960, Washington, D.C.: Government Printing Office, 1961, table 25, p. 487.

[2] Approximate cyclical peak.

[3] Approximate cyclical trough.

of the Federal Reserve System. In October, 1949, a cyclical trough, 38 percent of the marketable debt was due or callable within one year. During the next cyclical upswing the proportion of debt in this category should have declined. Actually, however, 54 percent of the marketable debt was due or callable within one year in July, 1953, the succeeding cyclical peak. By August, 1954, the next cyclical trough, debt in the one-year class had fallen to 41 percent. And so the pattern ran during the decade of the fifties.

TERM AND METHODS OF ISSUE OF THE MARKETABLE DEBT[32]

Because of their short maturity, the Treasury is most actively engaged in rolling over, that is, refunding, maturing bills.[33] The Federal Reserve banks, as fiscal agents for the Treasury, regularly receive tenders for Treasury bills. These are normally issued on a discount basis and

[32] On the subject of Treasury financing techniques, see Tilford C. Gaines, *Techniques of Treasury Debt Management,* New York: Graduate School of Business, Columbia University, and the Free Press of Glencoe, 1962; and Roland I. Robinson and Morris Mendelson, "The Market for United States Treasury Obligations" (Unpublished ms.).

[33] See appendix for a bibliography on Treasury bills.

are payable without interest within a period not exceeding one year.[34] The text of a United States Treasury bill appears in Exhibit 1-1. Bills are issued in denominations, that is, maturity values, of $1,000, $5,000, $10,000, $100,000, $500,000, and $1 million. The amount of the discount at which the bills are originally sold is considered to be interest for purposes of taxation.[35]

There are twenty-six outstanding issues of Treasury bills that are offered on a weekly basis. These consist of thirteen-week, or ninety-one-day, bills and twenty-six-week, or 182-day, bills. By Wednesday of each week, Treasury officials decide whether to increase or decrease the amount of bills for which tenders will be invited or simply to roll over the maturing issue.[36] A press release for the Thursday morning newspapers is then prepared. Each Federal Reserve bank next prepares a circular containing the text of the Treasury press release, which is mailed to all interested parties. An example of such a circular appears in Exhibit 1-2. In this circular, dated Wednesday, October 11, 1961, the Treasury invites tenders for the aggregate amount of $1.7 billion, or thereabouts, of ninety-one-day and 182-day Treasury bills, for cash or in exchange for Treasury bills maturing October 19, 1961, the following Thursday. The new ninety-one-day bills are to be issued on October 19, 1961, and represent an additional amount of bills dated July 20, 1961, and to mature January 18, 1962. The new 182-day bills are to be dated October 19, 1961, and to mature April 19, 1962.

The announcement further states that tenders will be received at Federal Reserve banks and branches up to 2 P.M., eastern daylight saving time on the following Monday, October 16, 1961. Noncompetitive tenders, for $200,000 or less in the case of ninety-one-day bills and $100,000 or less in the case of 182-day bills, but without a stated price, will be accepted in full from any bidder and will be awarded at the average price of accepted competitive bids. In the case of competitive tenders the bid price must be expressed on the basis of 100 with not

[34] 31 U.S.C. § 754. Any of the marketable instruments may be issued on an interest-bearing basis, on a discount basis, or on a combination of these. 31 U.S.C. § 754b.

[35] Treasury regulations governing the issue and sale of Treasury bills are published in *United States of America Treasury Bills*, Treasury Department Circular no. 418, revised Feb. 23, 1954.

[36] By increasing each 182-day issue $100 million, for example, $2.6 billion in new money can be obtained within six months.

THE
UNITED STATES
OF AMERICA

TREASURY BILL

On presentation of this Treasury bill to the Treasurer of
the United States or to any Federal Reserve Bank the United
States of America will pay to the bearer

DOLLARS

without interest on the due date hereon specified. This

Treasury bill is issued under authority of the Second

Liberty Bond Act, as amended, in accordance with, and

subject to, the provisions of Treasury Department Circular

No. 418, Revised, to which reference is made for a statement

of the rights of holders, as fully and with the same effect

as though herein set forth. This Treasury bill is issued by

a Federal Reserve Bank or Branch pursuant to a tender

accepted by the Secretary of the Treasury. It shall not be

valid unless the issue date and the maturity date are entered

hereon.

Issue Date

- - - - - - -
Due and Payable

- - - - - - -

Treasury Department   (facsimile signature)
  Washington   Secretary of the Treasury

Exhibit 1-1. Text, 1953 design, United States Treasury bill.

more than three decimals. Cash and exchange tenders will be treated
alike. Cash adjustments will be made in the event of differences between the par value of maturing bills accepted in exchange and the
issue price of the new bills.

Accompanying the circular announcing the offering are forms which
may be used for either competitive or noncompetitive bids. These are

FEDERAL RESERVE BANK OF NEW YORK

Fiscal Agent of the United States

[Circular No. 5095
October 11, 1961]

OFFERING OF TWO SERIES OF TREASURY BILLS

$1,100,000,000 of 91-Day Bills, Additional Amount, Series Dated July 20, 1961, Due Jan. 18, 1962

(To Be Issued October 19, 1961)

$600,000,000 of 182-Day Bills, Dated October 19, 1961, Due April 19, 1962

To All Incorporated Banks and Trust Companies, and Others Concerned, in the Second Federal Reserve District:

Following is the text of a notice issued by the Treasury Department, released for publication today at 4 p.m., Eastern Daylight Saving time:

The Treasury Department, by this public notice, invites tenders for two series of Treasury bills to the aggregate amount of $1,700,000,000, or thereabouts, for cash and in exchange for Treasury bills maturing October 19, 1961, in the amount of $1,600,399,000, as follows:

91-day bills (to maturity date) to be issued October 19, 1961, in the amount of $1,100,000,000, or thereabouts, representing an additional amount of bills dated July 20, 1961, and to mature January 18, 1962, originally issued in the amount of $499,904,000, the additional and original bills to be freely interchangeable.

182-day bills, for $600,000,000, or thereabouts, to be dated October 19, 1961, and to mature April 19, 1962.

The bills of both series will be issued on a discount basis under competitive and noncompetitive bidding as hereinafter provided, and at maturity their face amount will be payable without interest. They will be issued in bearer form only, and in denominations of $1,000, $5,000, $10,000, $100,000, $500,000 and $1,000,000 (maturity value).

Tenders will be received at Federal Reserve Banks and Branches up to the closing hour, two o'clock p.m., Eastern Daylight Saving time, Monday, October 16, 1961. Tenders will not be received at the Treasury Department, Washington. Each tender must be for an even multiple of $1,000, and in the case of competitive tenders the price offered must be expressed on the basis of 100, with not more than three decimals, e.g., 99.925. Fractions may not be used. It is urged that tenders be made on the printed forms and forwarded in the special envelopes which will be supplied by Federal Reserve Banks or Branches on application therefor.

Others than banking institutions will not be permitted to submit tenders except for their own account. Tenders will be received without deposit from incorporated banks and trust companies and from responsible and recognized dealers in investment securities. Tenders from others must be accompanied by payment of 2 percent of the face amount of Treasury bills applied for, unless the tenders are accompanied by an express guaranty of payment by an incorporated bank or trust company.

Immediately after the closing hour, tenders will be opened at the Federal Reserve Banks and Branches, following which public announcement will be made by the Treasury Department of the amount and price range of accepted bids. Those submitting tenders will be advised of the acceptance or rejection thereof. The Secretary of the Treasury expressly reserves the right to accept or reject any or all tenders, in whole or in part, and his action in any such respect shall be final. Subject to these reservations, noncompetitive tenders for $200,000 or less for the additional bills dated July 20, 1961 (91 days remaining until maturity date on January 18, 1962) and noncompetitive tenders for $100,000 or less for the 182-day bills without stated price from any one bidder will be accepted in full at the average price (in three decimals) of accepted competitive bids for the respective issues. Settlement for accepted tenders in accordance with the bids must be made or completed at the Federal Reserve Bank on October 19, 1961, in cash or other immediately available funds or in a like face amount of Treasury bills maturing October 19, 1961. Cash and exchange tenders will receive equal treatment. Cash adjustments will be made for differences between the par value of maturing bills accepted in exchange and the issue price of the new bills.

The income derived from Treasury bills, whether interest or gain from the sale or other disposition of the bills, does not have any exemption, as such, and loss from the sale or other disposition of Treasury bills does not have any special treatment, as such, under the Internal Revenue Code of 1954. The bills are subject to estate, inheritance, gift or other excise taxes, whether Federal or State, but are exempt from all taxation now or hereafter imposed on the principal or interest thereof by any State, or any of the possessions of the United States, or by any local taxing authority. For purposes of taxation the amount of discount at which Treasury bills are originally sold by the United States is considered to be interest. Under Sections 454(b) and 1221(5) of the Internal Revenue Code of 1954 the amount of discount at which bills issued hereunder are sold is not considered to accrue until such bills are sold, redeemed or otherwise disposed of, and such bills are excluded from consideration as capital assets. Accordingly, the owner of Treasury bills (other than life insurance companies) issued hereunder need include in his income tax return only the difference between the price paid for such bills, whether on original issue or on subsequent purchase, and the amount actually received either upon sale or redemption at maturity during the taxable year for which the return is made, as ordinary gain or loss.

Treasury Department Circular No. 418, Revised, and this notice, prescribe the terms of the Treasury bills and govern the conditions of their issue. Copies of the circular may be obtained from any Federal Reserve Bank or Branch.

This Bank will receive tenders for both series up to 2 p.m., Eastern Daylight Saving time, Monday, October 16, 1961, at the Securities Department of its Head Office and at its Buffalo Branch. Tender forms for the respective series are enclosed. Please use the appropriate forms to submit tenders and return them in an envelope marked "Tender for Treasury Bills." Tenders may be submitted by telegraph, subject to written confirmation; they may not be submitted by telephone. *Payment for the Treasury bills cannot be made by credit through the Treasury Tax and Loan Account. Settlement must be made in cash or other immediately available funds or in maturing Treasury bills.*

Results of the last offering of Treasury bills (90-day bills to be issued October 13, 1961, representing an additional amount of bills dated July 13, 1961, and maturing January 11, 1962; and 181-day bills dated October 13, 1961, maturing April 12, 1962) are shown on the reverse side of this circular.

Alfred Hayes,
President.

(OVER)

Exhibit 1-2. Federal Reserve Bank of New York Circular no. 5095, October 11 1961, offering of $1.1 billion of ninety-one-day bills and $0.6 billion of 182-day bills.

shown in Exhibits 1-3 and 1-4. Banks alone may submit tenders for the account of others. For this purpose, competitive tenders at the same price and noncompetitive tenders may be consolidated. However, each customer's name and the amount for which he is bidding must be divulged. More than one competitive bid may be submitted by a single institution.

Tenders will be received without deposit from incorporated banks, trust companies, and selected securities dealers. A payment of 2 percent of the face amount applied for must accompany other tenders. This payment need not be in Federal funds. However, full payment in cash, that is, Federal funds, must be made on Thursday when the bills allotted are delivered.

Tenders must be submitted in writing or by telegraph subject to written confirmation. They may not be submitted by telephone.

Immediately after the closing hour, bids are opened at the several Federal Reserve banks and branches. The quantity of bills bid for at each price and noncompetitive bids are totaled and the results wired to the Treasury Department. Then final totals are computed and the allotments made. First, allowance is made for the noncompetitive bids. Then competitive bids are accepted in descending order, with only that portion of the lowest acceptable competitive bid required to obtain the desired total being awarded. If the same price appears on more than one tender and only a part of the total can be accepted, the amount accepted at that price is prorated in accordance with the respective amounts applied for. The results of the offering are then reported to the Federal Reserve banks and branches, which in turn notify the individuals who had submitted bids.

A summary of the results of the offering is also released to the press for publication in the morning papers on Tuesday. The same summary usually appears on the reverse side of the Federal Reserve bank circular which announces the next bill offering. The reverse side of Federal Reserve Bank of New York Circular no. 5098, October 18, 1961, is shown in Exhibit 1-5. Applications were received for $2,220,864,000 of the January 18 bills; $1,100,033,000 in bids were accepted. This included $241,400,000 in noncompetitive bids, which were accepted in full at the average price. The highest bid was 99.405, equivalent to an annual rate of discount of approximately 2.354 percent. The low price was 99.395, a rate of discount of 2.393 percent per annum. Of the amount bid for at this price, 44 percent was accepted. The average[37] price was 99.398, or a 2.382 basis. Comparable information is provided for 182-day bills.

[37] Weighted by volume. See below, the last section of this chapter, for the method of interest computation.

The maturity of the bill will be changed in the case of holidays. For example, if the Thursday maturity date falls on a holiday, ninety-two-day or 183-day bills may be offered. When the usual Thursday issue date falls on a holiday, ninety-day bills will be issued on Friday. If a

---

No..................

TENDER FOR 91-DAY TREASURY BILLS

Additional Amount, Series Dated July 20, 1961, Maturing January 18, 1962

(To Be Issued October 19, 1961)

To FEDERAL RESERVE BANK OF NEW YORK,
Fiscal Agent of the United States.

Dated at ....

.........................., 19...

Pursuant to the provisions of Treasury Department Circular No. 418, Revised, and to the provisions of the public notice issued by the Treasury Department inviting tenders for the above described Treasury bills, the undersigned hereby offers to purchase such Treasury bills in the amount indicated below, and agrees to make payment therefor at your Bank on or before the issue date at the price indicated below:

COMPETITIVE TENDER [*Do not fill in both Competitive and Noncompetitive tenders on one form*] NONCOMPETITIVE TENDER

$............................(maturity value),
or any lesser amount that may be awarded.

Price: .... per 100.
(Price must be expressed with not more than three decimal places, for example, 99.925)

$.............................(maturity value).
(Not to exceed $200,000 for one bidder through all sources)

At the average price of accepted competitive bids.

Subject to allotment, please issue, deliver, and accept payment for the bills as indicated below:

Pieces	Denomination	Maturity value		Payment will be made as follows:
	$ 1,000		☐ 1. Deliver over the counter to the undersigned	☐ By charge to our reserve account
	5,000		☐ 2. Ship to the undersigned	☐ By cash or other immediately available funds
	10,000		☐ 3. Hold in safekeeping (for account of member bank only)	
	100,000		☐ 4. Allotment transfer (see list attached)	☐ By surrender of $............. (maturity value) of maturing Treasury bills. Pay cash adjustment, if any—
	500,000		☐ 5. Special instructions:	☐ By check
	1,000,000			☐ By credit to our reserve account
Totals—			*(No changes in delivery instructions will be accepted)*	*(Payment cannot be made through Treasury Tax and Loan Account)*

The undersigned (if a bank or trust company) hereby certifies that the Treasury bills which you are hereby instructed to dispose of in the manner indicated in item 3 above are solely owned by the undersigned.

[*Insert this tender in special envelope, marked "Tender for Treasury Bills"*]

Name of subscriber ....
(Please print)

By ....
(Official signature(s) required)

Title ...., Title ....

Address ....

(Banks submitting tenders for customer account must indicate name on line below, or attach a list)

....
(Name of customer) (Address)

INSTRUCTIONS:

1. No tender for less than $1,000 will be considered, and each tender must be for an even multiple of $1,000 (maturity value).

2. Others than banking institutions will not be permitted to submit tenders except for their own account. Banks submitting tenders for customer account may consolidate competitive tenders *at the same price* and may consolidate noncompetitive tenders, provided a list is attached showing the name of each bidder, the amount bid for his account, and method of payment. Forms for this purpose will be furnished on request.

3. If the person making the tender is a corporation, the tender should be signed by an officer of the corporation authorized to make the tender, and the signing of the tender by an officer of the corporation will be construed as a representation by him that he has been so authorized. If the tender is made by a partnership, it should be signed by a member of the firm, who should sign in the form ".., a copartnership, by ...., a member of the firm."

4. Tenders will be received without deposit from incorporated banks and trust companies and from responsible and recognized dealers in investment securities. Tenders from others must be accompanied by payment of 2 percent of the face amount of Treasury bills applied for, unless the tenders are accompanied by an express guaranty of payment by an incorporated bank or trust company.

5. If the language of this tender is changed in any respect, which, in the opinion of the Secretary of the Treasury, is material, the tender may be disregarded.

Exhibit 1-3. Tender for ninety-one-day Treasury bills, additional amount, series dated July 20, 1961, maturing January 18, 1962.

No................

TENDER FOR 182-DAY TREASURY BILLS

Dated October 19, 1961   Maturing April 19, 1962

To FEDERAL RESERVE BANK OF NEW YORK,   Dated at ....
Fiscal Agent of the United States.   ...., 19...

Pursuant to the provisions of Treasury Department Circular No. 418, Revised, and to the provisions of the public notice issued by the Treasury Department inviting tenders for the above described Treasury bills, the undersigned hereby offers to purchase such Treasury bills in the amount indicated below, and agrees to make payment therefor at your Bank on or before the issue date at the price indicated below:

COMPETITIVE TENDER   [*Do not fill in both Competitive and Noncompetitive tenders on one form*]   **NONCOMPETITIVE TENDER**

$....................(maturity value), $....................(maturity value).
or any lesser amount that may be awarded.   *(Not to exceed $100,000 for one bidder through all sources)*

Price: ....per 100.   At the average price of accepted competitive bids.
(Price must be expressed with not more than three decimal places, for example, 99.925)

Subject to allotment, please issue, deliver, and accept payment for the bills as indicated below:

Pieces	Denomination	Maturity value			Payment will be made as follows:
	$ 1,000			☐ 1. Deliver over the counter to the undersigned	☐ By charge to our reserve account
	5,000			☐ 2. Ship to the undersigned	☐ By cash or other immediately available funds
	10,000			☐ 3. Hold in safekeeping (for account of member bank only)	
	100,000			☐ 4. Allotment transfer (see list attached)	☐ By surrender of $............. (maturity value) of maturing Treasury bills. Pay cash adjustment, if any—
	500,000			☐ 5. Special instructions:	☐ By check
	1,000,000				☐ By credit to our reserve account
	Totals—			*(No changes in delivery instructions will be accepted)*	*(Payment cannot be made through Treasury Tax and Loan Account)*

The undersigned (if a bank or trust company) hereby certifies that the Treasury bills which you are hereby instructed to dispose of in the manner indicated in item 3 above are solely owned by the undersigned.

[*Insert this tender in special envelope marked "Tender for Treasury Bills"*]

Name of subscriber ....
                     (Please print)
By .... By ....
                 (Official signature(s) required)
Title ...., Title ....

Address ....

(Banks submitting tenders for customer account must indicate name on line below, or attach a list)

....
    (Name of customer)   *(Address)*

INSTRUCTIONS:

1. No tender for less than $1,000 will be considered, and each tender must be for an even multiple of $1,000 (maturity value).

2. Others than banking institutions will be not permitted to submit tenders except for their own account. Banks submitting tenders for customer account may consolidate competitive tenders *at the same price* and may consolidate noncompetitive tenders, provided a list is attached showing the name of each bidder, the amount bid for his account, and method of payment. Forms for this purpose will be furnished on request.

3. If the person making the tender is a corporation, the tender should be signed by an officer of the corporation authorized to make the tender, and the signing of the tender by an officer of the corporation will be construed as a representation by him that he has been so authorized. If the tender is made by a partnership, it should be signed by a member of the firm, who should sign in the form "..................................., a member of the firm."

4. Tenders will be received without deposit from incorporated banks and trust companies and from responsible and recognized dealers in investment securities. Tenders from others must be accompanied by payment of 2 percent of the face amount of Treasury bills applied for, unless the tenders are accompanied by an express guaranty of payment by an incorporated bank or trust company.

5. If the language of this tender is changed in any respect, which, in the opinion of the Secretary of the Treasury, is material, the tender may be disregarded.

Exhibit 1-4. Tender for 182-day Treasury bills dated October 19, 1961, maturing April 19, 1962.

holiday happens to fall on a Monday, bidding takes place on the preceding Friday, but the maturity of the bill is unaffected.[38]

[38] For an example of the offering of ninety-two-day and 183-day Treasury bills, see Federal Reserve Bank of New York, Circular no. 5070, Aug. 16,

Range of Accepted Competitive Bids

	91-Day Treasury Bills Maturing January 18, 1962		182-Day Treasury Bills Maturing April 19, 1962	
	Price	Approx. equiv. annual rate	Price	Approx. equiv. annual rate
High	99.405	2.354%	98.624[a]	2.722%
Low	99.395	2.393%	98.613	2.744%
Average	99.398	2.382%[1]	98.618	2.734%[1]

[a] Excepting three tenders totaling $960,000.

[1] On a coupon issue of the same length and for the same amount invested, the return on these bills would provide yields of 2.43 percent for the 91-day bills, and 2.81 percent for the 182-day bills. Interest rates on bills are quoted in terms of bank discount, with the return related to the face amount of the bills payable at maturity rather than the amount invested, and their length in actual number of days related to a 360-day year. In contrast, yields on certificates, notes, and bonds are computed in terms of interest on the amount invested, and relate the number of days remaining in an interest payment period to the actual number of days in the period, with semiannual compounding if more than one coupon period is involved.

(44 percent of the amount of 91-day bills bid for at the low price was accepted.)

(84 percent of the amount of 182-day bills bid for at the low price was accepted.)

Total Tenders Applied for and Accepted (By Federal Reserve Districts)

District	91-Day Treasury Bills Maturing January 18, 1962		182-Day Treasury Bills Maturing April 19, 1962	
	Applied for	Accepted	Applied for	Accepted
Boston	$ 33,449,000	$ 15,697,000	$ 3,744,000	$ 3,204,000
New York	1,645,453,000	714,015,000	899,723,000	457,613,000
Philadelphia	31,575,000	11,355,000	7,633,000	2,533,000
Cleveland	29,446,000	26,022,000	30,484,000	25,234,000
Richmond	10,620,000	10,320,000	7,758,000	7,758,000
Atlanta	18,855,000	15,485,000	5,739,000	4,939,000
Chicago	192,390,000	122,108,000	94,307,000	57,207,000
St. Louis	52,731,000	31,189,000	8,239,000	7,239,000
Minneapolis	25,924,000	14,944,000	6,229,000	3,379,000
Kansas City	45,896,000	36,049,000	15,818,000	6,928,000
Dallas	15,130,000	15,130,000	4,840,000	4,840,000
San Francisco	119,395,000	87,719,000	27,558,000	19,483,000
Total	$2,220,864,000	$1,100,033,000[b]	$1,112,072,000	$600,357,000[c]

[b] Includes $241,400,000 noncompetitive tenders accepted at the average price of 99.398.
[c] Includes $60,200,000 noncompetitive tenders accepted at the average price of 98.618.

Exhibit 1-5. Results of last offering of Treasury bills (two series issued October 19, 1961).

In addition, the Treasury has outstanding special one-year bills, which are being issued on a monthly basis. The bidding procedure is

---

1961, *Offering of Two Series of Treasury Bills.* In this case, ninety-one-day and 182-day bills would have matured on Thanksgiving Day and Washington's Birthday, respectively. An example of a ninety-day bill is contained in Federal Reserve Bank of New York, Circular no. 5256, Nov. 14, 1962, *Offering of Two Series of Treasury Bills.* In this instance, the regular issue date fell on Thanksgiving Day.

similar to that used in the regular weekly offerings, except that tenders are received on a day of the week other than Monday.[39]

The Treasury also issues strips of weekly Treasury bills. In these cases it is necessary for the investor to submit a single bid for each strip of bills. Each component of the strip increases the amount outstanding of an existing issue. Payment through credit to a Treasury Tax and Loan Account may be permitted.[40]

Finally, there are tax-anticipation bills, or TABs. These were introduced in order to offset fluctuations in Treasury receipts which were accentuated by the operation of the Mills Plan. Although the so-called Super-Mills Plan gradually restored much of the earlier pattern, the Treasury still employs this debt instrument as a means of reducing the effect of tax payments upon money-market conditions and for purposes of offsetting the seasonal pattern of budget receipts and outlays.[41]

Again, tender and acceptance procedures are similar to those of the weekly offering. The unique feature of the tax bill is the interest-rate adjustment. Though not maturing until a week following the tax date, TABs will be accepted at face value in payment of income and profits taxes due on the quarterly tax date. Taxpayers desiring to apply these bills in payment of taxes may surrender them to a Federal Reserve bank or branch or the Treasury not more than fifteen days before the date on which taxes are due. In exchange, they will receive receipts showing the face amount of the bills surrendered. These receipts, in turn, may be submitted in lieu of the bills on or before the tax date to the Director of Internal Revenue.[42]

[39] For an example of the offering of a one-year bill, see Federal Reserve Bank of New York, Circular no. 5054, July, 1961, *Offering of $2,000,000,000 of Special 365-day Treasury Bills, Dated July 15, 1961, Maturing July 15, 1962.*

[40] For a discussion of the value of a tax and loan account credit, see Chap. 3. For a description of a strip offering, see Federal Reserve Bank of New York, Circular no. 5043, June 2, 1961, *Offering of $1,800,000,000 Strip of Weekly Treasury Bills.* Since a single bid is accepted for a strip, the tax basis for taking each issue into position is according to ratio of market prices of the outstanding issues on a specified date. See Federal Reserve Bank of New York, Circular no. 5045, June 6, 1961, *Tax Basis for Purchase of Strips of Treasury Bills.*

[41] See appendix for a bibliography on factors affecting member bank reserves.

[42] For an example of a tax bill, see Federal Reserve Bank of New York, Circular no. 5058, July 13, 1961, *Offering of $3,500,000,000 of 240-day Tax Anticipation Treasury Bills, Dated July 26, 1961, Maturing March 23, 1962.*

Like the special offerings, certificates of indebtedness (C/Is), notes, and bonds require special procedures. The new issues may be for cash or for the purpose of refinancing maturing securities.[43] In each case, Treasury officials are waited upon by advisory committees representing such groups as the National Association of Mutual Savings Banks, the American Life Convention and Life Insurance Association of America, the American Bankers Association, and the Investment Bankers Association.[44] These committees express their views regarding market conditions and desires with respect to the price and maturity of the new issue.[45] If a certificate is issued, the decision is the responsibility

[43] The choice between a cash or exchange offering will depend upon several factors. A cash offering enables the Treasury to exert better control over speculation. It also eliminates the problem of attrition. On the other hand, some investors who might otherwise roll over their holdings may leave the market. On these issues, see "Margin Requirements," in Treasury Department and Board of Governors, Federal Reserve System, *Treasury–Federal Reserve Study of the Government Securities Market,* Washington, D.C., Feb. 1, 1960, part 3, pp. 47–66; Burton C. Hallowell and Kossuth M. Williamson, "Debt Management's Contribution to Monetary Policy," *Review of Economics and Statistics,* vol. 43, no. 1, February, 1961, pp. 81–84; and Goldsmith-Nagan Washington Service, *United States Government Securities,* Bulletin no. 643, Oct. 28, 1961. On the techniques for issuing certificates, notes, and bonds, see Tilford C. Gaines, *Techniques of Treasury Debt Management,* New York: Graduate School of Business, Columbia University, and The Free Press of Glencoe, 1962, pp. 153–196.

[44] See *Debt Management Advisory Committees (Treasury Department), Hearings before a Subcommittee of the Committee on Government Operations,* House of Representatives, 84th Congress, 2d Session, June 5, 7, 1956, Washington, D.C.: Government Printing Office, 1956; and *Conflicting Official Views on Monetary Policy: April 1956, Hearing before the Subcommittee on Economic Stabilization of the Joint Committee on the Economic Report,* 84th Congress, 2d Session, June 12, 1956, Washington, D.C.: Government Printing Office, 1956, pp. 13ff.

[45] The terms do not include fees for underwriters, since the Treasury does not ordinarily pay an underwriter's commission. Exceptions have occurred in the recent period when the Treasury has offered long-term bonds at competitive bidding.

The problem of setting the price of a new issue does not arise in the case of Treasury bills, since they are normally sold at auction. Other Treasury securities are usually offered at a price set by debt-management authorities after consultation with Federal Reserve officials and the private advisory committees. Many academic and congressional critics feel the problem of administrative pricing should be eliminated by selling all new securities for cash at auction. Treasury officials and market practitioners have felt that the regular

of the Secretary of the Treasury. Presidential approval is required for a note or a bond.[46] Certificates are payable in not more than one year from the issue date and are usually issued on a coupon basis.[47] Similarly, notes are issued on a coupon basis, but are payable in not less than one year nor more than five years from the issue date.[48] Bonds may be of any maturity, but are typically outstanding for a period in excess of five years and are issued on a coupon basis. The maximum coupon on a bond is $4\frac{1}{4}$ percent per annum.[49] Interest is paid semiannually on certificates of indebtedness, notes, and bonds.

Once the decision is made, a statement is released to the press and circulated by the Federal Reserve banks. Next, relevant circulars, application forms, and covering announcements are circulated. The deadline for receiving subscriptions is the close of business on a given day, although subscriptions received in the mail and postmarked by midnight of that day are acceptable. The books are normally open three days or longer on exchanges and one day on cash offerings. In the latter case, allotments are usually made the second day after the closing. The Secretary has wide discretionary authority in making allotments. Usually C/I allotments range from 50,000 to 100,000. Note allotments are smaller, and bonds are the smallest—from 5,000 to 10,-000. On subscriptions exceeding the minimum allotment, minimum allotments are awarded plus a certain percentage of the excess. This percentage, of course, is adjusted by the Treasury in order to cover the total issue.[50]

---

use of the auction technique would cost the Treasury money. See appendix for a bibliography on auctioning Treasury securities.

[46] Authority to issue notes and bonds with the approval of the President is found in 31 U.S.C. §§ 752 and 753, respectively.

[47] Authority to issue certificates is given in 31 U.S.C. § 754. As in the case of bills, tax-anticipation certificates (TACs) are sometimes issued.

[48] 31 U.S.C. § 735.

[49] 31 U.S.C. § 752. This statutory limitation has long been interpreted as an interest-rate ceiling. However, since bonds may be offered at a discount, this interpretation has been the subject of much controversy.

[50] Probably the biggest guessing game in Wall Street consists of predicting the magnitude of total subscriptions. For only with a foreknowledge of this figure can a subscriber determine the amount for which he must subscribe in order to be certain of being allotted a specific magnitude—an excellent example of Keynes's expectations of the third degree. As one specialist put it, "You might as well base your estimate on the number of windows you can count on the building next door."

Exchange offerings may take the form of advance refunding as well as the funding of maturing issues.[51] For example, the exchange offering of September, 1961, was of this kind. On September 7, 1961, the Treasury Department announced cash-borrowing plans and an advance-refunding offer to holders of the $2\frac{1}{2}$s of 1970/65 and March, 1971/66.[52] Four days later came the official offering in Treasury Department Circulars no. 1065, 1066, and 1067.[53] These circulars were legal documents governing the exchange procedures. Three circulars were issued because holders of the $2\frac{1}{2}$s had the option of accepting additional issues of the $3\frac{1}{2}$s of 1980, 1990, or 1998.[55]

A holder of the $2\frac{1}{2}$s of 1970/65 might, for example, exchange these for newly issued $3\frac{1}{2}$s of 1980. According to the Treasury circular, holders of the $2\frac{1}{2}$s might subscribe to the $3\frac{1}{2}$s at 102.25 percent of their face value. That is, an investor could exchange a $2\frac{1}{4}$ percent bond of, say, $1000 denomination plus $22.50 for a $3\frac{1}{2}$ percent bond of the same denomination. It was further declared that no gain or loss in the transactions would be recognized for income tax purposes. Payment for the face amount of the bonds allotted had to be made on or before September 29.

The subscriber was also instructed to detach coupons dated September 15, 1961, from the $2\frac{1}{2}$s. In the case of registered bonds, interest would be paid by check as usual. In addition to the $22.50 due the Treasury on account of the issue price of the new security, each subscription had to be accompanied by $11.69837 in interest accrued from May 15 to September 15, 1961.[56]

Finally, the investor was informed that he would have to reinvest

---

[51] See appendix for a bibliography on advance refunding.

[52] See Federal Reserve Bank of New York, Circular no. 5082, *Treasury Financing*, Sept. 7, 1961.

[53] These are reprinted in Federal Reserve Bank of New York, Circular no. 5083, *Treasury Offerings*, Sept. 11, 1961.

[55] For commentaries on the offerings, see Robert Van Cleave, *C. F. Childs and Company Review*, no. 365, Aug. 28, 1961; "Trying for a Stretchout," *Business Week*, Sept. 16, 1961; Goldsmith Washington Service, *United States Government Securities*, Bulletin no. 613, Oct. 1, 1960; Eugene Lerner, "The Public Debt and Monetary Policy," *Business Scope*, vol. 5, no. 9, Oct. 7, 1961; and David I. Fand, "The September Refunding" (Unpublished ms.).

[56] I.e., interest-payment dates on the $3\frac{1}{2}$s are May 15 and November 15. Thus interest at $0.0951087 had accrued for 123 days. For rules governing the computation of interest, see below, the final section of this chapter.

the proceeds of his $2\frac{1}{2}$ percent bond at maturity at a yield of approximately 4.31 percent in order to equal his gain from the exchange to the maturity of the $3\frac{1}{2}$ percent obligations.[57]

Each offering circular was accompanied by subscription forms. These completed forms would be received at the Federal Reserve banks and branches and at the Office of the Treasury of the United States during the period when the subscription books were open. Each form had to be accompanied by a check for moneys due the Treasury plus the securities to be surrendered.

On September 21, preliminary results were published, and the financing was proclaimed a success by the authorities.[58] On September 28, final results by Federal Reserve district were divulged.[59]

Since Treasury bonds are around for relatively long periods, they become old friends to the bond traders and are consequently given nicknames. The $2\frac{3}{4}$s of June 15, 1963/58, and December 15, 1965/60, are called the "PTEs," since they are partially tax-exempt. Practically all outstanding $2\frac{1}{2}$ percent bonds are called "Taps," since they were left on tap for some time by the Treasury.[60] The "Taps" are the $2\frac{1}{2}$s of June 15, 1972/67, December 15, 1968/63, June 15, 1969/64, December 15, 1969/64, March 15, 1970/65, March 15, 1971/66, June 15, 1972/67, and December 15, 1972/67. The "Taps" and the $2\frac{1}{2}$s of September 15, 1972/67, are also called the "optional $2\frac{1}{2}$s," since the Treasury has the option of calling these bonds prior to maturity. Individual issues also receive special designations. The $2\frac{1}{2}$s of June 15, 1972/67, are called the "Junes." The $2\frac{1}{2}$s of September 15, 1972/67, are called the "Banks," since they were exempt from the usual bank restriction. The $2\frac{1}{2}$s of December 15, 1972/67, are called the "Vics." The $3\frac{1}{4}$s of June 15, 1983/78, were dubbed the "Humphrey Dumpties," for the Secretary, because they fell out of bed [61] while being traded on a

---

[57] The terms of a refunding may be set so as to leave the investor indifferent with respect to the options provided. On the other hand, the Treasury may design a rate structure so as to achieve greater debt extension or to assure a tradable size to a particular issue.

[58] See Federal Reserve Bank of New York, Circular no. 5087, *Results of Current Treasury Offerings,* Sept. 21, 1961.

[59] See Federal Reserve Bank of New York, Circular no. 5089, *Final Results of Treasury's Current Advance Refunding,* Sept. 28, 1961.

[60] I.e., the subscription books remained open for an unusually long period of time.

[61] I.e., went below par.

"when-issued" basis. The $3\frac{1}{2}$s of 1990 are referred to as the "Gay Nineties"; the 3 percent bonds of June 15, 1995, are simply called the "3s."

By virtue of statutory provisions, all bonds bearing interest of more than 4 percent may be redeemed at par in the payment of Federal estate taxes.[62] With few exceptions, other outstanding bonds may be used for the same purpose by the terms of their issue.[63]

THE COMPUTATION OF INTEREST

When an investor or trader buys a Government security which has been issued on a coupon basis, he must add the accrued interest to the purchase price.[64] Consequently, such trading will usually involve the computation of one day's interest.

Computation of interest is made on an annual basis when it is payable in a single amount for the full term of the security, unless the term is an exact quarter-year (three months) or half-year (six months).[65] For a quarter-year term, interest is computed on a quarterly basis, for a half-year term, on a semiannual basis.

When the term of the security is exactly one year, interest is computed for the full period at the specified rate, regardless of the number of days in the year. If the term is less than one year, the annual interest period for purposes of computation is considered to be the full year from but not including the date of issue to and including the anniversary of the issue date. When the term exceeds one year, computation is based on the annual interest period ending with the maturity date and the fractional part of the preceding full annual interest period.

The computation of interest for a fractional part of an annual interest period is based on 365 days, or 366 days if February 29 falls within the annual period.

[62] 31 U.S.C. § 765.

[63] See Federal Reserve Bank of New York, Appendix to Operating Circular no. 17, revised Oct. 4, 1960, *Redemption of Treasury Bonds to Pay Federal Estate Taxes.* For the conditions prerequisite to the use of Treasury bonds for this purpose, see Treasury Department Circular no. 300, revised Apr. 30, 1955.

[64] Corporate stocks, on the other hand, are traded "flat."

[65] For a statement of rules to be followed in interest computations, see Treasury Department Circular no. 300, revised, *General Regulations with Respect to United States Securities,* 1955, pp. 27–29.

Computation of interest is made on a semiannual basis when interest is payable for one or more half-year (six-month) periods and a fractional part of a half-year period. A semiannual interest period is an exact half-year of six months and may consist of 181, 182, 183, or 184 days.

An exact half-year's interest at the specified rate is computed for each full period of exactly six months, regardless of the number of days in the half-year. If the initial interest covers a fractional part of a half-year, computation is based on the number of days in the half-year (exactly six months) ending on the day the initial interest payment is due. If the initial interest covers a period longer than six months, computation is based on the half-year period ending with the interest-due date, plus a fractional part of the preceding half-year period.

The computation of interest for a fractional part of a half-year period is based on the number of days in the full half-year period, including February 29 whenever it falls within the period.

Computation of interest is made on a quarterly basis when interest is payable for one or more quarter-year periods or for one or more quarter-year periods and a fractional part of a quarter-year period. A quarter-year period is an exact quarter-year of three months and may consist of eighty-nine, ninety, ninety-one, or ninety-two days.

An exact quarter-year's interest is computed for each quarter-year period, regardless of the number of days in the period. For a fractional part of any quarter-year, the interest computation is based on the number of days in the quarter-year, including February 29 if it falls within the period. When the initial interest covers a fractional part of a quarter-year preceding a full quarter-year period, computation is based on the number of days in the quarter-year (exactly three months) ending on the day the initial payment is due. If the interest payment covers a fractional part of a quarter-year following a full quarter-year period computation is based on the number of days in the quarter-year beginning on the day the final interest payment begins to accrue and ending exactly three months thereafter.

Bank discount is used in computing the discount rate on Treasury bills. Thus the amount of the discount is

$$d = f - p$$

where f is the face or maturity value and p is the price. Then the rate of discount in percentage terms is

$$r = \frac{d}{f} \cdot \frac{T}{t} \cdot 100$$

where t is the time to maturity in days and T is 360.[66] The average discount rate which applies to noncompetitive bids is

$$R = \frac{D}{F} \cdot \frac{T}{t} \cdot 100$$

where

$$D = F - P$$

and F represents the face value of the total number of bills awarded and P is the total payment for these bills received by the Treasury.[67]

[66] The true discount rate is $R = (d/p)\ (T/t)\ (100)$, where T is 365 or 366.

[67] In effect, the yield which applies to noncompetitive bids is an average of the yields of the accepted competitive bids weighted by volume.

chapter 2

INVESTMENT IN GOVERNMENT SECURITIES

Especial attention will be given to the operations and position policy of the dealers who make the market for Government securities. However, the market they make reflects the forces of supply and demand originating primarily in the investment activities of the great financial intermediaries. Consequently, these investment activities and the role of Government securities in institutional portfolios will be reviewed briefly.[1]

POSTWAR SHIFTS IN OWNERSHIP OF THE FEDERAL DEBT

On December 31, 1946, there was outstanding $259.5 billion in securities issued or guaranteed by the United States Government, excluding guaranteed securities held by the Treasury. At the end of 1960, the debt stood at $290.4 billion. (See Table 2-1.) During this fourteen-year period, massive shifts occurred in the ownership of the Federal debt.

[1] For a general coverage of this subject, see Tilford C. Gaines, *Techniques of Treasury Debt Management,* New York: Graduate School of Business, Columbia University, and The Free Press of Glencoe, 1962, chaps. 4, 5, pp. 93–152; Michael E. Levy, *Cycles in Government, I. Federal Debt and Its Ownership,* New York: National Industrial Conference Board, 1962; and Roland I. Robinson and Morris Mendelson, "The Market for United States Treasury Obligations" (Unpublished ms.), chap. 4.

TABLE 2-1   Estimated ownership of Federal securities[1]

	1946		1951		1960	
	Amt.	%	Amt.	%	Amt.	%
Total Federal securities outstanding[2]	259.5	100	259.5	100	290.4	100
Total held by banks	97.9	38	85.4	33	89.5	31
Commercial banks	74.5	29	61.6	24	62.1	22
Federal Reserve banks	23.3	9	23.8	9	27.4	9
U.S. Government investment accounts	30.9	12	42.3	16	55.1	19
Total held by private nonbank investors	130.7	50	131.8	51	145.8	50
Total held by individuals	64.2	25	64.6	25	64.7	23
Savings bonds	44.2	17	49.1	19	45.6	16
Other	20.1	8	15.5	6	19.1	7
Insurance companies	24.9	9	16.5	6	11.9	4
Mutual savings banks	11.8	5	9.8	4	6.3	2
Corporations	15.3	6	20.7	8	20.1	7
State and local governments	6.3	2	9.6	4	18.7	6
Miscellaneous investors[3]	8.1	3	10.6	4	24.2	8

[1] SOURCE: Treasury Bulletin. Amounts are in billions of dollars. Percentages have been computed and are based on total Federal securities outstanding. Data are for Dec. 31 of year indicated. Components may not add totals because of rounding.

[2] Securities issued or guaranteed by the United States Government, excluding guaranteed securities held by the Treasury.

[3] Includes savings and loan associations, nonprofit institutions, corporate pension trust funds, dealers and brokers, and investment of foreign balances in this country.

Commercial banks reduced their holdings from 29 to 22 percent of the outstanding debt. Insurance companies and mutual savings banks also markedly reduced their ownership of the debt. Insurance companies reduced their share from 9 to 4 percent. Mutual savings bank holdings declined from 5 to 2 percent.

The Federal Reserve System, individuals, and corporations maintained about the same relative positions, with 9, 23, and 7 percent, respectively, in 1960.

The securities which were sold or allowed to run off by the banks and insurance companies were absorbed by the United States Government investment accounts, state and local governments, and miscellaneous investors. The share of the United States Government investment accounts grew from 12 to 19 percent. State and local governments increased their share from 2 to 6 percent, and the miscellaneous-investor group increased its holdings from 3 to 8 percent.

The investment activities of financial intermediaries are determined by the complex of factors affecting the profitability possibilities and risk exposure of various asset and liability combinations within constraints imposed by law and the regulations of supervisory authorities. Typically these constraints severely restrict the choice of liabilities. These in turn influence the process of asset selection by affecting the investor's risk position. Operating constraints imposed by various governmental bodies may also restrict directly, or indirectly through the tax system, the choice of assets from among the array of anticipated earning possibilities appearing in the market place.[2]

Each asset holder is confronted by a unique environment. There is, on the other hand, a common characteristic among these environments, namely, that uncertainty necessarily attaches to the cash flows of financial intermediation. Successful management entails the minimization of the cost of synchronizing these cash flows. Holding a stock of cash increases costs in terms of investment earnings forgone. Holding zero cash increases investment returns, but it may also increase costs if relatively illiquid assets have to be liquidated unexpectedly. The crucial task of management, therefore, is to find the most profitable array of assets, an array which will consist of assets of varying degrees of earning capacity and liquidity. Relatively liquid investment media will be sought in place of cash so long as the interest return exceeds or, at the margin, just compensates for the increase in the cost of the uncertainty involved plus the cost of investment. Because they are relatively liquid, Government securities play a unique role in this process of portfolio selection. In the following discussion, this role will be considered for each of the major institutional investors.

COMMERCIAL BANKS

Commercial banks comprise the largest single investor group among institutional holders of Government securities.[3] At the end of the calendar year 1960, 23.7 percent of commercial bank assets were so invested.[4] (See Table 2-2.)

[2] See appendix for bibliographies on institutional portfolio policy and on the role of the Government securities portfolio in transmitting the effects of monetary policy.

[3] See appendix for a bibliography on commercial banks.

[4] Comparable data are not available for foreign agency banks. However, see Andrew F. Brimmer, "Foreign Banking Institutions in the United States Money Market," *Review of Economics and Statistics,* vol. 44, no. 1, February, 1962, pp. 76–81.

TABLE 2-2   Principal assets and liabilities of commercial banks[1]

	Amount	Percentage of total assets
Mortgages	28.8	
Other loans	91.7	
Total loans, gross	120.5	
Total loans, net of valuation reserves	118.1	45.7
Cash	52.2	20.2
Obligations of the U.S. Government	61.1	23.7
State and local obligations	17.6	6.8
Other securities	3.3	1.3
Real estate	3.2	1.2
Miscellaneous assets	2.7	1.1
Total assets	258.4	100.0
Demand deposits	156.8	60.7
Time deposits	73.7	28.5
Miscellaneous liabilities	6.8	2.6
Capital accounts	21.1	8.2
Total liabilities and capital accounts	258.4	100.0

[1] SOURCE: Federal Deposit Insurance Corporation, Report no. 54, Assets, Liabilities and Capital Accounts, Commercial and Mutual Savings Banks, Dec. 31, 1960. Amounts are in billions of dollars. Figures are for all commercial banks and nondeposit trust companies. Components may not add to totals because of rounding.

The impact of the nature of commercial bank liabilities upon the structure of commercial bank assets is immediately apparent. With minor exceptions, commercial banks are the only financial institutions which are permitted by law to accept deposits subject to sight drafts. About 60 percent of commercial bank liabilities fall into this category. The demand nature of these liabilities plus the existence of legal cash-reserve requirements largely account for the fact that cash assets and Government securities combined amount to about 44 percent of commercial bank assets.

Specifically, Government securities perform four important roles in commercial bank portfolio policy, namely, in serving as pledged assets, in meeting solvency standards, in making money-position adjustments, and in providing a medium for tax switching.

Commercial banks are required by law to put up collateral in numerous instances. In each case Government securities are acceptable, and more often than not they are preferred, as pledged assets. The primary use of Governments in this regard is to collateralize the deposits of the United States Treasury. To act as a Treasury depositary, a commercial bank must place in the hands of the district Federal Reserve bank or branch a block of securities whose discounted value for pledging purposes is equal to the deposit liability.[5] Similar requirements exist in the case of trust-account deposits or public deposits owned by a state or one of its political subdivisions. Finally, although the locale of the borrowing transaction is still called the discount window, rediscounting is practically a lost art. With few exceptions, member banks "go into the Fed" by borrowing on their own notes with Government securities, acceptable at par, as collateral. Thus the Government securities which serve as pledged assets form the basic part of a commercial bank's Government portfolio.

The second basic function performed by the Government securities portfolio is to shore up the capital position in defense of a commercial bank's solvency. Prior to World War II, supervisory authorities regularly appraised a bank's position by applying, among other measures, the 10 percent capital-deposit ratio as a standard for solvency. With the expansion of the banking system provided by the Federal Reserve System to enable the banks to do the major share of World War II financing, the capital-deposit ratio fell rapidly below the conventional norm. Wisely as well as expeditiously, examiners incorporated the Government portfolio into their measure of a bank's defensive position. At year-end, 1960, the ratio of capital to total assets other than cash and United States Government securities stood at a healthy 14.5 percent level.[6]

The third and most important function performed by the Government securities portfolio is its utilization in the adjustment of a commercial bank's money position. A commercial bank is subject to a wide variety of cash flows. Cash inflows may take the form of new deposits due to transfers from another bank, a currency inflow, the calling of a loan, the maturing of a loan or security, the amortization of a term loan, the sinking-fund retirement of a bond, sales of own or portfolio securities, borrowing, and dividend and interest receipts. A release of existing cash

[5] See appendix for a bibliography on Treasury Tax and Loan Accounts.

[6] According to the "Form for Analyzing Bank Capital" developed by the Board of Governors of the Federal Reserve System, capital requirements vary according to the quality and maturity of the asset. For the approach employed by the Federal Reserve Bank of New York, see Howard D. Crosse, *Management Policies for Commercial Banks*, Englewood Cliffs, N.J.: Prentice-Hall, Inc., 1962, pp 169–173.

occurs as the result of the extinguishment of existing liabilities. Cash outflows take the form of a loss of deposits due to the commitment of existing cash through the creation of new liabilities in making a loan, purchasing a security or mortgage, or settling a debt; a currency drain; the payment of operating costs including taxes; and dividend and interest payments. Some of these flows can be controlled by the bank, while others are beyond its control. Those whose net sum measures the magnitude of the necessary adjustment in the money position are of both kinds. Trend factors aside, there are three purposes for which adjustments must be made, namely, seasonal, contingency, and speculative.

A number of the cash flows affecting the money position over time tend to manifest a seasonal pattern. The most important seasonal factors are loan demand and currency drains.[7] The time patterns of each of these factors can be predicted with a reasonable degree of accuracy on the basis of a knowledge of the business characteristics and currency-using habits of the bank's customers. Once the time-path forecast is made, it is incumbent upon the manager of the bank's money position to have the cash available according to schedule. To some degree, this may be accomplished by synchronizing the maturity of investment securities with the need for cash. Government securities are ideal for this purpose because of the wide range of maturities available in both the new-issue and secondary markets and because of the ease[8] with which they may be acquired if recourse is had to the secondary market.

The second important adjustment role of the Government securities portfolio is in providing a potential source of cash to meet unforeseen contingencies. When such a contingency arises, the money manager may have four alternative courses of action. First, he may buy Federal funds.[9] That is, a bank may borrow the deposits which other banks have with a Federal Reserve bank. These are funds which are cash today in the sense that clearinghouse funds may not become cash, as far as a Federal Reserve bank is concerned, until tomorrow.[10]

Second, a bank in need of cash may refuse to renew repurchase agreements (RPs) with Government securities dealers or loans to

---

[7] See appendix for a bibliography on factors affecting member bank reserves.

[8] That is, relatively large blocks of Government securities may be purchased without driving up the price.

[9] See appendix for a bibliography on the Federal funds market.

[10] This is the case in New York City.

securities dealers or brokers.[11] Though RPs are made with a definite maturity date, there is typically a tacit understanding that they carry a two-way call option. Loans to brokers and dealers partake of the nature of customer loans; but they are, in fact, call loans. Moreover, the terms are subject to daily renegotiation; and a substantial hike in the interest rate is an effective substitute for an outright call.

Third, a member bank may seek accommodation at the discount window.[12] With the exception, perhaps, of the money-market banks, going into the Federal involves all the anxieties connected with being in debt to the central bank. Presumably, continuous resort may not be had to the lender of last resort!

The adjustment which occurs with any sense of finality consists of sales from the investment portfolio, typically Government securities. *Ceteris paribus,* short-term obligations are the most satisfactory adjustment media.[13] Thus, 13 percent of commercial bank holdings of marketable Government securities are in Treasury bills; 29 percent mature within one year. (See Table 2-3.)

[11] See appendix for a bibliography on dealer financing.

[12] See appendix for a bibliography on discount policy.

[13] The greater liquidity of shorter-term securities is demonstrated by the following example.

Assume a ninety-day bill with a 0.75 discount. Then $r = (dT/ft) (100)$ (see Chap. 1 for an explanation of this formula), or

$$r_s = \frac{(0.75)\ (360)\ (100)}{(100)\ (90)} = 3 \text{ per cent.}$$

Also assume a 360-day bill with a 3.00 discount. In this case

$$r_t = \frac{(3)\ (360)\ (100)}{(100)\ (360)} = 3 \text{ per cent.}$$

Now suppose that the price of each bill declines by 1.00 on the issue date. Then

$$r_s = \frac{(1.75)\ (360)\ (100)}{(100)\ (90)} = 7 \text{ per cent,}$$

and

$$r_t = \frac{(4)\ (360)\ (100)}{(100)\ (360)} = 4 \text{ per cent.}$$

This example shows that for a given price decline, the interest rate increases more for the short-term bill. Consequently, lenders will normally prevent such a rise in yield and decline in price for the shorter security. Thus the slope of the demand curve facing the seller of a block of short-term securities tends to be relatively small numerically. Consequently, they may be said to be relatively liquid.

TABLE 2-3 Composition of institutional portfolios of marketable Government securities[1]

Security classifications	Total amount outstanding		6,314 commercial banks[2]		512 mutual savings banks[3]		307 life insurance companies		529 fire, casualty, and marine insurance companies	
	Amt.	% of total	Amt.	% of total	Amt.	% of total	Amt.	% of total	Amt.	% of total
Type of security:										
Treasury bills	39,446	20.9	6,976	12.9	144	2.4	137	3.0	204	4.7
Certificates of indebtedness	18,442	9.7	2,573	4.7	143	2.4	37	0.8	109	2.5
Treasury notes	51,284	27.1	16,947	31.2	1,190	20.0	282	6.1	1,093	24.9
Treasury bonds	79,794	42.2	27,754	51.1	4,466	74.9	4,161	89.9	2,970	67.7
Panama Canal bonds	50	[5]	9	[5]			3		5	0.1
Guaranteed by U.S. Government	155	0.1	9	[5]	17	0.3	9	0.2	4	0.1
Total	189,170		54,269		5,961		4,630		4,384	
By call classes:										
Within 1 year	84,028	44.4	19,843	36.6	620	10.4	289	6.2	1,138	26.0
1–5 years	75,274	39.8	29,838	54.9	2,987	50.1	1,465	31.6	2,416	55.1
5–10 years	16,552	8.7	3,896	7.2	932	15.6	1,068	23.1	528	12.0
10–15 years	1,123	0.6	84	0.2	142	2.4	32	0.7	33	0.8
15–20 years	3,126	1.7	159	0.3	181	3.0	311	6.7	85	1.9
20 years and over	8,911	4.7	441	0.8	1,083	18.2	1,456	31.4	179	4.1
Guaranteed securities	155	0.1	9	[5]	17	0.3	9	0.2	4	0.1
By maturity classes:										
Within 1 year	75,315	39.8	16,002	29.4	480	8.1	222	4.8	748	17.1
1–5 years	70,812	37.4	30,291	55.8	1,544	25.9	401	8.7	2,078	47.4
5–10 years	18,684	9.9	5,654	10.4	1,849	31.0	1,172	25.3	903	20.6
10–15 years	11,697	6.2	1,670	3.1	770	12.9	1,052	22.7	381	8.7
15–20 years	1,527	0.8	106	0.2	127	2.1	220	4.8	49	1.1
Over 20 years	10,979	5.8	538	1.0	1,174	19.7	1,553	33.5	222	5.1
Guaranteed securities	155	0.1	9	[5]	17	0.3	9	0.2	4	0.1
By tax status:										
Exempt from U.S. income tax	50	[5]	9	[5]	[6]		3	0.1	5	0.1
Partially exempt from U.S. income tax	1,485	0.8	1,305	2.4	[6]		6	[5]	30	0.7
Subject to U.S. income tax	187,635	99.2	52,955	97.6	5,961	100.0	4,626	99.9	4,349	99.2

[1] SOURCE: Treasury Bulletin and Federal Reserve Bulletin. Amounts are in millions of dollars. Figures are for Dec. 31, 1960.
[2] Excludes trust departments, but includes trust companies and stock savings banks.
[3] Excludes trust departments.

54

TABLE 2-3   Composition of institutional portfolios of marketable Government securities (continued)

Security classifications	489 savings and loan associations Amt.	% of total	497 corporations Amt.	% of total	Federal Reserve banks Amt.	% of total	U.S. Government investment accounts Amt.	% of total	Held by all other investors[4] Amt.	% of total	Memo item: 12,490 corporate pension funds Amt.	% of total
Type of security:												
Treasury bills	163	6.6	5,599	52.1	3,217	11.7	591	7.2	22,415	31.5	333	19.5
Certificates of indebtedness	57	2.3	1,331	12.4	9,082	33.2	461	5.6	4,649	6.5	63	3.7
Treasury notes	510	20.7	1,712	15.9	12,519	45.7	1,770	21.6	15,260	21.4	423	24.7
Treasury bonds	1,724	70.1	2,099	19.5	2,566	9.4	5,294	64.6	28,758	40.4	889	52.0
Panama Canal bonds									32	[5]	[6]	[5]
Guaranteed by U.S. Government	6	0.2					81	1.0	29	[5]	2	0.1
Total	2,460		10,741		27,384		8,198		71,143		1,710	
By call classes:												
Within 1 year	451	18.3	8,747	81.4	16,237	59.3	1,727	21.0	34,977	49.2	572	33.5
1–5 years	1,000	40.7	1,911	17.8	10,869	39.7	3,367	41.1	21,421	30.1	666	38.9
5–10 years	520	21.1	39	0.4	250	0.9	1,543	18.8	7,776	10.9	174	10.2
10–15 years	42	1.7	10	0.1			203	2.5	577	0.8	29	1.7
15–20 years	83	3.4	1	[5]			384	4.7	1,922	2.7	87	5.1
20 years and over	358	14.6	32	0.3	28	0.1	893	10.9	4,441	6.2	180	10.5
Guaranteed securities	6	0.2					81	1.0	29	[5]	2	0.1
By maturity classes:												
Within 1 year	324	13.2	8,366	77.9	15,223	55.6	1,482	18.1	32,467	45.6	523	30.6
1–5 years	856	34.8	2,243	20.9	10,711	39.1	2,431	29.7	20,259	28.5	554	32.4
5–10 years	473	19.2	58	0.5	1,179	4.3	1,601	19.5	5,794	8.1	238	13.9
10–15 years	351	14.3	39	0.4	243	0.9	1,224	14.9	5,967	8.4	116	6.8
15–20 years	45	1.8	6	[5]			237	2.9	744	1.0	37	2.2
Over 20 years	406	16.5	33	0.3	28	0.1	1,140	13.9	5,886	8.3	241	14.1
Guaranteed securities	6	0.2					81	1.0	29	[5]	2	0.1
By tax status:												
Exempt from U.S. income tax									32	[5]	[6]	[5]
Partially exempt from U.S. income tax	2	0.1	26	0.2	6	[5]	6	[5]	122	0.2	[6]	[5]
Subject to U.S. income tax	2,459	99.9	10,715	99.8	27,384	100.0	8,198	100.0	70,989	99.8	1,710	100.0

[4] Includes banks, insurance companies, savings and loan associations, and corporations not reporting in the Treasury Survey of Ownership. Also includes holdings of the corporate pension funds appearing in the memo item.
[5] Less than 0.05 percent.
[6] Less than $500,000.

In the event there is a surfeit of cash, each of these actions may be reversed. The bank may sell funds, it may negotiate RPs or make call loans, indebtedness to the Federal may be extinguished, or Government securities may be acquired. In any case, the choice of the means of adjustment when a bank is confronted by an unforeseen contingency is affected by the interest cost involved, the expected duration of the need for funds, the degree of credit rationing by the regional Federal Reserve bank, and the predilections of bank management.

The third purpose of a portfolio adjustment is speculative in nature and is undertaken in a cyclical context. Typically, the process is described by some statement to the effect that a commercial bank always takes care of loan demand first. Then, if unused resources remain, investment securities are acquired. This, however, is a superficial description of a complicated portfolio decision involving an interest-rate forecast. More precisely, it involves an expected-returns forecast. In other words, there is always a surfeit of loan demand in the sense of borrower needs and willingness to pay, especially during cyclical lows, when demand is said to be lacking. Unfortunately, the prospective borrower's evaluation of the marginal efficiency of capital tends, in those times, to be more sanguine than the banker's. Thus if a banker rejects a borrower's request and buys a Government security instead, he is implicitly assuming a higher return on the latter investment. Moreover, his choice of maturity clearly involves a forecast of the duration of the cyclical decline.

Bankers have sometimes been counseled to defend their liquidity position by shortening the maturity of the Government securities portfolio as investments give way to loans in the cyclical upswing. In fact, they may sell off their Treasury bills first. This procedure makes sense, however, if it is felt that the peak in interest rates has been attained. In this case, the rational policy consists, precisely, of lengthening the term structure of the portfolio.[14]

Finally, Government securities perform a unique function in commercial bank portfolios as a medium for tax switching. A commercial

[14] Some aspects of this issue are dealt with, inferentially at least, in the literature on the availability doctrine. (See appendix for a bibliography on the role of the Government securities portfolio in transmitting the effects of monetary policy.) In this literature, however, the maturity parameter is invariably suppressed. In other words, to treat the problem in full compass, one must introduce the term structure of potential portfolio inputs before solving for the ideal liquidity-yield mix.

bank is, in general, taxed in the same manner and at the same rates as other corporations.[15] However, net capital losses realized from the sale of securities may be deducted from taxable income.[16] Capital gains, on the other hand, when realized from securities held more than six months and in excess of realized capital losses, are subject to only a 25 percent tax.[17] These rules apply only to securities initially issued at par. Capital gains realized from securities issued at a discount, such as Treasury bills, are subject to regular income tax rates.[18]

As a consequence of these provisions of the tax law, commercial banks may reduce their taxable income, in those years when they do not realize capital gains, by deliberately selling securities in order to incur a capital loss.[19] This operation is distinct from the decision either to slough a Government security for the purpose of acquiring a more profitable loan or to shift the maturity composition of the portfolio in order to take advantage of expected changes in interest rates. Such exchanges of assets are, of course, encouraged by the provisions of the tax law now being discussed. But suppose that all such exchanges which appear profitable have been accomplished. Then, on top of these operations, a commercial bank may still engage in tax switches that will improve its after-tax profit position. This is true because tax switches do not entail any fundamental shift in portfolio composition. Indeed, were it permitted to do so by the Bureau of Internal Revenue, a bank would sell and repurchase precisely the same security. Such a transaction would, of course, be too much of a good thing; so the Bureau of Internal Revenue has issued rulings designed to prevent such wash sales.[20] It is then the job of the portfolio manager to find, within the

[15] Sec. 11, Internal Revenue Code of 1954, as amended and in force on Jan. 3, 1961.

[16] Sec. 582, Internal Revenue Code of 1954, as amended and in force on Jan. 3, 1961.

[17] Secs. 1201 and 1222, Internal Revenue Code of 1954, as amended and in force on Jan. 3, 1961.

[18] See Chap. 1. On the other hand, if a security is purchased at a premium, the premium may be amortized on a straight-line basis, and the amortizable premium is tax-deductible.

[19] See, e.g., L. W. Seidman, "Proper Handling of Bond Account Can Yield Better Income for Banks through Lower Tax," *American Banker,* Nov. 22, 1957.

[20] See, e.g., "Loss from Wash Sales of Stock or Securities," *Internal Revenue Bulletin,* no. 1958–19, May 12, 1958, pp. 23–33. Also see sec. 1091(a), Internal Revenue Code of 1954, as amended and in force on Jan. 3, 1961. The Internal

constraints imposed by the Treasury Department, securities for purchase which closely resemble those sold but are sufficiently differen-
tiated to meet the standards required to avoid the wash-sale indict-
ment.

Government securities are preeminently desirable media for tax
switching because of the relatively good market which they command.
If, for example, corporate or municipal obligations were employed, it
is possible that the market would move so markedly against the bank,
both as buyer and seller, that the loss directly involved in the exchange
would wipe out the gain from the tax switch. In other words, a successful tax switch requires the sale—albeit at less than the original purchase price—and repurchase of a similar security at about the same
price.

Since commercial banks are subject to the corporate income tax,
they are especially interested in the tax-exempt feature. Consequently,
they hold the lion's share of available partially exempt Governments
and a substantial portion of wholly exempt Governments. (See Table
2-3.) For the same reason, they are heavily invested in state and local
obligations.[21] Commercial banks are permitted a tax-deductible allocation to a reserve for bad debts equal to a proportion, not exceeding 5
percent, of eligible loans based on its loss experience of any twenty
consecutive years after 1927.[22]

Revenue Service has ruled that no loss may be deducted if, within a period
beginning thirty days before the sale and ending thirty days afterward (a
period of sixty-one days), the taxpayer has acquired substantially identical
securities. Prior rulings indicate that differences with respect to eligibility
for purchase by commercial banks and with respect to payment of Federal
estate taxes are considered substantial. At the same time, the following differences have been considered unsubstantial: differences in interest-payment
dates, denominations, form (i.e., registered or coupon), call provisions, maturity, and issue dates. It is possible that differences in type (i.e., note, bond,
etc.), yield, and coupon rates may be considered substantial.

[21] See Table 2-2. Another reason for holding municipals, at least temporarily, is that restrictions against commercial bank underwriting apply only to
corporate obligations. See 12 U.S.C. § 378. The rule against commercial bank
underwriting is also usually interpreted so as to include state and local revenue
bonds, as opposed to general-obligation issues.

[22] See Commissioner of Internal Revenue, Com. Mimeograph Coll. no.
6209, *Reserve Method of Accounting for Bad Debts in the Case of Banks,*
Washington, D.C.: Treasury Department, Dec. 8, 1947; and Internal Revenue
Service, IR-mimeograph no. 54–55, *Reserve Method of Accounting for Bad*

INSURANCE COMPANIES

Second in importance among private financial institutions as holders of Government securities are the insurance companies.[23] In the case of life companies, 5.4 percent of total assets are in Government securities. (See Table 2-4.) This relatively low proportion may be attributed

TABLE 2-4   Principal assets and liabilities of life insurance companies[1]

	Amount	Percentage of total assets[2]
Obligations of the U.S. Government	6.4	5.4
State and local obligations	4.6	3.8
Other securities	52.5	43.9
Mortgages	41.8	34.9
Real estate	3.8	3.1
Miscellaneous assets	10.5	8.8
Total assets	119.6	100.0
Policy reserves	98.5	82.4
Policy-dividend accumulations	3.4	2.8
Set aside for policy dividends	1.8	1.5
Other obligations	6.3	5.3
Capital and surplus	9.6	8.0
Total liabilities and capital accounts	119.6	100.0

[1] SOURCE: Institute of Life Insurance, Life Insurance Fact Book, 1961. Amounts are in billions of dollars. Figures are for Dec. 31, 1960
[2] Percentages may not add to 100 because of rounding.

to the nature of life company liabilities and to the fact that cash flows tend to be positive and may be predicted with some degree of accuracy. Since life policies are usually purchased relatively early in the period of life expectancy, the obligation to make a benefit payment is long-term in nature. The major cash inflows of life companies are due to premium receipts, calls and maturing loans and securities, the amortization of direct placements and mortgages, sinking-fund retirement of bonds, sales of portfolio and own securities, and interest and dividend receipts. The chief outflows are due to benefit payments, making direct

Debts in the Case of Banks, Washington, D.C.: Treasury Department, Apr. 18, 1954.
[23] See Table 2-1. See appendix for a bibliography on insurance companies.

placements and policy loans, the purchase of securities and mortgages, operating costs including taxes, and dividend payments.

Cash outflows due to benefit payments may be predicted on the basis of mortality tables. Cash inflows that are the result of premium receipts, the amortization of direct-placement and mortgage loans, and corporate bond sinking-fund payments may also be predicted fairly accurately. These facts plus the positive nature of the net cash flow would seem to eliminate the need for Government securities as a source of liquidity. Only 3 percent of the marketable Government securities portfolio is in Treasury bills, and only 4.8 percent mature within one year. (See Table 2-3.) The chief reason for holding any Governments at all is to compensate for the errors made in synchronizing the actual inflow of cash with commitments made to take up mortgage loans and to meet the takedown on direct placements.

Life companies are subject to a complicated tax formula involving four components of income. The first is investment income. The policyholders' share of investment income is nontaxable. The company's share—subject to the corporate income tax—is the excess of actual investment income over the interest return required to maintain reserves when reserves are valued at the lower of the company's earned interest rate and the average interest rate earned over the past five years.

The second component of taxable income consists of underwriting gains. These are defined as the net return from operations less taxable investment income.

Step three in the tax computation applies only to stock companies. At this point are added distributions to stockholders out of earnings retained formerly on a tax-exempt basis. The final step consists of computing capital gains subject to the usual capital gains tax.[24]

The impact of this tax formula, introduced in 1959, is not yet apparent. But the relatively light tax burden borne by life companies prior to the 1959 law is evident in their lack of interest in tax-exempt securities. (See Tables 2-3 and 2-4.)

The classification of the cash flows of property insurance companies is similar to that of the life industry. On the other hand, the maturity of liabilities is more uncertain, and related cash flows are difficult to predict.

[24] Secs. 801, 802, 804, 805, 806, 809, 810, 811, 812, 815, and 817, Internal Revenue Code of 1954, as amended and in force Jan. 3, 1961.

Investments of property insurance carriers, therefore, are more liquid in character than those of life companies. Property companies normally reinsure in order to spread the risk of localized disasters. Still, they must be prepared to meet possibly large though random and non-cumulative demands from policyholders. Liquidity is therefore more important to them than to life companies. Fire, casualty, and marine insurance companies have 4.7 percent of their Treasuries in bills, and 17.1 percent mature in less than one year. (See Table 2-3.)

The tax status of property insurers differs from that of life companies. For property companies, contributions to reserves are not allow-

TABLE 2-5   *Principal assets and liabilities of fire, casualty, and marine insurance companies*[1]

	Amount	Percentage of total assets[2]
Cash	1.4	4.7
Obligations of the U.S. Government	5.7	19.0
State and local obligations	5.1	17.0
Other bonds	4.9	16.5
Common stock	8.6	28.9
Preferred stock	0.8	2.7
Mortgages	0.1	0.3
Real estate	0.5	1.7
Miscellaneous assets	2.7	9.1
Total assets	29.8	100.0
Losses-adjustment expense	7.8	26.2
Unearned premiums	8.4	28.2
Other liabilities	1.8	6.1
Surplus and capital paid in	9.9	33.2
Voluntary reserves	1.9	6.4
Total liabilities and capital accounts	29.8	100.0

[1] SOURCE: Adapted by the Treasury Department from Alfred M. Best and Company, Aggregates and Averages, 1961. Amounts are in billions of dollars. Figures are for Dec. 31, 1960, and cover stock, mutual, Lloyds, and reciprocal companies.
[2] Percentages may not add to 100 because of rounding.

able. Premiums and investment income, as well as underwriting income, are fully taxable. Payoffs for losses are deductible, however.[25] Hence property carriers are more sensitive than life companies to the tax status of investment securities. (See Tables 2-3 and 2-5.)

[25] Secs. 831 and 832, Internal Revenue Code of 1954, as amended and in force Jan. 3, 1961.

MUTUAL SAVINGS BANKS

Mutual savings banks rank next among private financial institutions as holders of Government securities.[26] Savings banks normally do not accept demand deposits. Hence their Government securities portfolio, which amounts to 15.3 percent of total assets, is less important than in the case of commercial banks. (See Tables 2-2 and 2-6.) On the other

TABLE 2-6   *Principal assets and liabilities of mutual savings banks*[1]

	Amount	Percentage of total assets
Cash	0.9	2.2
Obligations of the U.S. Government	6.2	15.3
State and local obligations	0.7	1.7
Other securities	5.1	12.6
Mortgages	26.7	65.8
Real estate	0.3	0.7
Miscellaneous assets	0.7	1.7
Total assets	40.6	100.0
Demand deposits	[2]	[2]
Time deposits	36.3	89.4
Miscellaneous liabilities	0.7	1.7
Reserve accounts	3.6	8.9
Total liabilities	40.6	100.0

[1] SOURCE: Federal Deposit Insurance Corporation, Report no. 54, Assets, Liabilities and Capital Accounts, Commercial and Mutual Savings Banks, Dec. 31, 1960. Amounts are in billions of dollars. See also National Association of Mutual Savings Banks, Mutual Savings Banking Annual Report, May, 1961.

[2] Demand deposits are $33,251, a negligible proportion of total assets.

hand, savings bank deposit liabilities are usually met upon presentation of the depositor's passbook and must ordinarily be met in full after a maximum of thirty days' notice. The Government securities position is thus strong relative to that of nonbanking institutions.

The cash flows of savings banks are similar in many respects to those of commercial banks. Inflows are primarily due to new deposits, maturing bonds and mortgages, amortization of mortgages and sinking-fund payment of bonds, sales of portfolio securities, and dividend and in-

[26] (See Table 2-1.) See appendix for a bibliography on mutual savings banks.

terest receipts. Outflows, in the main, are due to the loss of deposits, the purchase of mortgages and bonds, operating costs including taxes, and interest payments.

These flows can be predicted fairly accurately, with the important exception of deposit losses. Moreover, even though deposits are not subject to sight drafts, savings bankers prefer to keep sufficiently liquid to meet customer withdrawals on demand, withdrawals which might be large and cumulative. This fact further explains the importance of the Government securities portfolio, as well as its structure. Of total mutual savings bank holdings of marketable Government securities, 2.4 percent are in Treasury bills, and 8.1 percent mature within one year. (See Table 2-3.)

Mutual savings banks are taxed in the same manner as commercial banks except with regard to allocations to loss reserves. Under the statutory formula,[27] additions to reserves for bad debts are limited to (1) an amount based on the loss experience for unsecured loans, plus (2) an amount not exceeding the greatest of (a) 60 percent of income less the amount of (1) above, but limited to a magnitude that would not increase the reserve for secured loans above 6 percent of such loans; (b) the difference between 3 percent of secured loans at the end of the year and the reserve for secured loans at the beginning of the year less losses charged to reserves during the year; and (c) an amount based upon loss experience for secured loans. In addition, there is an over-all limitation to the effect that such allocations may be made on a tax-deferred basis only so long as total reserves, including undivided profits and surplus, do not exceed 12 percent of deposit liabilities. As a result of their relatively favorable tax status, mutual savings banks have not been attracted by the lower yields obtainable from tax-exempt securities. (See Tables 2-3 and 2-6.)

SAVINGS AND LOAN ASSOCIATIONS

Among private financial institutions, savings and loan associations had the smallest holdings of Government securities at the end of calendar year 1960.[28] These accounted for 6.4 percent of total savings and loan

[27] See sec. 6, Public Law 87–834, 87th Congress, H.R. 10650, Oct. 16, 1962. This section amends sec. 593, Internal Revenue Code of 1954, as amended and in force Jan. 3, 1961.

[28] See appendix for a bibliography on savings and loan associations.

association assets. (See Table 2-7.) The relatively unimportant role given the Government securities portfolio is explained by the fact that these savings institutions do not accept deposits. Rather, savings capital consists of shares of ownership or fractions of shares.

TABLE 2-7   *Principal assets and liabilities of savings and loan associations*[1]

	Amount	Percentage of total assets[2]
Cash	2.7	3.8
Obligations of the U.S. Government	4.6	6.4
Mortgages	60.1	84.0
Real estate	0.1	0.1
Miscellaneous assets	4.0	5.6
Total assets	71.5	100.0
Savings capital	62.1	86.9
Miscellaneous liabilities	4.4	6.1
Reserve accounts	5.0	7.0
Total liabilities	71.5	100.0

[1] SOURCE: Federal Home Loan Bank Board, Chart Book, 1963, no. 8. Amounts are in billions of dollars. Figures are for Dec. 31, 1960.
[2] Percentages may not add to 100 because of rounding.

The chief cash inflows of savings and loan associations consist of receipts from the sale of shares or fractions of shares, the maturing of mortgages and bonds, the amortization of mortgages, sales of portfolio securities, borrowing, and interest receipts. The outflows are due to the repurchase of own shares or fractions thereof, the purchase of mortgages and securities, the repayment of debt, operating costs including taxes, and dividend payments.

Although they are not required to do so, savings and loan associations emulate banking institutions by repurchasing outstanding shares or fractions thereof whenever a customer wants cash. This is the chief factor among savings and loan association cash flows which gives rise to a demand for liquidity. And it accounts for the relatively high proportion of savings and loan association holdings in short-term instruments. Treasury bills account for 6.6 percent, maturities with one year

13.2 percent, of their marketable Government securities portfolio.[29] (See Table 2-3.)

The tax treatment accorded savings and loan associations is similar to that of the mutual savings banks.[30]

CORPORATE PENSION TRUST FUNDS

Corporate pension trust funds are rapidly growing newcomers to the area of financial intermediation.[31] Although solid information on the corporate pension field is still hard to come by, it is thought that the bulk of these schemes are of the level-of-benefit variety. Under such schemes, a specific level of benefits will be paid to employees as service requirements are fulfilled. These obligations may be insured, but more often they are funded through a bank-administered trust. Although there is no guarantee that the trust fund will produce sufficient income to make all benefit payments, it is incumbent upon a going concern to meet any deficiencies.

The stream of cash flowing into a pension fund is composed principally of employer and employee contributions, maturing securities, sinking-fund payments on bonds, sales of securities, and dividend and interest receipts. Benefit payments, the acquisition of securities, and operating costs comprise the outflow. Insured plans are subject to the same restrictions on investment outlets as are insurance companies. Trusteed plans, on the other hand, enjoy a relatively high degree of freedom in their investment activities.

Investment-policy constraints plus the contingency that benefit payments might exceed investment income apparently explain the demand for Government securities. Thus 7 percent of the total assets of corporate pension funds are allocated to the Government sphere. (See Table 2-8.) Of the marketable Government securities portfolio, 19.5 percent is in Treasury bills, and 30.6 percent matures within a year.

---

[29] In the case of member institutions, the demand for Governments as a source of liquidity is reduced by the availability of loans from the Federal Home Loan Bank System.

[30] Sec. 6, Public Law 87–834, 87th Congress, H.R. 10650, Oct. 16, 1962, amending sec. 593, Internal Revenue Code of 1954, as amended and in force Jan. 3, 1961.

[31] See appendix for a bibliography on private pension funds.

(See Table 2-3.) These proportions would seem, in view of the relatively recent popularity of retirement systems, to indicate that fund managers attach a high priority to the early provision for a defensive liquidity position. Since the investment income of pension funds is not subject to tax,[32] few of their resources are allocated to the tax-exempt securities. (See Tables 2-3 and 2-8.)

TABLE 2-8   Assets of corporate pension funds[1]

Assets	Amount	Percentage of total assets[2]
Cash	0.4	1.4
Obligations of the U.S. Government	2.1	7.1
Mortgages	0.9	3.0
Corporate obligations	25.6	84.3
Other assets	1.3	4.3
Total	30.3	100.0

[1] SOURCE: Securities and Exchange Commission. Amounts are in billions of dollars. Figures are for Dec. 31, 1960.
[2] Percentages do not add to 100 because of rounding.

NONFINANCIAL CORPORATIONS

The largest private institutional holders of Government securities outside the commercial banking sector are the nonfinancial corporations.[33] Holdings of $20.1 billion by these institutions account for 7 percent of the total outstanding at the end of calendar year 1960. (See Table 2-1.) The growing importance as suppliers of funds of these traditional occupants of the demand side of the money and capital markets has been a concomitant of the attempt to perfect techniques of cash management by corporate treasurers and comptrollers. The inflow of corporate cash stems from product sales, the sale of the corporation's own securities, the maturity of, and sinking-fund payments on, portfolio securities, the maturity of loans, sales of portfolio securities, and interest and dividend receipts. An outflow of corporate cash results from operating costs including taxes, outlays on capital goods, sinking-fund and installment payments on outstanding obligations, the ma-

[32] Sec. 501, Internal Revenue Code of 1954, as amended and in force on Jan. 3, 1961.
[33] See appendix for a bibliography on corporate cash management.

turity and repurchase of outstanding own securities and obligations, making loans and the purchase of portfolio securities, and dividend and interest payments.

The dimensions of these cash flows are variegated with respect to size and geographical pattern, and they present a fascinating challenge in economy. Outlays can be predicted with a fair degree of accuracy; receipts are more haphazard. Their failure to mesh over time, along with the costs of securities transactions, gives rise to a need for a stock of cash. Why, then, is there a need for Governments or other liquid investment media? A stock of cash of given size will prevent embarrassing calls for bank accommodation. That is, cash, as usual, is a good antidote for uncertainty. Corporate interest in short-term investment media, as in the case of other asset holders, can be explained in part by an interest return which more than compensates or, at the margin, just compensates for the modest increase in the cost of uncertainty involved in substituting relatively liquid securities for cash. In part, also, the demand for such securities is due to known needs for cash whose time dimensions are such that more profitable uses of existing funds are lacking. Such needs arise in anticipation of payments, say, to shareholders, bondholders, contractors, or the tax collector.

The importance of Government securities as a short-term investment outlet is reflected in the fact that over 86 percent of the total short-term securities portfolios of 276 large corporations were Government obligations in 1955. (See Table 2-9.) The short-term nature of corporate demand for noncash liquidity explains the fact that 52.1 percent of their marketable Government securities portfolio is in Treasury bills and 77.9 percent is in maturities of less than one year. (See Table 2-3.)

UNITED STATES INVESTMENT ACCOUNTS

In addition to private institutions, public pools of investable funds share in the demand for Government securities. Such are the United States Government accounts.[34] These funds held $55.1 billion in Governments, or 19 percent of the outstanding debt, at the end of 1960. (See Table 2-1.) Treasury bills accounted for 7.2 percent and maturities within one year 18.1 percent of their Government holdings.

[34] See appendix for a bibliography on the United States investment accounts.

TABLE 2-9   Short-term investment portfolio of 276 large
nonfinancial corporations[1]

	Amount	Percentage of total securities
Government securities:		
91-day bills	3,177.0	26.9
180 days or less	2,809.3	23.8
181 days–1 year	2,461.9	20.9
1–2 years	888.8	7.5
2–3 years	572.1	4.9
3 years and over	306.5	2.6
Total Governments	10,215.6	86.6
Securities held under RPs		
(mostly Treasuries)	643.8	5.5
Agencies	118.6	1.0
Tax-exempts:		
1 year or less	224.5	1.9
Over 1 year	15.9	0.1
Foreign government securities	81.3	0.7
Finance company paper	280.9	2.4
Commercial paper	163.3	1.4
All other securities	45.9	0.4
Total securities	11,789.8	100.0
Cash	6,418.6	
Other current assets	27,814.8	
Total current assets	46,023.2	

[1] SOURCE: Charles E. Silberman, "The Big Corporate Lenders," Fortune, vol. 54, no. 2, August, 1956, pp. 111–114. Amounts are in millions of dollars. Data are for Nov. 30 or Dec. 31, 1955.

(See Table 2-3.) There are fifty-two trust funds and other accounts managed by the Treasury Department in addition to those few handled by the agencies themselves. Eight of the Treasury-managed funds account for $51.1 billion out of the total of $55.1 billion in Governments. (See Table 2-10.) Unlike most other investor groups, the United States investment accounts are, for the most part, restricted by law to Government obligations. Moreover, in managing these accounts, the Secretary of the Treasury is duty-bound to do the best he can for those who own the funds. He is therefore handicapped in performing his function as chief manager of the public debt. Within limits, however, these funds can be, and have been, employed as an instrument of debt-management policy. It must be understood, of course, that even though temporary objectives in the debt-management area may be achieved,

TABLE 2-10   Treasury-managed trust funds with holdings of Government securities in excess of $1 billion[1]

Trust fund	Total Government holdings	Public issues	Special issues
Federal Old-age and Survivors Insurance Trust Fund	19,128	3,346[2]	15,782
Federal Employees Retirement Funds	10,407	633	9,774
National Service Life Insurance Fund	5,760		5,760
Railroad Retirement Account	3,591	256	3,335
Federal Deposit Insurance Corporation	2,319	1,701	618
Federal Disability Insurance Trust Fund	2,180	87[2]	2,093
Government Life Insurance Fund	1,078		1,078
Unemployment Trust Fund	6,638	1,091[2]	5,547
Total	51,101	7,114	43,987

[1] SOURCE: Treasury Bulletin, Federal Reserve Bulletin, and Annual Report of the Secretary of the Treasury. Amounts are in millions of dollars, for Dec. 31, 1960.
[2] Carried net of unamortized premium and discount.

no permanent effects on the money supply are thereby produced. For example, if public holdings of cash are reduced by increments to a trust fund and these, in turn, are invested in special Treasury issues, public holdings of cash nevertheless benefit because public holdings of other forms of the Government debt will be commensurately less. In other words, what the Treasury does not sell to the trust funds, it must sell to somebody else.

STATE AND LOCAL GOVERNMENTS

We are a federal system. Consequently, the sovereign states and their political subdivisions enjoy the power to tax, collect social-security payments, and so on. These fund-collecting capacities give rise to investment pools which, in turn, have an impact on the government securities market. Holdings of Government securities by state and local governments account for no less than 6 percent of the total.[35] (See Table 2-1.)

State and local investment funds are diverse in kind. They include the general-fund account plus funds for retirement, industrial accidents and sickness, highway and construction, debt service and retirement, and schools. Aggregate figures, in addition, reflect the degree to

[35] See appendix for a bibliography on state and local investment funds.

which portfolio managers are restricted by their respective legislative enactments. Nevertheless, funds subject to the control of fifteen state governments have allocated 58.5 percent of their assets to United States Government securities.[36] (See Table 2-11.) This high proportion re-

TABLE 2-11   Investment portfolios of fifteen state governments[1]

	Percentage of total portfolio
Obligations of the U.S. Government	58.5
State and local obligations	21.3
Corporate stocks and bonds	9.3
Mortgages	5.9
Certificates of deposit	1.6
FHA and other nonguaranteed Federal securities	1.3
Other securities[2]	2.1
Total	100.0

[1] SOURCE: Joseph L. Bower, "Investment in United States Government Securities by State Governments," National Tax Journal, vol. 13, no. 2, June, 1960, table II, p. 133. The states are Arkansas, Connecticut, Maine, Maryland, Massachusetts, Nevada, New Mexico, New York, North Carolina, North Dakota, Oregon, Rhode Island, South Dakota, Tennessee, and Vermont. Figures are for June 30, 1958, for all states except New York. For New York, figures are for Mar. 31, 1958.

[2] Primarily obligations of the Canadian government and the International Bank for Reconstruction and Development.

flects the fiduciary role of portfolio managers as well as the conservative predilection of legislative bodies.

The composition of the United States Government securities portfolio reflects, also, the desire for a liquidity medium, since 15.5 percent is in Treasury bills and at least 29 percent matures within one year. (See Table 2-12.)

FEDERAL RESERVE SYSTEM

Last but hardly least as an institutional investor in Governments is the central bank. Holdings allocated to the various Federal Reserve banks accounted for 9 percent of outstandings at the end of calendar year 1960. (See Table 2-1.) Though once considered solely a source of

[36] They also assign 21.3 percent of their resources to municipals. This, in view of the tax status of municipals *and* state and local funds, is uneconomic portfolio management. See Roland I. Robinson, *Postwar Market for State and Local Government Securities,* Princeton, N.J.: Princeton University Press, 1960, pp. 158–201.

TABLE 2-12   United States Government securities portfolios of fifteen state governments[1]

	Percentage of U.S. Government securities portfolio[2]		
Marketable:			
Bills		15.5	
Certificates		9.7	
Notes:			
Within 1 year	1.9		
1–5 years	1.1		
Total notes		3.0	
Bonds:			
Maturity unknown	4.8		
Within 1 year	1.9		
1–5 years	5.1		
5–10 years	3.3		
Over 10 years	38.0		
Total bonds		53.1	
Total marketable			81.4
Convertible bonds, Investment Series B			13.6
Nonmarketable:			
Investment Series A		0.4	
Savings bonds		4.4	
Total nonmarketable			4.8
			100.0

[1] SOURCE: Joseph L. Bower, "Investment in United States Government Securities by State Governments," National Tax Journal, vol. 13, no. 2, June, 1960, table IV, p. 136.
[2] Percentages do not add precisely because of rounding.

earnings, the central bank's portfolio is now the primary instrument of monetary policy.[37] The composition of the Government securities portfolio, of course, depends upon the central bank's policy with respect to operating in various maturities.[38] (See Table 2-3.)

[37] See, e.g., E. A. Goldenweiser, *American Monetary Policy*, New York: McGraw-Hill Book Company, 1951; *Federal Reserve Bank of Chicago Annual Report*, 1955, p. 40; Robert V. Roosa, *Federal Reserve Operations in the Money and Government Securities Markets*, Federal Reserve Bank of New York, July, 1956; "The Fed Is in the Market," *Federal Reserve Bank of Philadelphia Business Review*, December, 1960; A. C. L. Day and Sterie T. Beza, *Money and Income*, Fair Lawn, N.J.: Oxford University Press, 1960; *Federal Reserve System Purposes and Functions*, Washington, D.C.: Board of Governors of the Federal Reserve System, 1961; and Lester V. Chandler, *Economics of Money and Banking*, New York: Harper & Row, Publishers, Incorporated, 1964.

[38] See appendix for a bibliography on the bills-only policy.

Whatever this policy may be, it is uninteresting as portfolio policy. This is due to the suppression of profit-maximizing motives by the modern central bank often burdened with major responsibility for over-all economic stability. Thus, from the viewpoint of the Government securities market, the central bank must be considered primarily in terms of its role in the determination of the structure, as well as the level, of interest rates.

OTHER INVESTORS

The other-investor category in the Treasury Survey of Ownership accounts for about 38 percent of the total outstanding direct and guaranteed, interest-bearing marketable debt. (See Table 2-3.) This classification includes corporate pension trust funds, and those banks, insurance companies, savings and loan associations, and corporations not reporting in the Treasury Survey. Banks and insurance companies reporting in the Survey account for about 95 percent of total Governments held by

TABLE 2-13   Assets of personal trust funds[1]

Assets	Amount	Percentage of total assets
Cash	0.5	0.8
Obligations of the U.S. Government	2.8	4.5
State and local obligations	9.1	14.6
Mortgages	0.8	1.2
Corporate obligations	44.3	71.1
Participation in common trust funds	2.5	4.1
Other assets	2.3	3.7
Total	62.3	100.0

[1] SOURCE: "Assets in Personal Trust Accounts Top $62 Billion in 1960," Trusts and Estates, vol. 100, no. 10, October, 1961, p. 852. Amounts are in billions of dollars. Figures are for reporting dates near at year-end, 1960.

these financial institutions. Reporting savings and loan associations and corporations account for about 50 percent of the total holdings of these institutions. The other-investor class also includes individuals, who hold $19.1 billion in Governments other than savings bonds.[39]

[39] See Table 2-1. These securities are mostly marketables. See appendix for a bibliography on individual portfolio policies.

Part of individual holdings show up in personal trust funds administered by commercial banks and trust companies.[40] Governments account for 4.5 percent of total personal trust accounts.[41] (See Table 2-13.) A small amount of individual holdings appear in the portfolios of common trust funds. (See Table 2-14.)

TABLE 2-14   Assets of common trust funds[1]

	Amount	Percentage of total assets
Cash	21.9	0.8
Obligations of the U.S. Government		
Marketable		
Within 1 year	20.8	0.7
After 1 year	185.3	6.6
Nonmarketable	14.4	0.5
State and local obligations	45.4	1.6
Mortgages	45.9	1.6
Corporate obligations	2,372.1	84.3
Other assets	106.8	3.8
Total assets	2,812.6	100.0

[1] SOURCE: "Survey of Common Trust Funds, 1960," Federal Reserve Bulletin, May, 1961, table 3, p. 527. Amounts are in millions of dollars. Figures are for reporting dates near or at year-end 1960.
[2] Percentages do not add to 100 because of rounding.

Individual portfolio policies are difficult to summarize. This is especially true of trust accounts, since investment policies will vary with the size and purpose of the trust. Moreover, individuals in the lower-income classes tend to prefer nonmarketables, while high-income groups favor tax-exempts. On the other hand, the financial response of individuals to changes in interest rates on marketable Governments can be dramatic.[42] There is also strong evidence of individual reactions

[40] See appendix for a bibliography on trust funds.
[41] An unknown portion of this percentage is in nonmarketable obligations.
[42] For example, the public's reaction to the "Magic 5s" (5 percent notes of August 15, 1964), dubbed the "Tragic 5s" by thrift institutions. See Robert Van Cleave, C. F. Childs and Company Review, no. 322, Oct. 12, 1959; " 'Magic Fives,' " Business Week, Oct. 17, 1959; Charls E. Walker, "Problems of Treasury Debt Management," address before the annual convention of the U.S. Savings and Loan League, Dallas, Texas, Nov. 11, 1959; and "Government Issues Attract Personal Savings," Federal Reserve Bank of Chicago Business Conditions, January, 1960. Note also the role of the residual (individuals

in the Government securities market to changes in interest-rate expectations.[43] It may be inferred, therefore, that the liquidity and credit-risk attributes of Government securities are of importance to individual, as well as to institutional, investors.

and others) as an interest-rate indicator. See Bankers Trust Company, Economics Department, "Technical Notes," *Investment Outlook*, New York, 1962, and William C. Freund and Edward D. Zinbarg, "Application of Flow-of-Funds to Interest Rate Analysis," *Journal of Finance*, vol. 18, no. 2, May, 1963, pp. 231–248.

[43] Cf. Joseph R. Slevin, *Speculation in U.S. Bonds*, New York: *New York Herald Tribune*, 1958; and *Treasury–Federal Reserve Study of the Government Securities Market*, Washington, D.C.: Treasury Department and Board of Governors, Federal Reserve System, July, 1959, part 1, p. 9.

chapter 3

DAY-TO-DAY OPERATIONS
OF A GOVERNMENT
SECURITIES DEALER

The debt-management operations of the United States Treasury, the open-market operations of the Federal Open Market Committee, and the Government securities transactions of the great financial intermediaries, nonfinancial corporations, and individual investors are all centered upon the dealers who make the market in Government securities.[1] These dealer houses stand with the money-market banks at the apex of the money and capital markets. As, for example, local business activity increases and the pressures of loan demand expand, the Government securities portfolios of local lending institutions will be reduced. Initially, these securities may be absorbed by the larger correspondent banks in the regional money-market center. But eventually the pressure will be felt in New York as these larger banks trim the size of their portfolios through adjusting sales to the Government securities dealers. Dealers will find the flow of offers exceeding the flow of bids. They will reduce their bid quotations to prevent an undue expansion in their portfolios. The rising yield structure will stimulate the inward flow of funds from other regions. Thus from the money-market center the stringency will be spread through the rest of the economy. In this manner, a more profitable use of resources locally will

---

[1] See appendix for a bibliography on the Government securities dealers.

attract funds from far-flung regions, with the dealers providing a crucial link.

From the viewpoint of both the execution of stabilization policy and the day-to-day smoothing of money-market pressures, a critical dealer function involves the trading arm of the Federal Open Market Committee (FOMC), the Trading Desk of the Securities Department of the Federal Reserve Bank of New York. If, for example, the trading account wishes to offset some factor which is momentarily pushing free reserves beyond the current target level, it will solicit dealer bids. Payment is made by nonbank dealers through debits to the reserve account of the money-market bank that serves as their clearing agent. Payment is made by bank dealers by drawing on their reserve accounts directly. In each case, therefore, member bank reserves are reduced, and the level of free reserves is kept under control.

If the FOMC institutes a policy of increased restraint, the trading account will follow a similar procedure. In this case, however, the action will exert an effect more far-reaching than that of simply offsetting an unwanted increase in reserves. As dealers take on additional securities from the trading account and from the money-market banks, they gradually lower their bid and offer quotations. At the same time, the dealers step up their selling efforts through branch offices and correspondent banking connections all over the country. These efforts, combined with the rise in yields, lead to widely dispersed sales. As the securities are taken up by banks and local investors, local member bank reserves decline. As member banks find their reserves are under greater pressure, they will borrow temporarily in the Federal funds[2] market or from the Federal Reserve bank of their district. Or they may sell Government securities, chiefly to dealers. In this manner —and again with the dealers providing the connecting link—the contraction of bank reserves directly due to the open-market sale is spread throughout the economic system.[3]

In similar fashion the dealers participate in the underwriting and distribution of new Treasury issues. Accordingly, if the Treasury changes the maturity structure of the debt, the dealers aid in communicating the shift in yield structure to the outstanding Government debt and other investment media. The Government securities dealers,

---

[2] See appendix for a bibliography on the Federal funds market.

[3] See Ira O. Scott, Jr., "The Regional Impact of Monetary Policy," *Quarterly Journal of Economics*, vol. 69, no. 2, May, 1955, pp. 280–282.

therefore, provide the channel through which the effects of monetary and debt-management policy are transmitted to the economy, and they supply a constant means of communication for participants in the money and capital markets.

THE ORGANIZATION OF A DEALER FIRM

At present, there are twenty primary dealers in Government securities. Six are commercial banks. The other fourteen dealers are securities houses, some of which conduct a wide range of investment banking activities. Others handle Government securities almost exclusively. Four of the bank dealers are in New York City. Two are in Chicago, though their securities transactions may in some instances be executed in New York. The head offices of all but one of the nonbank dealers are located in New York. One nonbank dealer firm, the oldest in the business, has its head office in Chicago; but its securities operations are conducted in New York. Two of the nonbank dealers are members of the New York Stock Exchange. Some of them have branches in leading metropolitan centers. All of the bank dealers and eleven of the nonbank dealers are incorporated. The rest are organized as partnerships.

The range of securities in which these dealers operate and the extent to which they are willing to make a market in each maturity varies considerably. The larger firms are active in all maturities. A few of the smaller firms restrict their operations, for the most part, to Treasury bills. However, all of the primary dealers have one feature in common. The Securities Department of the Federal Reserve Bank of New York will do business with them. Any prospective dealer may apply to the Federal Reserve Bank of New York for the privilege of participating in its operations. The firm's reputation, its capital position, and its willingness to make a market are the primary criteria used in judging its suitability as a dealer. Of course, any investor who wishes to do so and who has sufficient capital may make a market in Government securities. Many commercial banks do so for their correspondents, and even some nonfinancial corporations will participate in limited transactions. However, being admitted to the group of dealers with whom the Federal Reserve Bank of New York will trade has several important advantages. First, the business which this bank gives the dealers can be substantial. These transactions include not only those executed for the FOMC, but also for Treasury-managed investment funds, foreign central banks, various international financial organizations, and smaller member banks that do not have good access to the dealer market. Second, nonbank dealers in this group are eligible for repurchase-money accommodation at the Federal Reserve Bank of New York, the timing and magnitude of which may be of crucial importance for the success of the dealer operation. Finally, the primary dealers are usually permitted to subscribe to Treasury offerings without a down payment and also may borrow against Government securities from national banks without having to meet the usual margin requirements for such borrowings.

The dealer organization may be broken down into five functions, namely, trading, sales, the cage, computations, and research.[4] The trading room is the heart of the dealer operation, for the traders are those plucky individuals who make the market. The essence of successful trading is knowledge, a knowledge of the terms according to which securities may be bought and sold. This knowledge is provided through incessant telephonic communication with all of the sensitive points in the market. Thus the hot seat, on which the trader sits, faces a bank of telephone switches and indicator lights. With the flick of a key, the trader is placed in immediate contact with his counterpart in other dealer firms, the trading room at 33 Liberty Street,[5] or the great money-market banks. By this means, he maintains a continuous knowledge of the terms on which business can be done. Armed with this information, he can adjust the terms according to which *he* will do business in order to accomplish his position objectives in face of the forces of supply and demand that converge upon his firm.

Interrupting the trader's routine are the periodic inquiries of salesmen regarding the acceptability of offers or bids and requests for a market quotation.[6] If a deal is concluded, the salesman reports it back to the trader, who makes the necessary change in the record of his position. As market forces tend to widen the gap between his actual and desired position, the trader will change his terms. New prices will

[4] The extent to which these functions are performed by different individuals or departments, of course, varies with the size of the firm.

[5] The address of the Federal Reserve Bank of New York.

[6] This is no market for dullards. The author has stood many times at a trader's side discussing complex questions of economic policy and watched him, without a moment's hesitation, shout his approval or disapproval of a suggested deal or the best quotations he is willing to state and then return immediately to the question at hand.

be sent electronically or by the board boy to the giant quotation board that covers one end of the trading room.

From 10 A.M. to 3:30 P.M., the trader is buffeted by market developments—a large institutional portfolio shift, a press release by the Treasury Department, election results, news of war and peace, views expressed by a congressman, a Government official, or the author of a market letter, and so on. He takes his lunch—bites of a cold sandwich and gulps of black coffee—while the battle rages on. He takes dessert—tidbits of gossip and a spicy story from another trader whom he knows very well but may not have met—while an itinerant bootblack shines his shoes. At 2:30 P.M., the trader dashes off a list of quotations for the computational department. After the market close and a post-mortem on the events of the day, he grabs his hat and makes for the 4:30 train.

A trader will specialize in a particular maturity sector of the marketable debt. Typically, there will be a bill trader, a trader in certificates, notes, and short bonds, and a trader in intermediate and long-term bonds. The degree of autonomy exercised by the trader—the extent to which he may commit the firm's capital—will be determined by the senior partners or officers of the firm. Deals involving trades which exceed the limits of the trader's discretion are referred to these partners or officers for decision. Traders are often partners or officers themselves; and in any case, their counsel is weighed heavily in making decisions regarding commitments undertaken by the firm.

The sales department, of which the firm's branches are essentially outlying appendages, forms a network of communication links between the dealer firm and other participants in the capital market. In the home office, the salesmen are normally seated in close proximity to the trader. Before them also lies a bank of telephone keys, in this instance connecting the firm with the portfolio and money-position managers of leading financial institutions and nonfinancial corporations. The salesman's day is spent in going through his list of accounts, soliciting customers—chiefly by telephone but sometimes through personal visits or over the luncheon table—suggesting profitable portfolio adjustments and tax and arbitrage switches, computing the basis at which a longer bill can be sold and have the same yield in the holding period that a shorter bill has to maturity, passing along and picking up market information, and polishing a personal contact that may produce some business at a later date. The successful salesman not only must master the Government securities market; he must also have a detailed knowledge of institutional portfolio practices, the institution's tax status, and the idiosyncrasies of each portfolio manager and his board of directors.

Communication with out-of-town customers and branches is maintained by both teletype and telephone. There are individual teletype machines connecting the home office with each branch and a master machine for all messages. The branch notifies the home office of what its customer wishes to buy or sell and receives approval, disapproval, or acceptable terms from the trader in charge of the relevant position. If the deal is brought to a successful conclusion, the trader is notified so that he can change his records accordingly. Negotiations which are too complicated to handle by teletype are completed over the telephone.

Thus the over-the-counter market in Government securities is primarily an over-the-telephone market. A dealer's word is as good as his bond. Obviously, it must be so, or the market would collapse. For the sake of record keeping, confirmation of the terms of a transaction is made by letter.

The cage houses the last of the three crucial operating units in the dealer firm, a unit which is responsible for the related functions of financing, clearing, and accounting. It is upon the cage that the flurry of sales and purchase tickets falls almost like confetti. It is in the cage that the physical side of these myriad transactions must be unraveled, coordinated, and netted out. From the cage, runners are dispatched to make local deliveries or pickups, telephonic or teletype instructions are given for out-of-town transactions, the country is scoured for funds to finance the dealer's position, institutional investors are canvassed for securities which must be borrowed in order to make delivery, appeals are made to the Fed for repurchase accommodation, and last-minute overnights must be negotiated with the money-market banks. Long after the din of the market place has died and the trading room has been invaded by cleaning women wielding swishing mops and whirring waxing machines, the lights burn on in the cage. For after the last bond has been delivered or financed, entries for the day's transactions must be made in the firm's permanent records. The chief cashier hurries to catch the last train home.

Computations are made in the P and S (purchase and sales) department, which is in juxtaposition to both trading room and cage. P and S is staffed by attractive comptometrists, whose nimble fingers unobtrusively and interminably convert prices into yields, yields into prices, market returns into after-tax returns, and flat quotations into receipts or outlays gross of interest sold or acquired. Their precision is matched only by that of the machines they manipulate.

Last but not least is the research department. The head of the research staff is the first to arrive, hours before the market opens. He has already, on his way home the night before, digested all relevant developments reported in the evening press. On his way to the office he has gathered all of the morning dailies. These he hurriedly scans before tackling the morning mail and its ration of money-market letters. By 9:30 A.M., he has culled from these many sources the material required for the premarket policy meeting, where he, the senior partners, and chief traders will chart the firm's position policy for the day ahead. As trading progresses, the director of research turns to the problem of longer-run forecasting for the investment account, the computation of the value of a tax and loan account deposit, the supervision of chart construction, and, perhaps, the preparation of his own firm's money-market letter. He regularly, over the telephone and luncheon table, exchanges views with top staff and policy makers at the Fed and Treasury and with other market analysts. As he learns of shifts in market forces, whether reported by word of mouth or over a news-service teletype outlet, he immediately informs the traders and policy makers affected. And so his day goes. It ends with a brief case bulging with half-digested market reports, records of congressional hearings, and addresses by Federal Reserve spokesmen.

The passage of a Government security through a dealer firm can best be described in terms of tickets and accounts.[7] Assume, to begin with, that a customer, a representative of the XYZ National Bank, wishes to sell 1 myn Treasury bills.[8] He calls the firm's contact man, or salesman, and states his intentions. The salesman, with the seller on the line, asks the bill trader for a bid for the block of bills. He receives the bid from the trader and reports it to the customer, who finds it acceptable. The salesman then fills in certain basic information identifying the transaction on a purchase ticket. (See Exhibit 3-1.)

This information includes the following:

date—9/19/61
type of security—bills
number of securities (par or maturity value $1,000)—1,000

---

[7] For this description, the author is indebted to Charles Giamondi.
[8] A block of bills whose maturity value is $1 million.

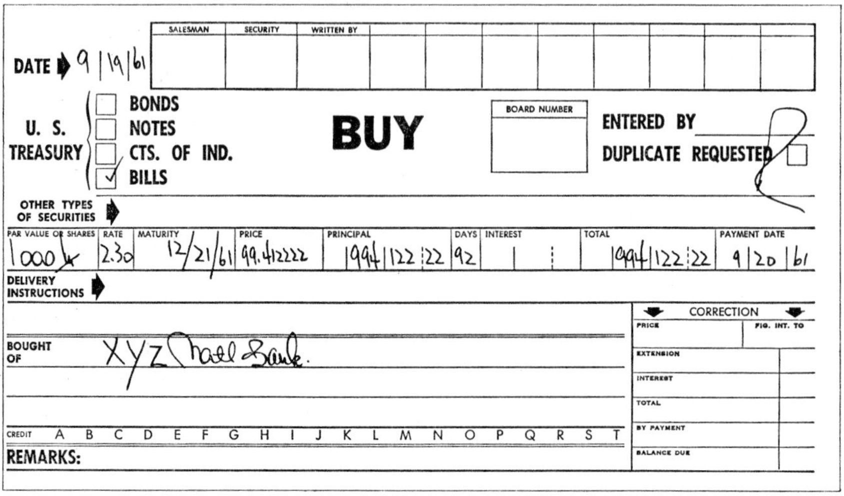

Exhibit 3-1. Buy ticket showing purchase of 1 myn Treasury bills from XYZ National Bank.

rate—2.30

maturity—12/21/61

days (to maturity from payment date)—92

payment date—9/20/61

seller—XYZ National Bank

The salesman then informs the trader of the conclusion of the deal. The latter enters the transaction in his ledger, so that the record of his trading position is always kept up to the minute.

The ticket is next sent to the P and S department, where the price, principal (extension),[9] and total due the customer are calculated and added to the ticket.[10] Then the ticket is typed for confirmation to the customer.[11] The confirmation contains the same information as the purchase ticket. (See Exhibit 3-2.) A record of the purchase is then entered in the daily blotter. The purpose of this entry is to provide a record of all of the day's transactions as a guide for the cage in clearing the securities the next day.

[9] Principal and extension are synonymous and equal to par value times the price.

[10] Note from Chap. 1 that $d = f - p$, and $r = (d/f)(T/t)(100)$; or $2.30 = (d/100)(360/92)(100)$, $d = 5.877778$, and $p = 99.4122222$. At this price, 1 myn bills costs the dealer \$994,122.22.

[11] Copies of the confirmation ticket also serve as a messenger receipt, a part of the salesman's volume record, and the record of the transaction in the company's file for the particular customer.

The daily purchase blotter shows debits to the securities accounts and interest on bonds, and credits to cash according to the bank from which money is drawn to make payment. At the end of the day, a balance is struck so that individual purchases made with checks drawn on a particular bank sum to equal the total withdrawn from that bank. In proof, the information appearing on the blotters is posted onto the bond ledger. This ledger shows securities bought and sold— the par amount, price, extension, and the purchase and sale of interest —the balance, and profit and loss.

Next, suppose that an inquiry is received from the Last National Bank regarding the purchase of 2 myn 3⅝s of 1967, and an offer of 98.27 is accepted. (See Exhibits 3-3 and 3-4.) At this price, the dealer will receive a principal amount of $1,976,875 for the block of securities.[12] The payment date shown on the ticket is September 26, 195 days after the security was issued, March 15, and prior to the payment of any interest. Therefore the buyer must pay the dealer 195 days' interest, or $38,616.31,[13] making a total of $2,015,491.31 due on September 26 from the Last National Bank. (See Exhibit 3-5.) As in the case of the purchase ticket, the information appearing on the sales ticket is transcribed to the daily blotter and finally to the bond ledger.

[12] I.e., $(0.98)(\$2,000,000) = \$1,960,000$, and $(27/32)(\$20,000) = \$16,875$, or a total of $1,976,875. Thus, the figures after the decimal point represent 32d's of a point.

[13] I.e., $(1/2)(61/181 + 134/184)(\$2,000,000)(0.03625) = \$38,616.31$. Interest-payment dates, May 15 and November 15, account for distribution of the 195 days' interest. (See Chap. 1.) Most interest computations will be for a half-year or less. The present example is an exception and has what is known as a *long* coupon period.

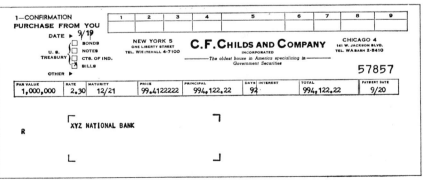

Exhibit 3-2. Confirmation of purchase of 1 myn bills from XYZ Bank.

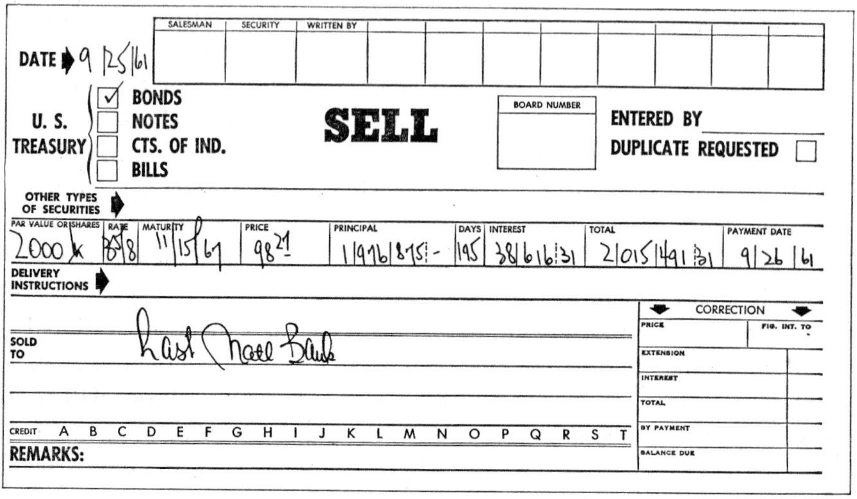

SALESMAN | SECURITY | WRITTEN BY

DATE ➧ 9/25/61

U. S. TREASURY
☑ BONDS
☐ NOTES
☐ CTS. OF IND.
☐ BILLS

SELL

BOARD NUMBER

ENTERED BY

DUPLICATE REQUESTED ☐

OTHER TYPES OF SECURITIES ➧

PAR VALUE OR SHARES	RATE	MATURITY	PRICE	PRINCIPAL	DAYS	INTEREST	TOTAL	PAYMENT DATE
2000 M	3 5/8	11/15/67	98 21/32	1,976,875.–	195	38,616.31	2,015,491.31	9/26/61

DELIVERY INSTRUCTIONS ➧

SOLD TO Last National Bank

CORRECTION
PRICE | FIG. INT. TO
EXTENSION
INTEREST
TOTAL
BY PAYMENT
BALANCE DUE

CREDIT A B C D E F G H I J K L M N O P Q R S T

REMARKS:

Exhibit 3-3. Sell ticket showing sale of 2 myn $3\frac{5}{8}$s to Last National Bank.

MAKING A MARKET

The nominal market made by a Government securities dealer is depicted in his quotation sheet. The quotations appearing in Exhibit 3-6 (pages 88–89) were set by the appropriate traders at 2:30 P.M. on September 12, 1961. Within an hour or so, the sheets had been dispatched by mail to all of the firm's customers.

United States Treasury bills head the list. For each issue is reported the amount outstanding, the number of days to maturity, bid and asked, and yield after corporate income tax. There is, for example, $1,701,000,000 of the short bill outstanding. It matures in seven days, September 21. It is bid on a 1.80 basis, with 1.70 asked.[14] Its after-tax yield is 0.81.[15] In addition to the ninety-one-day variety, the list includes TABs and other longer maturities.

[14] Treasury bills are auctioned and quoted on a bank, rather than true, discount basis. (See Chap. 1 for formulas.) Thus the true rate earned by the investor is greater than the quoted rate because the latter is based on par, or 100, while the true rate is based on the actual investment. The true rate also exceeds bank rate because the former is based on a 365- or 366-day year, while bank rate is based on a 360-day year. This means that the amount of interest received is, in the case of true rate, earned during a smaller fraction of the whole year, making the interest rate on an annual basis larger. The Treasury bill calculation, on the other hand, ignores the result of compounding for bills maturing in excess of six months.

[15] Although bills are sold on a discount basis, interest earned is treated

Then, in chronological order by final maturity date, are quotations for certificates, notes, and bonds. For example, there is $1,819,000,000 of the $2\frac{1}{2}$ of 68/63 outstanding. This bond, with a $2\frac{1}{2}$ percent coupon, was callable in 1963 and matures in 1968. It is bid at 90.14, with 90.22 asked. This represents a 2/32 decline in bid price from the previous day's quotations. On the basis of the asked quotation, the investor's yield to the nearest call date, with semiannual compounding, is 7.04 percent; to maturity, 3.99 percent. Yield after corporate income tax is 2.31.[16] The 1961 range in asked quotations was 93.22 to 89.4.[17]

Toward the bottom of the quote sheet, it is stated that yields[18] are computed for delivery on September 14, 1961. In other words, the

---

as ordinary income. (See Chap. 1.) Assuming the investor pays 1.70 for the bills and that he is in the 52 percent bracket, his after-tax yield = (0.48)(1.70) = 0.81.

[16] When issues are quoted at par or above or when they mature in six months or less, the after-tax yield is computed on the basis of the 52 percent bracket. If the security is quoted below par and has more than six months to run, allowance is made for the lower tax rate on capital gains. Thus after-tax yield = $y - 0.52c - 0.25(y - c) = 0.75y - 0.27c$, where y represents yield to maturity and c denotes the coupon. In the example of the $2\frac{1}{2}$s or 68/63, the after-tax yield = $(0.75)(3.99) - (0.27)(2.5) = 2.31$.

This calculation, allowing for the lower tax rate on capital gains, is useful to investors generally if their net long-term capital gains exceed their net short-term losses. A banking institution or savings and loan association will not wish to experience long-term capital gains at the same time it is realizing capital losses, since the latter, in excess of capital gains, can be deducted from ordinary income. (See Chap. 2.) On the other hand, individual investors, who can usually offset ordinary income with capital losses only up to a maximum of $1,000, and nonbanking corporations, which are not permitted such a deduction at all, may find it desirable to offset net losses with capital gains. Unused net losses may be carried forward for five years. Thus when capital gains are offset by unused capital losses, the effective capital gains rate is zero. In any case, the tax rate or rates used in computing the relevant tax-adjusted yield will vary widely according to the investor's tax status.

When a security is quoted at a premium above par, the after-tax yield is computed on the basis of the yield to the next call date. This will be the next interest-payment date if the first call date has already passed.

A partially tax-exempt security is exempt from the 30 percent normal tax but subject to the 22 percent surtax. Thus, the after-tax yield is computed by multiplying the appropriate yield by 0.78.

[17] Quotations for the special series of $1\frac{1}{2}$ percent notes are presented on the reverse side of the quotation sheet (not shown) along with the list of Federal agency obligations.

[18] I.e., bond yields.

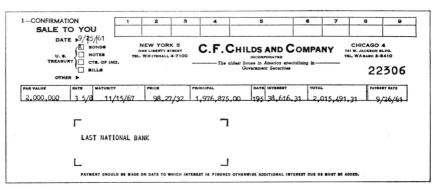

Exhibit 3-4. Confirmation of sale of 2 myn 3⅝s to Last National Bank.

quotation sheet, prepared toward the closing of the market on September 12, will be read by investors on September 13. Securities purchased on that day for regular delivery will be paid for and become a part of the investor's portfolio on September 14.

At the end of the sheet is a table showing the dollar value of thirty-seconds of a point. It is stated, for example, that 1/32 is equal to 0.03125. Thus if the asked price is 98.01, an investor must pay $980.3125 for a $1,000 bond.

At 3:30 P.M., the key is closed, and everything is on the wire. Late inquiries may still come from Western branches and customers. The evening press may contain items of interest, and the morning press is scrutinized. Barring influential happenings, closing quotes are used at the start. Then the feel of the market is gauged as soon as possible. At 10 A.M., or soon thereafter the traders start calling each other asking for runs, usually of the latest three- and six-month bills, the last two one-year bills, the most recent TAB, and the certificate, note, and bond list. Inquiries are watched carefully.

If there is buying interest, the asked is raised. With a short position, there is a scramble to cover. If the market is down, inquiries may be planted so as to buoy the list while a long position is unwound. If some issue seems out of line, the trader starts out bidding or offering, as the case may be.[19]

[19] See C. F. Childs and Company, *Price Spreads of Selected U.S. Government Securities*, New York. An investor may compare this source, published monthly, with current quotations to see whether the current spread between the prices of any two securities is markedly different from their historical relationship.

CHICAGO 4, ILL.
141 W. JACKSON BLVD.
TEL. WABASH 2-5410
TELETYPE CG 17

CLEVELAND 14, OHIO
UNION COMMERCE BUILDING
TEL. MAIN 1-8086

Treas. 4s	Treas. 4¼s	Treas. 3½s	Treas. 3¾s	Treas. 3⅜s	Treas. 3⅝s
1980	1985/75	1980 1998	1966	1966 Dated Mar. 15, 1961	1967 Dated Mar. 15, 1961
February 15 August 15	May 15 November 15	May 15 November 15	May 15 November 15	May 15 November 15	May 15 November 15
1.84782605	12.58831517	10.36684830	11.10733653	15.68375808	16.84551719
1.95652170	12.70380430	10.46195700	11.20923870	15.77547004	16.94402262
2.17391300	12.93478256	10.65217440	11.41304304	15.95889396	17.14103348
2.28260865	13.05027169	10.74728310	11.51494521	16.05060592	17.23953891
2.39130430	13.16176082	10.84239180	11.61684738	16.14231788	17.33804434
2.49999995	13.28124995	10.93750050	11.71874955	16.23402984	17.43654977
2.60869560	13.39673908	11.03260920	11.82065172	16.32574180	17.53505520
2.71739125	13.51222821	11.12771790	11.92255389	16.41745376	17.63356063
2.93478255	13.74320647	11.31793530	12.12635823	16.60087768	17.83057149
3.04347820	13.85869560	11.41304400	12.22826040	16.69258964	17.92907692
3.15217385	13.97418473	11.50815270	12.33016257	16.78430160	18.02758235
3.26086950	14.08967386	11.60326140	12.43206474	16.87601356	18.12608778
3.36956515	14.20516299	11.69837010	12.53396691	16.96772552	18.22459321
3.47826080	14.32065212	11.79347880	12.63586908	17.05943748	18.32309864
3.69565210	14.55163038	11.98369620	12.83967342	17.24286140	18.52010950
3.80434775	14.66711951	12.07880490	12.94157559	17.33457336	18.61861493
3.91304340	14.78260864	12.17391360	13.04347776	17.42628532	18.71712036
4.02173905	14.89809777	12.26902230	13.14537993	17.51799728	18.81562579
4.13004370	15.01358690	12.36413100	13.24728210	17.60970924	18.91413122
4.23913035	15.12907603	12.45923970	13.34918427	17.70142120	19.01263665
4.45652165	15.36005429	12.64945710	13.55298861	17.88484512	19.20964751
4.56521730	15.47554342	12.74456580	13.65489078	17.97655708	19.30815294
4.67391295	15.59103255	12.83967450	13.75679295	18.06826904	19.40665837
4.78260860	15.70652168	12.93478320	13.85869512	18.15998100	19.50516380
4.89130425	15.82201081	13.02989190	13.96059729	18.25169296	19.60366923
4.99999990	15.93749994	13.12500060	14.06249946	18.34340492	19.70217466

22	23	24	25	26	27	28	29	30	31	32
.68750	.71875	.75000	.78125	.81250	.84375	.87500	.90625	.93750	.96875	1.00000

SEPTEMBER 1961

NEW YORK 5, N. Y.
ONE LIBERTY STREET
TEL. WHitehall 4-7100
TELETYPE NY 1-2340

BOSTON 10, MASS.
50 FEDERAL STREET
TEL. HAncock 6-9500

ST. LOUIS 2, MO.
314 NORTH BROADWAY
TEL. GArfield 1-5115
TELETYPE SL 295

PITTSBURGH 19, PA
UNION TRUST BUILDIN
TEL. ATlantic 1-617

INTEREST TABLE FOR U. S. TREASURY BONDS

C. F. CHILDS AND COMPANY

The oldest house in America specializing in
Government Securities

Accrued interest during the month of September, 1961, on each different $1000. U. S. Treasury Bond.

U. S. TREASURY BONDS

September	Treas. 2¾s 1961 March 15 / September 15	Treas. 2¾s 1965/60 June 15 / December 15	Treas. 2½s 1967/62 1968/63 1969/64 1972/67 June 15 / December 15	Treas. 2½s 1970/65 1971/66 1972/67 March 15 / September 15	Treas. 2¼s 1962/59 June 15 / December 15	Treas. 3¼s 1983/78 June 15 / December 15	Treas. 2½s 1961 May 15 / November 15	Treas. 2½s 1963 February 15 / August 15	Treas. 4s 1969 April 1 / October 1	Treas. 3⅞s 1968 1974 May 15 / November 15	Treas. 3s 1964 1966 1995 February 15 / August 15	Treas. 3½s 1990 February 15 / August 15	Treas. 2⅝s 1965 February 15 / August 15	N.
Friday 1	12.70380420	5.86065558	5.32786878	11.54891260	4.79508198	6.92622918	7.40489102	1.15489126	16.72131186	11.47758119	1.38586958	1.61684790	1.21263584	9.
Saturday 2	12.77853246	5.93579219	5.39617479	11.61684738	4.85655739	7.01502699	7.47282580	1.22282604	16.83060148	11.58288010	1.46739132	1.71195660	1.28396736	9.
Monday 4	12.92798898	6.08606541	5.53278681	11.75271694	4.97950821	7.19262261	7.60869536	1.35869560	17.04918072	11.79347792	1.63043480	1.90217400	1.42663040	9.
Tuesday 5	13.00271724	6.16120202	5.60109282	11.82065172	5.04098362	7.28142042	7.67663014	1.42663038	17.15847034	11.89877683	1.71195654	1.99728270	1.49796192	9.
Wednesday 6	13.07744550	6.23633863	5.66939883	11.88858650	5.10245903	7.37021823	7.74456492	1.49456516	17.26775996	12.00407574	1.79347828	2.09239140	1.56929344	10.
Thursday 7	13.15217376	6.31147524	5.73770484	11.95652128	5.16393444	7.45901604	7.81249970	1.56249994	17.37704958	12.10937465	1.87500002	2.18750010	1.64062496	10.
Friday 8	13.22690202	6.38661185	5.80601085	12.02445606	5.22540985	7.54781385	7.88043448	1.63043472	17.48633920	12.21467356	1.95652176	2.28260880	1.71195648	10.
Saturday 9	13.30163028	6.46174846	5.87431686	12.09239084	5.28688526	7.63661166	7.94836926	1.69836950	17.59562882	12.31997247	2.03804350	2.37771750	1.78328800	10.
Monday 11	13.45108680	6.61202168	6.01092888	12.22826040	5.40983608	7.81420728	8.08423882	1.83423906	17.81420806	12.53057029	2.20108698	2.56793490	1.92595104	10
Tuesday 12	13.52581506	6.68715829	6.07923489	12.29619518	5.47131149	7.90300509	8.15217360	1.90217384	17.92349768	12.63586920	2.28260872	2.66304360	1.99728256	10.
Wednesday 13	13.60054332	6.76229490	6.14754090	12.36412996	5.53278690	7.99180290	8.22010838	1.97010862	18.03278730	12.74116811	2.36413046	2.75815230	2.06861408	10.
Thursday 14	13.67527158	6.83743151	6.21584691	12.43206474	5.59426231	8.08060071	8.28804316	2.03804340	18.14207692	12.84646702	2.44565220	2.85326100	2.13994560	10.
Friday 15	13.75000000	6.91256812	6.28415292	12.50000000	5.65573772	8.16939852	8.35597794	2.10597818	18.25136654	12.95176593	2.52717304	2.94836970	2.21127712	10.
Saturday 16	....	6.98770473	6.35245893	.06906077	5.71721313	8.25819633	8.42391272	2.17391296	18.36065616	13.05706484	2.60869568	3.04347840	2.28260864	10.
Monday 18	....	7.13797795	6.48907095	.20718231	5.84016395	8.43579195	8.55978228	2.30978252	18.57923540	13.26766266	2.77173916	3.23369580	2.42527168	11
Tuesday 19	....	7.21311456	6.55737696	.27624308	5.90163936	8.52458976	8.62771706	2.37771730	18.68852502	13.37296157	2.85326090	3.32880450	2.49660320	11
Wednesday 20	....	7.28825117	6.62568297	.34530335	5.96311477	8.61338757	8.69565184	2.44564208	18.79781464	13.47826048	2.93478264	3.42391320	2.56793472	11
Thursday 21	....	7.36338778	6.69398898	.41436462	6.02459018	8.70218538	8.76358662	2.51358686	18.90710426	13.58355939	3.01630438	3.51902190	2.63926624	11
Friday 22	....	7.43852439	6.76229499	.48342539	6.08606559	8.79098319	8.83152140	2.58152164	19.01639388	13.68885830	3.09782612	3.61413060	2.71059776	11
Saturday 23	....	7.51366100	6.83060100	.55248616	6.14754100	8.87978100	8.89945618	2.64945642	19.12568350	13.79415721	3.17934786	3.70923930	2.78192928	11
Monday 25	....	7.66393422	6.96721302	.69060770	6.27049182	9.05737662	9.03532574	2.78532598	19.34426274	14.00475503	3.34239134	3.89945670	2.92459232	11
Tuesday 26	....	7.73907083	7.03551903	.75966847	6.33196723	9.14617443	9.10326052	2.85326076	19.45355236	14.11005394	3.42391308	3.99456540	2.99592384	11
Wednesday 27	....	7.81420744	7.10382504	.82872924	6.39344264	9.23497224	9.17119530	2.92119554	19.56284198	14.21535285	3.50543482	4.08967410	3.06725536	11
Thursday 28	....	7.88934405	7.17213105	.89779001	6.45491805	9.32377005	9.23913008	2.98913032	19.67213160	14.32065176	3.58695656	4.18478280	3.13858688	12
Friday 29	....	7.96448066	7.24043706	.96685078	6.51639346	9.41256786	9.30706486	3.05706510	19.78142122	14.42595067	3.66847830	4.27989150	3.20991840	12
Saturday 30	....	8.03961727	7.30874307	1.03591155	6.57786887	9.50136567	9.37499964	3.12499988	19.89071084	14.53124958	3.75000004	4.37500020	3.28124992	12

32nds			1	2	3	4	5	6	7	8	9	10	11	12	13	14	15	16	17	18	19	20
DECIMAL EQUIVALENT per $100 Bond			.03125	.06250	.09375	.12500	.15625	.18750	.21875	.25000	.28125	.31250	.34375	.37500	.40625	.43750	.46875	.50000	.53125	.56250	.59375	.62500

For U. S. Treasury Notes and Certificates of Indebtedness Table, see other side.

Exhibit 3-5. Table of accrued interest for bonds during September, 1961.

Whether a particular price is out of line is not always apparent to the uninitiated. Investors may, for example, prefer a security selling at par because they want the current income of a higher coupon even though this security yields less on an after-tax basis than a similar security selling at a discount. Dealers themselves prefer to have higher-coupon securities in long position and lower-coupon securities in short position because their net interest costs are thereby reduced.

The price of a dollar-quoted security selling at a discount will normally drop perceptibly when the security falls below the six-month maturity level, since investors can no longer use it to qualify for long-term capital gains.

Nor are investors indifferent between the certificate and a bill of the same maturity. If the C/I sells below par, its price would have to increase every day—that is, quotations would have to be raised each day—to keep the yield constant, whereas bills kept at the same yield every day still approach par with the passage of time.

Bills which mature around a tax date or on a corporate dividend date usually yield less, as do those maturing at year-end, window-dressing time.

Finally, it may be noted that since Governments are not dealt in flat, a coupon instrument does not actually yield its coupon at 100 except on the interest-payment date. On other dates, as seen in the example of a bond sale, the buyer must pay the accrued interest, which he does not receive back until the next interest-payment date.

There is a markdown in long-term quotations if word comes that an AA corporate has just been floated at an unexpectedly high yield. There is a sell-down as an issue being dumped by an institutional investor is digested by the market.

Quotes change when there seems to be a preponderance of sellers or buyers. If the market shift is precipitate, only one side of the market is quoted.

If a trader has to bid to take care of a customer, he may hedge by selling a similar issue. A trader open-ends his position when he wants to take a stand on the market, either by selling his long position and remaining short or by covering his short position and remaining long. When uncertain, he hedges his position or withdraws. If he does not wish to open-end a tax swap, he tries to find a matching customer in broker fashion. It might be argued that a reluctant trader should be willing to make a bid at some point below the current market and

C. F. CHILDS AND COMPANY

NEW YORK 5, N.Y.
ONE LIBERTY STREET
TEL. WHITEHALL 4-7100
TELETYPE NY 1-2340

BOSTON 10, MASS.
50 FEDERAL STREET
TEL. HANCOCK 6-9500

ST. LOUIS 2, MO.
314 NORTH BROADWAY
TEL. GARFIELD 1-5115

PITTSBURGH 19, PA.
UNION TRUST BUILDING
TEL. ATLANTIC 1-6171

CHICAGO 4, ILL.
141 W. JACKSON BLVD.
TEL. WABASH 2-5410
TELETYPE CG 17

CLEVELAND 14, OHIO
UNION COMMERCE BUILDING
TEL. MAIN 1-8086

The oldest house ... specializing in Government ... securities

SEPTEMBER 12, 1961

Quotations —

U. S. TREASURY BILLS

Outstand. (Millions)	Days to Mat'y	Maturity	2:30 P.M. Bid	Asked	Corp. Yield Aft. Tax	Outstand. (Millions)	Days to Mat'y	Maturity	2:30 P.M. Bid	Asked	Corp. Yield Aft. Tax
1701	7	9/21 1961	1.80	1.70	.81	500	105	12/28 1961	2.30	2.20	1.05
1503	8	9/22 1961	1.75	1.50	.72	500	112	1/4 1962	2.40	2.30	1.10
1700	14	9/28 1961	1.80	1.70	.81	500	119	1/11 1962	2.45	2.35	1.12
1600	71	11/24 1961	2.25	2.22	1.06	600	175	3/ 8 1962	2.67	2.64	1.26
1600	77	11/30 1961	2.30	2.27	1.08	600	181	3/15 1962	2.69	2.67	1.28
1601	84	12/ 7 1961	2.29	2.27	1.08	3503	190	3/23 1962	2.73	2.71	1.30
1600	91	12/14 1961	2.32	2.30	1.10	2000	213	4/15 1962	2.78	2.76	1.32
501	98	12/21 1961	2.30	2.20	1.05	2004	304	7/15 1962	2.88	2.86	1.37

U. S. TREASURY BONDS, NOTES, CERTIFICATES

Outstand. (Millions)	Rate	Maturity	2:30 P.M. Bid	Asked	Change	Notations	Yield to Call	Yield to Mat.	Corp.Yield Aft.Tax	Range 1961 High	Low
2239	2¾	9/15 1961	99.31	100.1	—	——			—	100.10	99.29
6963	2½	11/15 1961	100.	100.2	—	——		2.11	1.01	100.5	99.23
647 N	3⅝	2/15 1962	100.12	100.14			2.00	2.56	1.22	101.1	100.11

4195 N	$4\frac{7}{8}$	11/15 1964	103.6	103.10	-	———		3.76	1.80	105.26	102.28
6896	$2\frac{5}{8}$	2/15 1965	96.2	96.6	-	———		3.83	2.16	98.8	95.23
2113 N	$4\frac{5}{8}$	5/15 1965	102.18	102.22	-	———		3.83	1.83	105.11	102.16
*1485	$2\frac{1}{4}$	12/15 65/60	100.14	100.18	-	———	2.00	2.62	1.56	100.27	100.10
1213	$3\frac{3}{4}$	5/15 1966	99.27	99.31	-	———		3.75	1.80	102.14	99.10
1484	3	8/15 1966	96.28	97.	-	———		3.67	1.94	99.5	96.12
2438	$3\frac{3}{8}$	11/15 1966	97.27	97.31	-	———		3.80	1.94	100.10	97.12
1464	$2\frac{1}{2}$	6/15 67/62	92.14	92.22	-	———	12.75	3.93	2.28	95.22	91.20
3604	$3\frac{5}{8}$	11/15 1967	98.9	98.13	-	———		3.91	1.95	100.27	97.15
2136	$3\frac{7}{8}$	5/15 1968	99.9	99.13	-	———		3.97	1.93	102.8	98.14
1819	$2\frac{1}{2}$	12/15 68/63	90.14	90.22	-2	———	7.04	3.99	2.31	93.22	89.4
2638	$2\frac{1}{2}$	6/15 6 /64	8 .26	90.2	-2	———	6.50	4.00	2.32	92.20	88.16
1424	4	10/ 1 1969	100.24	101.	-2			3.85	1.84	103.8	99.20

470	$4\frac{1}{4}$	5/15 85/75	101.26	102.6	-	———	4.04	4.09	1.96	106.4	101.22
2719	$3\frac{1}{2}$	2/15 1990	88.22	88.30	-4	———		4.17	2.18	96.6	88.26
2695	3	2/15 1995	85.8	85.16	-4	———		3.77	2.01	89.18	84.22
2343	$3\frac{1}{2}$	11/15 1998	87.22	87.30	-4	———		4.14	2.09	95.22	87.26

FEDERAL NATIONAL MORTGAGE ASS'N. COMMON STOCK

78 BID   79 1/2 OFFERED   4.08 YIELD

Yields computed for delivery— SEPTEMBER 14, 1961   # 1 1/2% NOTES SHOWN ON REVERSE SIDE AT BOTTOM.

*** Exempt from 30% normal tax but subject to 22% surtax**

DOLLAR VALUE OF 32nds.

1/32— .03125	5/32— .15625	9/32— .28125	13/32— .40625	17/32— .53125	21/32— .65625	25/32— .78125	29/32— .90625
2/32— .06250	6/32— .18750	10/32— .31250	14/32— .43750	18/32— .56250	22/32— .68750	26/32— .81250	30/32— .93750
3/32— .09375	7/32— .21875	11/32— .34375	15/32— .46875	19/32— .59375	23/32— .71875	27/32— .84375	31/32— .96875
4/32— .12500	8/32— .25000	12/32— .37500	16/32— .50000	20/32— .62500	24/32— .75000	28/32— .87500	32/32—1.00000

Exhibit 3-6. C. F. Childs quote sheet for September 12, 1961.

that such a bid is the true market. But if the dealer did this, the market would be down, and he could not unload at a profit. Hence, the work-out arrangement is employed to keep the securities moving.

If the trader likes a salesman's proposition, he hits the bid or takes the offer with the flick of a finger. If he receives an offer and a bid at the same price, he is locked.

The trader may take a "$\frac{1}{2}$," that is, a half-million. He may bid 22 to $22\frac{1}{2}$ split, which means he is buying half of a block at _____.22 and half at _____45/64. A bill trader will usually sell with a rise in the price of bills because there is a new supply of bills coming into the market each week. This makes a difference even though the total volume of outstanding bills does not change, because the new bills must find a home.

If a trader wants to do business, he closes up his spreads. Whether he raises his bid or lowers his asked depends on which way the market is going. Typically, spreads vary with the maturity of the issue. This relationship is apparent in going down the bill list.

Market considerations apart, there is a mechanical reason for the fact that bill spreads widen as maturities become shorter. In order to explain this relationship, it is necessary to compute the dollar equivalent of an .01. (See Table 3-1.) Suppose that a one-year bill is bid 3.45. The price of a $1,000 denomination is then $965.50.[20] Now suppose the bill sells down to 3.46. The price drops to $965.40. Thus the dollar equivalent of an .01 on a $1,000 bill which has one year to run is 0.100000 (=$0.10). Alternatively, if the bill is quoted at 3.45 and matures tomorrow, its price is $999.904187. Now if the bill drops to 3.46, its price falls only to $999.903889. Therefore, if a bill has only one day to run, a 1-basis-point[21] change in the yield is equivalent to a change of $0.000278 in the price of a $1,000 instrument. In other words, the value of an .01 on a $1,000 denomination with 360 days to run is $0.10; with one day to run it is 1/360 of $0.10, or $0.000278.[22] This characteristic of the price-yield-maturity relationship follows from the fact that with a longer maturity, a discount instrument must appreciate more in price to gain a given annual interest return. Hence the spread in yield

---

[20] I.e., the discount $D = Frt = (\$1,000)(0.0345)(1) = \$34.50$. The price $P = F - D = \$1,000 - \$34.50 = \$965.50$.

[21] A basis point is 1/100 of 1 percent, or 0.01 percent.

[22] I.e., $\Delta D = F \cdot \Delta r \cdot t$; or $\Delta D = F(0.10)(1)$ for a one-year security, and $\Delta D = F(0.01)(1/360)$ for a one-day security. See Chap. 1 for a reference to the effect of this relationship on the relative liquidity of short-dated instruments.

TABLE 3-1   Dollar equivalent of an .01 from one day to one year for a $1,000 bill

Days	Equivalent	Days	Equivalent	Days	Equivalent
1	0.000278	32	0.008889	63	0.017500
2	0.000556	33	0.009167	64	0.017778
3	0.000833	34	0.009444	65	0.018056
4	0.001111	35	0.009722	66	0.018333
5	0.001389	36	0.010000	67	0.018611
6	0.001667	37	0.010278	68	0.018889
7	0.001944	38	0.010556	69	0.019167
8	0.002222	39	0.010832	70	0.019444
9	0.002500	40	0.011111	71	0.019722
10	0.002778	41	0.011389	72	0.020000
11	0.003056	42	0.011667	73	0.020278
12	0.003333	43	0.011944	74	0.020556
13	0.003611	44	0.012222	75	0.020833
14	0.003889	45	0.012500	76	0.021111
15	0.004167	46	0.012778	77	0.021389
16	0.004444	47	0.013056	78	0.021667
17	0.004722	48	0.013333	79	0.021944
18	0.005000	49	0.013611	80	0.022222
19	0.005278	50	0.013889	81	0.022500
20	0.005556	51	0.014167	82	0.022778
21	0.005833	52	0.014444	83	0.023056
22	0.006111	53	0.014722	84	0.023333
23	0.006389	54	0.015000	85	0.023611
24	0.006667	55	0.015278	86	0.023889
25	0.006944	56	0.015556	87	0.024167
26	0.007222	57	0.015833	88	0.024444
27	0.007500	58	0.016111	89	0.024722
28	0.007778	59	0.016389	90	0.025000
29	0.008056	60	0.016667	91	0.025278
30	0.008333	61	0.016944		
31	0.008611	62	0.017222		

6 months (180 days)	0.050000
9 months (270 days)	0.075000
1 year (360 days)	0.100000

quotations on a shorter maturity must be greater in order to give the dealer the same dollar spread as on a larger maturity.[23] Thus spreads will vary from 10 to 40 basis points on the short bill and from 1 to 4 basis points on the long bill.

[23] The trader must also have a feel for the dollar value of an .01 when a salesman pleads for a shading of a bill quotation. Only by this means can he evaluate the dollar equivalent of the implied change in the quotation.

The rest of the list is quoted in thirty-seconds of a point.[24] As maturities increase, spreads typically increase, too. Normally they will vary from 1/32 on shorter-term issues to 8/32 on longer-term securities. These may narrow to 1/64 as buying and selling interest increases. On inactive issues, they may widen to a $\frac{1}{2}$ point. If the market fluctuates erratically or shifts precipitately, spreads will increase, particularly in the longer sector.

In buying a dollar bond [25] for delayed delivery, a trader is interested in knowing the number of days interest required to equal 1/32. (See Table 3-2.) For example, if he sells a security carrying a $2\frac{1}{2}$ per-

TABLE 3-2   Number of days interest, on a
365-day basis, required to equal $\frac{1}{32}$

Coupon, percent	Days	Coupon, percent	Days
$\frac{1}{4}$	45.63[1]	$1\frac{7}{8}$	6.08
$\frac{3}{8}$	30.42	2	5.70
$\frac{1}{2}$	22.81	$2\frac{1}{4}$	5.07
$\frac{5}{8}$	18.25	$2\frac{1}{2}$	4.56
$\frac{3}{4}$	15.21	$2\frac{3}{4}$	4.15
$\frac{7}{8}$	13.04	3	3.80
1	11.41	$3\frac{1}{4}$	3.51
$1\frac{1}{8}$	10.14	$3\frac{1}{2}$	3.26
$1\frac{1}{4}$	9.13	$3\frac{3}{4}$	3.04
$1\frac{3}{8}$	8.30	4	2.85
$1\frac{1}{2}$	7.60	$4\frac{1}{4}$	2.68
$1\frac{5}{8}$	7.02	$4\frac{1}{2}$	2.53
$1\frac{3}{4}$	6.52	$4\frac{3}{4}$	2.40

[1] $\frac{1}{32}$ = 0.03125 on the basis of 100. If 0.25 in interest is earned in one 365-day year, it takes 45.63 [= (0.03125/0.25)(365)] days to earn $\frac{1}{32}$.

cent coupon short and the price rises 1/32, it will require 4.56 days of interest to compensate for the price change. But if it is a $4\frac{1}{4}$ percent issue, only 2.68 days are required.

The quotations given by a trader do not necessarily represent a commitment. "Who is it?" he will ask the salesman waiting for a quotation with someone on the wire. If it is a valued customer, the trader may quote an inside market, for example, "dollar less to plus." [26]

[24] A point is equal to $10 on a $1,000 bond.
[25] A security quoted in terms of price.
[26] This is 0.31 + 1/64 bid, 100 + 1/64 asked; or 100 − 1/64 bid, 100 + 1/64 asked.

The administrative cost of processing an order is about the same regardless of its size. Hence dealers may charge an odd-lot fee. This fee may vary from 8/32 on orders for one to five bonds down to 1/32 on orders for fifty to one hundred bonds. These charges vary from firm to firm and among customers of the same firm. Dealers are essentially wholesalers, but the nonbank dealers get an odd-lot business because commercial banks may pass along the relatively small orders of their customers without combining them into larger blocks. In addition, trades up to, say, twenty-five bonds, may be executed for interest and delivery on the second business day from the date of the contract rather than the first business day as is usually the case.

With customers, quotations are usually firm for $5 million in bills, from $1 million to $5 million in certificates, and $1 million in notes and short bonds. Under normal market conditions, quotations for long bonds are good for $100,000 to $250,000. In a thin[27] market, the quantity for which a quotation is firm tends to decline or vanish altogether, so that the amount of individual negotiation increases. In many cases, an offer of long-term bonds will be accepted only on a work-out basis.[28]

In transactions with other dealers, a trader may begin with, "Have you got a trading market?" Quotations in this case are usually good for $1 million in bills and $250,000 in certificates, notes, and short bonds. Dealers often refuse to give one another firm quotations for long bonds.

If a dealer is confronted by a customer with a proposition involving a sizable block of an inactive issue, he may ask for a stock bid or offer—the best price the customer will state to induce the dealer to put the block in position.

If a dealer wishes to conduct business with other dealers without revealing his identity, he will place his order with one of the five brokers that specializes in matching dealer trades. A broker does not take a position but usually charges a commission of 1/64 of 1 point.[29] When a trade is concluded, its terms are reported by the broker to all of the dealers. A broker's activities are concentrated in the note and bond sector, and they are often relied upon if a dealer wants to trade an inactive issue.

[27] Thinness implies a relatively large change in price as the result of the sale of a block of given size.

[28] I.e., the dealer essentially becomes a broker. The price he pays for the bonds depends upon the price at which he is able to sell them.

[29] $15.63 for 100 bonds.

There are three kinds of delivery, namely, cash, regular, and delayed. Treasury bills are typically traded for cash, that is, for payment in Federal funds today, the day the trade is agreed upon. On a Friday, a dealer prefers not to make cash bids, particularly late in the day, though there is no attempt made to shave the portfolio over the weekend. Regular delivery involves delivery tomorrow, the day after the deal is made, and is typically for cash, that is, Federal funds, on that day. Relatively few contracts call for delayed delivery at some point in time after tomorrow. Delayed-delivery contracts, although infrequent, may serve a number of purposes. By this means, a buyer may establish a speculative position which is financed by the dealer. Corporations that expect a large block of funds in from a capital emission may begin to buy Governments in advance so as not to disrupt the market. Financial institutions may desire such contracts for similar reasons.

The FOMC regularly conducts its business with the dealer fraternity.[30] When the Fed, that is, the Securities Department of the Federal Reserve Bank of New York, wants to do an open-market operation in bills, it does a go-around of the dealers.[31] Each dealer is called and asked whether he wishes to show something, that is, make a firm offer or bid, specifying at the same time the quantity he wishes to trade.[32] Upon receiving the dealer's bid or offer, the Fed trader says, "Let me keep it for twenty minutes." During this period he queries the remaining dealers. Then he will come back to those dealers offering the best quotations to conclude the transaction.

When the Federal deals in issues other than bills, the operation is somewhat different. In these cases, Fed traders may contact immediately those dealers who have already shown their offerings without solicitation. The Fed will inquire whether the securities are still available and on what terms. If these dealers can fulfill the Fed's needs, other dealers may not be approached and never know that the Fed has been in the market.

A dealer is not required to make a market every time the Fed does

---

[30] See appendix for a bibliography on open-market operations.

[31] This is the usual procedure. Sometimes, on the other hand, bills will be purchased or sold on the basis of unsolicited offerings or bids from the dealers.

[32] The Fed trader specifies whether the transaction is to be on a cash- or regular-delivery basis. Normally, a cash-delivery basis is required; though the dealer may be given an option.

a go-around. But if he should stay out of the market for a prolonged period either by refusing to bid or offer or by maintaining unusually wide spreads, he would probably be dropped from the Fed's list. A dealer would not ordinarily go short to the Fed, for he would not wish to risk the possibility of a fail in delivery.

When the Fed comes around with bills to offer, a dealer will probably take $5 million to $10 million at the market. If certificates or notes are offered, a dealer may take $1 million to $2 million. If the Fed starts selling longer stuff, some dealers may withdraw on the second or third day, even at scaled prices.

The Fed also conducts business for Treasury-managed trust funds, foreign central banks, certain international organizations, and small member banks which do not have good access to the dealer market. In these cases, the Fed trader may not do a go-around. Rather, he may choose the best market from recently sampled quotations. Normally, the Fed trader will ask for a recapitulation of the transaction when representing a foreign institution, a practice not usually followed when acting for the FOMC. However, the fact that no recap may be requested when serving the Treasury prevents the use of this device as a sure means of identifying the intervention of the Open Market Account.

In its role as fiscal agent for the Treasury, the Federal Reserve System manages many of the technical aspects of debt-management operations. The New York Government bond houses, of course, deal with the Federal Reserve Bank of New York. Each Monday, the bill trader is preoccupied with the Treasury bill auction. About 12:30, he starts checking the market. To get the feel of the market, he calls other dealers, the banks, and important customers. "Will holders let their bills run off?" "Is the Fed bidding for Treasury or foreign accounts?"

Market trends and expectations will, of course, influence the bidding. But as a rule of thumb, in the case of the ninety-one-day issue, 2 or 3 basis points may be added to the quotation on the bill sold in the previous week's auction. If the new bill comes out at dividend, tax, or Christmas Club payment time, 5 to 7 basis points may be added.

At 1:25, the bid is called in to the dealer's runner, who is posted in a telephone booth, at a desk, or possibly in a broom closet near the Fed. At 1:30, the bill trader calls the other dealers for their bids. The greater the uncertainty in the market, the greater the scale-out of the bids. (For examples of actual dispersions of dealer bids for ninety-one-

TABLE 3-3   An actual dispersion of selected dealer ninety-one-day bill bids[1]

Price	Dealer													
	A	B	C	D	E	F	G	H	I	J	K	L	M	N
266								30						
265	40			50	10		50							
264		50			20	100	25						5	
263		25	50		10		25						5	5
262					10						100	10	5	
261									15	30		15	5	

[1] Prices are the three decimal places permitted by the Treasury. That is, the actual prices bid are 99.266, 99.265, etc. Amounts are in millions of dollars.

day bills, see Tables 3-3 and 3-4.) Normally, some scale-out results from throwaway bids,[33] which may appear despite relative unanimity in the market. There is always a chance that a dealer may get his hands on some cheap bills!

Unless it wishes to tighten up the money market by letting its bills run off, the System will tender also. Its tender is placed close to the deadline after sampling market sentiment. In this way the System is able to place a bid that will not be unnecessarily high but will be reasonably sure to win bills.

By checking the breakoff point in the Tuesday morning papers, each bill trader knows what he and the other dealers got. And then trading in the new bill begins. Since buyers usually dominate the market for a new bill, traders close up their spreads. If the System has missed, which rarely happens, it may have been that the market was aggressive. By the time Thursday, the payment day, rolls around, the dealer's inventory of new bills may well have all been sold.

Nondealer as well as dealer banks advise their correspondents on the bill tender, but the latter tender at their own Federal Reserve banks. The banks do tender, however, for their nonbank customers. Usually such customers leave competitive bids to the discretion of the tendering bank. Moreover, in this case, the customer does not have to put up a down payment. Also, the bank is obligated to deliver the bills. If it misses, the bank must go to the market in order to make delivery. If the customer designates the bid price, the bank is not responsible for the success of the tender.

[33] Sometimes these are euphemistically called underwriting bids.

TABLE 3-4   An actual dispersion of selected dealer ninety-one-day bill bids[1]

Price	Dealer													
	A	B	C	D	E	F	G	H	I	J	K	L	M	N
241						5								
240						5								
239						5	5							
238						5		5			10			
237			15		5		5			30				
236	5			10		5						5		
235					5		5					5		
234						5		5			10	5		
233	5			5	5		5					5		
232		5	10	10		5						5		5
231				5	5		5					10		
230	5					5		5			10			
229					5		5		5					
228						5					10			
227	5						5				5			
226					5	5					5			
225							5				5			
224											5			
223					5						5		5	
222											5			
221											5			
220					5						25			
219														
218	5												5	
217					5									

[1] Prices are the three decimal places permitted by the Treasury. That is, the actual prices are 99.241, 99.240, etc. Amounts are in millions of dollars.

If TABs or other securities issued against tax and loan account credit are offered, the nonbank dealers stand on the sidelines. They cannot compete with the banks in this case.

In a cash offering, the dealers join the large investors in trying to guess allotments. Their eagerness depends on their evaluation of the terms set by the Treasury. In case of an exchange offering, the Treasury announcement is first checked to see what the Fed can bid on. If the Fed holds a large block of rights, it is more difficult to judge the tender situation, although the Fed usually goes for the "anchor" issue. If the terms seem favorable, dealers will bid aggressively for rights. If not, participation will be reduced to a polite minimum. Depending upon their expectations regarding market trends, the dealers will act to push the market down to the new-issue yield or to push the new security to a premium when the offering is made at a yield above the current yield pattern.

When a dealer buys rights from an investor who wishes to do his own refunding, the dealer may dispose of the rights in one of three ways. He may sell the rights to another investor who wants the exchange issue. He may proceed to sell the new security on a when-issued basis while the subscription books are open. Or he may position the new security himself. In any case, making a market for rights smooths the digestion process involved in distributing a new security in place of one about to mature.

It is estimated that dealers, on the average, take about 20 percent of the regular ninety-one-day bill issue and from 25 to 30 percent of the regular 182-day bills. They take from 5 to 20 percent of the public awards of longer-term securities not offered on a tax and loan account basis.

To some extent there is a tendency for bank dealers to concentrate more heavily upon the short end of the market. This reflects, of course, the over-all investment philosophy of the commercial banking industry. To some extent, also, a dealer bank may deal on more favorable terms in order to avoid losing a depositor. In this case, the dealer operation becomes something of an additional service for a depositor.

DEALER POSITIONS

As the name implies, a Government securities dealer acts as a principal rather than simply as a broker. The extent to which a market will be made throughout the list of outstanding securities varies from dealer to dealer. But as noted earlier, the FOMC will do business with the twenty firms designated as primary dealers. Thus they have met the minimum standards set by the FOMC for making markets. In making a market, the dealer may take either a long or a short position. In the former case, the dealer buys the securities and owns them outright. In the case of a short position, the dealer sells securities he does not own. He therefore borrows the securities in order to make delivery.

The willingness of a dealer to make a market, then, implies a willingness to narrow his spreads for the purpose of taking securities into position. His willingness to take a position in the market depends, for the most part, upon the expected profitability of doing so. And these expectations vary according to economic conditions and the complexion of monetary and debt-management policy. The process by which these expectations are formulated and the variety of factors taken into account are exceedingly complex. All available information is sifted carefully. Each new piece of information carries some weight. Out of the mass of detail comes a consensus, but a consensus which, with the rush of events, is immediately succeeded by another.

Dealer positions reflect the dominant view of the trend of economic forces. But within this broad framework, they reflect the often inexplicable forces of the market, whose pressures, in centripetal fashion, converge upon the dealer firm. For this reason, the trader flies by the seat of his pants more often than not, making his way into the unknown future on the basis of what he feels.

In any case, it is the dealer's position that reflects his view of the market and its potentialities. The bulk of a dealer's holdings is in his trading position, which includes securities that are immediately available or will soon be available for sale plus those which have been borrowed to make delivery. In addition, a dealer may own an investment portfolio, set aside in the hope of long-term capital gains or of making money on the difference between interest returns and financing costs. But these securities are not available for trading purposes. Hence they are of peripheral importance to the dealer operation.

Between positions, dealers are more prone to the long side. There are important asymmetries that account for this preference. The primary ones are relative financing costs, the difficulty of borrowing securities, and market inelasticity in covering the short sale. Never mentioned but of doubtless importance is the vague feeling that it is easier to do something with what you have than with something you do not possess—a variant of the bird-in-the-hand theme. Whatever the attempted rationalization, dealers are more often long than short. In bad times, they move toward zero but not far beyond. During the 1948–1958 period, for example, net positions were relatively high in December, 1949, June and December, 1952, December, 1953, June, 1954, December, 1957, and June, 1958. (See Table 3-5.) These peaks correspond roughly with periods of monetary ease and reflect the dealers' attempts to reap speculative gains in a buoyant bond market.

TABLE 3-5   *Dealer net positions*[1]

Year	Number of firms	June	December
1948	13	877.1	790.2
1949	14	233.9	891.4
1950	14	458.2	693.0
1951	14	624.7	724.7
1952	14	1,261.6	1,166.1
1953	14	404.7	1,505.7
1954	14	1,377.8	748.8
1955	14	393.9	764.1
1956	14	532.8	660.3
1957	14	541.4	1,511.2
1958	14	1,415.4	1.048.4

[1] SOURCE: Allan H. Meltzer and Gert von der Linde, A Study of the Dealer Market for Federal Government Securities, materials prepared for the Joint Economic Committee, 86th Congress, 2d Session, Washington, D.C.: Government Printing Office, 1960, table III-6, p. 41. Amounts are in millions of dollars.

FINANCING AND CLEARANCE

Oftentimes, the chief cashier is the unsung hero of the dealer drama. The leading role is played by the trader, whose exuberance may project him into the position of one who is hoist with his own petard. When the shouting is over and the din of the fray subsides, it is the cashier who must pick up the pieces. He must deliver the securities sold. He must find the wherewithal to pay for those which have been bought.

Probably in no phase of the dealer operation is human ingenuity more manifest than in the financing and clearing operation. It includes buy-backs, RPs, resales, borrowed securities, fails, Fed funds transactions, the tailoring of contracts, and a coverage of sources of supply wherever money can be found.[34]

Operations with narrow spreads can be profitable only if the dealer can achieve a high leverage factor on his capital base, a factor which, incidentally, not only increases the opportunity for gain but also the danger of loss. Dealers in Governments are able to achieve a high leverage factor primarily because of the gilt-edge quality of their assets. In addition, they must submit regular financial reports to the Federal Reserve Bank of New York. The fact that they qualify for RP

[34] See appendix for a bibliography on dealer financing.

accommodation by the Fed speaks well for their credit standing. The fact that a majority of the dealer firms are limited-liability corporations is not a relevant consideration.

Thus dealers operate on a very low margin of invested capital. Accommodation by money-market banks may be obtained on a margin as low as 2 percent in the case of bonds, 1 percent for intermediate maturities, and zero for Treasury bills.[35] For nonbank dealers, positions have been as much as twenty-six times net worth during the postwar period.[36] In 1953, when this was so, the aggregate of dealer net positions in Governments and agencies was seventy-two times total cash balances.[37]

A dealer's chief financing worry concerns the financing of his long position. For this purpose, dealers rely primarily upon collateralized call loans and repurchase agreements (RPs). There are two kinds of call loans, namely, day loans and overnight loans. Day loans must be repaid the same day they are made. These loans are used to pay off a loan for which the securities have been used as collateral or to pay for securities being delivered. The day loan, therefore, is used to finance the securities until they can be sold for cash or until an overnight loan or other financing can be arranged so as to pay off the day loan. The day loan is in clearinghouse funds. That is, it is a credit to the borrower's bank account which he can draw upon. If the loan is to be used to carry securities being delivered against Fed funds, the dealer must make other arrangements to acquire the Federal funds.[38] No

[35] See testimony by Girard L. Spencer, *Employment, Growth, and Price Levels, Hearings before the Joint Economic Committee,* 86th Congress, 1st Session, Aug. 5, 6, 7, 1959, Washington, D.C.: Government Printing Office, 1959, part 6B, pp. 1558–1559.

[36] Allan H. Meltzer and Gert von der Linde, *A Study of the Dealer Market for Federal Government Securities,* materials prepared for the Joint Economic Committee, 86th Congress, 2d Session, Washington, D.C.: Government Printing Office, 1960, table VI-2, p. 101.

[37] Based on *ibid.,* table III-2, p. 37, and table VI-5, p. 103.

[38] Federal funds are deposit liabilities of the Federal Reserve banks. Like currency, a draft on a Federal Reserve bank is cash in the sense that it can be immediately converted into deposits at a Federal Reserve bank. Clearinghouse funds, by contrast, are cash tomorrow. In other words, a draft on a Federal Reserve bank gives the holder immediate ownership of Federal funds. The holder of a check drawn on a commercial bank member of the New York Clearing House Association cannot acquire Federal funds until the next day. This is due to the fact that a bank presenting a check at the clearing will not

margin is required on day loans. In a sense, day loans amount to additional working capital that is used to clear the day's transactions. The rate of interest charged is usually 1 percent. Nor does the lender have possession of the securities. However, the loan is safeguarded by a lien or chattel mortgage on the securities being financed, and a list of the securities may be attached to the borrower's note. (For a sample day-loan agreement, see Exhibit 3-7.)

An overnight loan is used to carry the long position overnight. (For a sample overnight-loan agreement, see Exhibit 3-8.) These loans are made with the New York money-market banks on an overnight or over-the-weekend basis. The securities being financed are put up as collateral for the loan. The loans, referred to as call loans, are made in clearinghouse funds, or Federal funds if they are required to pay for the securities being taken into position. Hence the dealer is only charged the call-loan rate for one day, or for three days if it is an over-the-weekend loan.

As noted above, margin requirements are relatively low. However, in periods of rapidly deteriorating markets, the lending bank may issue a margin call. The rate of interest charged on call loans varies with the availability of funds. In periods of tight money, it tends to reduce and sometimes makes negative the carry on the dealer's position.[39] One might suppose that a call loan, collateralized by Treasury securities, would be more liquid than the underlying collateral and hence involve an interest charge which is lower than the yield of those securities.[40] However, there is some tendency on the part of the dealer to develop a customer relationship with the lending bank. Therefore the loans do not have the impersonal nature of the traditional call loan. Hence their rates tend to be more competitive with customer loans. In the event a dealer cannot find accommodation elsewhere, he can always have recourse to his clearing bank even though the loan forces the bank into the Fed. In this sense, the clearing bank acts as a lender of last resort.

It has been the negative carry on call-loan financing that has induced the dealers to seek RP accommodation. *Ceteris paribus,* a dealer

---

receive credit for the check in his account at the Federal Reserve Bank of New York until the following day. See appendix for a bibliography on the Federal funds market.

[39] Carry is equal to the coupon less financing costs.

[40] Such is the case in Great Britain and Canada.

DAY NOTE AND PLEDGE AGREEMENT

New York,⸺⸺⸺⸺⸺⸺, 19⸺⸺

The undersigned having applied to the MANUFACTURERS TRUST COMPANY, 55 Broad Street, New York, New York (hereinafter called the "Trust Company"), for a loan of⸺⸺⸺⸺⸺⸺⸺⸺⸺⸺⸺⸺⸺⸺⸺⸺Dollars ($⸺⸺⸺⸺⸺⸺⸺⸺), to be credited to the account of the undersigned, upon the terms and conditions below stated, and in consideration of such loan the undersigned agree(s).

1. To repay this loan at or before the close of business this day, with interest at the rate of ⸺⸺⸺⸺⸺% per annum.

2. That the avails of said loan shall be used only for the following purposes:
    (a) To pay, in whole or in part, the purchase price of, and thus to obtain, securities which the undersigned has contracted to purchase and receive; or
    (b) To pay, in whole or in part, another loan or other loans heretofore made to the undersigned, and thus to release to the undersigned securities held as collateral for such other loan or loans.

3. That as security for the payment of this loan, the Trust Company shall have (in addition to any and all liens provided for in any general loan and collateral agreement, note or other instrument heretofore or hereafter executed by the undersigned) a lien upon:
    (a) All securities received by the undersigned (or to which the undersigned may be entitled) by the use of the avails of this loan; and
    (b) All securities received by the undersigned (or to which the undersigned may be entitled) by the use of any other funds withdrawn by the undersigned from the Trust Company during this day.

4. That the undersigned shall keep the securities described in paragraph 3 above separate and apart from all other securities in trust for and as the property of the Trust Company, shall keep and maintain a complete record of said securities, and shall deliver the said securities to the Trust Company before the close of business this day, unless this loan shall have been repaid to the Trust Company. The undersigned may, however, before the close of business this day, sell, transfer or exchange or pledge for cash contemporaneously loaned, any or all of the said securities, but the proceeds of any such sale, transfer or loan or the securities acquired in exchange shall forthwith become subject to lien as collateral security for this loan and shall be held by the undersigned in trust for the Trust Company and the undersigned shall account therefor to the Trust Company and shall pay and/or deliver to the Trust Company the said proceeds and avails of such sale, transfer, loan or the exchanged securities before the close of business this day, unless this loan shall have been paid to the Trust Company.

5. To further secure the Trust Company, the undersigned hereby assigns to the Trust Company, its successors and assigns, all of the right, title and interest of the undersigned to and in any and all claims of the undersigned against third parties now existing, and that may be created this day for the purchase price or any present unpaid balance thereof, of any of the securities sold, transferred, exchanged or pledged by the undersigned, and to and in all claims of the undersigned against customers of the undersigned for the balance due or to become due for the purchase price of any of said securities, or the proceeds thereof, delivered or deliverable to such customers.

6. That the Trust Company's lien on securities carried for the account of any customer of the undersigned, which secure this loan, shall not be greater at any particular time than the amount of the funds withdrawn from the Trust Company by the undersigned during this day and used for the purpose of acquiring securities for or on behalf of customers of the undersigned. The terms "customer" and "securities carried for the account of any customer" are used herein as the said terms are defined in Rules X-8C-1(b)(1)(2) and X-15C2-1(b)(1)(2) of the Securities and Exchange Commission which appear on the reverse side hereof.

7. That the provisions of this agreement shall supersede any contrary or inconsistent provision of any collateral loan agreement heretofore or hereafter executed by the undersigned and delivered to the Trust Company.

⸺⸺⸺⸺⸺⸺⸺⸺⸺⸺⸺⸺⸺⸺⸺⸺⸺⸺⸺⸺⸺⸺⸺

By⸺⸺⸺⸺⸺⸺⸺⸺⸺⸺⸺⸺⸺⸺⸺⸺⸺⸺⸺

1276   3-55

Exhibit 3-7. Sample day-loan agreement.

would prefer to finance his portfolio with the money-market banks. Scouring the country for funds entails time and telephone expense, and the processing of repurchase-money contracts involves extra handling and clearance charges. In addition, the call loan usually permits greater flexibility than the RP in such matters as the maturity range

C. F. CHILDS & COMPANY
INCORPORATED

ONE WALL STREET
NEW YORK 5. N. Y.

New York 5, N. Y.,_____

THE CHASE MANHATTAN BANK

Under the terms of your form of General Loan and Collateral Agreement
which we have signed and is on file with you, we hereby deliver you the
securities listed below against which please lend us $
with interest at   % per annum, payable on demand.

C. F. CHILDS & COMPANY
INCORPORATED

_____   _____
VICE PRESIDENT   ASST. TREASURER
ASST. TREASURER   ASST. SECRETARY

COLLATERAL	PRICE	MARKET VALUE
TOTAL		

Exhibit 3-8. Sample overnight-loan agreement.

acceptable by the lender and the substitution of collateral. But the difference in interest cost has been of paramount importance.

RPs are made primarily with nonfinancial corporations[41] and out-of-town banks. Other sources of repurchase money include the Federal Home Loan banks, state and local governments,[42] foreign agency

[41] See appendix for a bibliography on corporate cash management.
[42] See appendix for a bibliography on state and local investment funds.

banks,[43] mutual savings banks,[44] savings and loan associations,[45] and last but not least, the Federal Reserve Bank of New York.

According to the terms of a repurchase contract, a dealer will sell a block of securities to the lender, agreeing to repurchase the same block of securities at the same price at an appointed time in the future and to pay a specified rate of interest on the borrowed funds. The rate of interest is normally less than the call-loan rate. The maturity of the contract varies from overnight to several weeks or months. Longer-term contracts may provide for a double call option and for the substitutability of collateral. Both sale and repurchase are against Fed funds.

Nonfinancial corporations find the RP a desirable investment medium because the term of the contract may be tailored to meet the corporation's need for funds, and capital-value risk is practically nil.

Commercial banks find the RP a suitable short-term investment for several reasons. First, the rate of return often exceeds that on Federal funds. Second, the size of the transaction may be more convenient. On the one hand, the amount of lendable funds may be less than $1 million, which is the basic trading unit in Fed funds, but still large enough to be of interest to a Government securities dealer. On the other hand, the amount of available funds may exceed the bank's loan limit. With certain exceptions, a national bank is not permitted to lend to a single borrower an amount in excess of its capital and surplus.[46] An important exception is made in the case of repurchase agreements involving Government securities. In this case, a national bank may lend any amount to a single borrower provided the loan is secured by United States obligations having maturities not greater than eighteen months.[47] This means that a bank which is not permitted to lend a block of Federal funds in an amount exceeding the statutory limit governing straight loans can accomplish the same objective by entering into a repurchase agreement.

For the Federal Reserve Bank of New York, the repurchase agree-

[43] See Andrew F. Brimmer, "Foreign Banking Institutions in the United States Money Market," *Review of Economics and Statistics,* vol. 44, no. 1, February, 1962, pp. 76–81.

[44] See appendix for a bibliography on mutual savings banks.

[45] See appendix for a bibliography on savings and loan associations.

[46] 12 U.S.C. § 84. State banks operate under similar limitations.

[47] Comptroller of the Currency, *Regulation Regarding National Bank Loans Secured by Direct Obligations of the United States,* Apr. 17, 1958.

ment is an important instrument of monetary policy, one which contributes additional flexibility to its management of the money market. If the Fed wishes to act in a way which contributes marginal ease to the market, it makes outright purchases of Government securities. If it wishes to impart market ease of a more temporary nature, the Fed will enter into repurchase contracts with Government securities dealers.[48] (For a sample repurchase agreement with the Federal Reserve Bank of New York, see Exhibit 3-9.) These new reserves thus injected into the market are said to be on a string, because they are automatically extinguished at the termination of the contract. New reserves may be created under even more stringent conditions by forcing into the discount window the money-market bank that accommodates the dealer as a lender of last resort.[49]

RPs are only made by the Fed with nonbank dealers.[50] The contract may run up to fifteen days but is callable both ways. The instrument is particularly useful as an aid to heavily stocked dealers during a Treasury exchange offering. It also lends precision to the allocation of new money, inasmuch as the dealers under heaviest pressure may be given direct assistance, instead of being forced to capture the aid indirectly as in the case of outright purchases by the Federal Reserve from other dealers. The amount of repurchase money made available to a particular dealer[51] depends upon the dealer's financial capacity as well as the Fed's objective with respect to conditions in the money market. In accepting Federal Reserve aid by this means, a dealer is also limited by the fact that the securities involved are normally valued slightly below the market. This means that the dealer's capital is encumbered to the extent of the difference between the valuation assigned by the Trading Desk and the cost of the securities to the dealer. The rate of interest charged by the Fed is usually the same as its discount rate, though this need not be the case.[52]

[48] Dealers may request repurchase money, but accommodation is at the initiative of the Fed. RPs are not participated in by other Federal Reserve banks as is the Open Market Account.

[49] There is also greater statistical stringency in this case, since RPs are not added to member bank borrowing in the calculation of free reserves.

[50] Bank dealers have access to the discount window.

[51] These funds are credited to the account of the dealer's bank.

[52] During periods of easy money when the Fed is eager to put out reserves by this means, a rate lower than the discount rate may be charged in case the dealers would not find financing at the discount rate particularly attractive.

_____
(Date)

Federal Reserve Bank of New York,
New York 45, N. Y.

Gentlemen:

      We hand you herewith United States Government securities (with
all unmatured coupons, if any, attached), having a total par value of
$_____, listed below, which we have today sold to you for
$_____. In consideration of the purchase by you of such secu-
rities, we hereby agree to repurchase them from you at any time at your
or our option on or before_____, at the same price plus
interest thereon at the rate of ___ % per annum for the number of days
that said securities are held by you. It is understood that, if any of
the attached coupons mature before we repurchase the securities as provided above, you will, upon notice by us, deliver such coupons to us or
collect them for our account. Our obligations hereunder are secured by
and subject to the terms and conditions of our general collateral agreement with you.

Very truly yours,

_____
(Name of dealer)

By_____
(Signature)

_____
(Title)

SCHEDULE OF SECURITIES COVERED BY ABOVE AGREEMENT

Description of issue	Maturity	Amount (Par Value)

Exhibit 3-9. Sample repurchase agreement with the Federal Reserve Bank of New York.

Similar to the RP, but infrequently used, is the buy-back, or overnight. This method of borrowing Federal funds differs in two respects
from the repurchase agreement. First, two separate contracts are involved. Second, the buy-back normally involves the sale of a bundle
of securities at one price and its repurchase at a different price. Since

the tax effects of the capital gains and losses resulting from such trades make it difficult to compute the effective yield on the loan, it is customary to restrict the use of this instrument to the financing of tax-exempt securities or Treasury bills, whose price changes are not treated as capital gains or losses for tax purposes.

The available evidence[53] indicates that the nonbank dealers, in their search for repurchase money, perform an important function in equalizing money-market pressures throughout the country. As money becomes tight in New York, the dealers seek funds elsewhere. In the process of substituting RPs for collateral loans, funds are drawn from outlying regions to the center,[54] thus easing the money shortage in New York and spreading the stringency to other areas.

Short positions are, of course, taken for their own sake. But they may be used as a means of financing a long position. When a dealer sells short, he is immediately put in funds. These funds can then be used to finance a long position. Whether this is worthwhile, of course, depends upon the balance of costs and returns involved. For example, a dealer may sell a 2 percent note short and go long $2\frac{1}{2}$ percent bonds with the proceeds of the short sale. His running, or out-of-pocket, costs[55] will then be the 2 percent coupon on the note plus a $\frac{1}{2}$ of 1 percent borrowing fee. To offset this, he will have the $2\frac{1}{2}$ percent coupon of the bonds held in long position.[56]

A dealer may do a short sale for any one of three reasons. First, as just suggested, a short position may be employed as an integral part of the financing apparatus. Second, a short position may be under-

[53] See *Treasury-Federal Reserve Study of the Government Securities Market,* Washington, D.C.: Treasury Department and Board of Governors, Federal Reserve System, February, 1960, part II, table C-3, pp. 142–143; and Meltzer and von der Linde, *A Study of the Dealer Market for Federal Government Securities,* pp. 71–95.

[54] It has erroneously been stated by some New York bankers that the development of the repurchase agreement has cost them deposits. This may be true, of course, on an individual-bank basis. But in the aggregate, the use of repurchase agreements by nonbank dealers has brought money to New York, not the reverse.

[55] There will also be the opportunity cost of the capital involved in meeting the margin requirements for the borrowed notes.

[56] This example assumes either that there are no losses or gains in covering his short position or in unwinding his long position or that a gain and a loss are equal to each other.

taken for speculative purposes. Difficulties and costs involved in borrowing securities[57] must be weighed in the balance with bearish expectations. Many portfolio managers are not permitted to lend securities. Moreover, in a demoralized market, institutional investors may be "locked in," thus inhibiting the covering of a short sale. But if a short sale of long-term securities is made for speculative reasons, financing costs may be reduced in either of two ways. A long position in bills or relatively short-term securities, whose prices are unlikely to fall as much as the longs, may be acquired. Alternatively, the dealer may do a resale agreement, say, with a commercial bank. Under the terms of such a contract, the dealer buys at a rate of interest a shade lower than the discount rate a block of securities which he then pledges as collateral for the borrowed issue. The bank, in turn, agrees to repurchase the securities at the time that the dealer wishes to cover his short position. The dealer, therefore, is able to reduce his financing costs, to the extent of his interest earnings from the bank, and at the same time to eliminate the capital-value risk associated with the long position in pledged securities.

Finally, a dealer may do a short position, irrespective of market expectations, in order to meet the needs of a valued customer. In this event, especially in the face of considerable uncertainty, the dealer may hedge his position by going long a similar issue, assuming he cannot buy the issue he sold on favorable terms. The latter may not only be used as collateral to reduce financing costs. It will also serve to offset possible capital losses entailed in covering the short position.

An integral part of the trading operation is the provision for the physical transfer of securities. Nonbank dealers, for the most part, rely heavily upon one of the large money-market banks as clearing agent.[58] For this clearing service, the dealers may be charged $10 for $1 million in Treasury bills, $15 for $1 million in certificates, and $35 for $1 mil-

---

[57] It is quite possible that the cashier may find it impossible to borrow the securities sold short, though he makes it his business to know what securities various investors have available to lend. In case he cannot find the necessary securities, the liability "fails" is credited, rather than the usual "borrowed bonds." In any case, interest on the securities must be paid to the purchaser by the dealer, even though the buyer does not put up cash until the securities are actually delivered.

[58] Two other money-market banks also perform the clearing function, and one nonbank dealer does its own clearing.

lion in longer maturities.[59] Deliveries involved in trades with customers in New York are made by messenger. Delivery is also accomplished by personal messenger when the securities are transferred to a New York bank performing a custody function for an out-of-town customer. The physical delivery of securities to and by out-of-town customers is achieved over the Commissioner of the Public Debt (CPD) wire-transfer system. By means of this facility, a seller can present his securities at practically any Federal Reserve bank or branch and have them transmitted by wire to virtually any other Federal Reserve bank or branch. No charge is made for securities maturing or called within one year. In other cases, a charge of $5 is made for transfers of amounts up to $50,000 in face value, and $10 for amounts of $50,000 and over.[60]

VOLUME AND COMPOSITION OF TRADING, AND DEALER PROFITS

The relative importance of dealer volume is highlighted by a comparison with activity on an organized exchange. During 1958, $34.1 billion in stocks and bonds was sold on the New York Stock Exchange. During the same year, sales of Government securities through the dealer market amounted to $176.5 billion.[61] The average of annual ratios of dealer sales to outstanding securities for the 1948–1958 period was 0.79 for bills, 0.56 for certificates, and 0.33 for notes and bonds.[62] In addition to the size and composition of the outstanding marketable

[59] Meltzer and von der Linde, *A Study of the Dealer Market for Federal Government Securities,* p. 25. Clearing charges for some dealers run lower than those cited in this study.

[60] In each instance, the transfer must be a single issue and to a single recipient. Most Federal Reserve banks and branches will also make denominational exchanges (DXs), supplying securities in units of $1,000, $10,000, $100,-000, and $1 million.

The Helena Branch of the Federal Reserve Bank of Minneapolis does not participate in this system, nor can securities be transferred to the Buffalo Branch of the Federal Reserve Bank of New York. See Robert V. Roosa, *Federal Reserve Operations in the Money and Government Securities Markets,* Federal Reserve Bank of New York, July, 1956, pp. 41–42.

[61] Total dealer volume, i.e., dealer purchases and sales, was $353,005,000,000. The sales figure quoted above was gotten by dividing the volume figure by 2. See Meltzer and von der Linde, *A Study of the Dealer Market for Federal Government Securities,* pp. 49–69, 105–140; table IV-2, p. 58; and pp. 59, 68.

[62] Quarterly sales were used in computing the ratio for bills. See *ibid.,* table IV-3, p. 59, and table IV-4, p. 60.

debt, changes in monetary policy and Treasury debt-management operations appear to be important factors influencing dealer trading volume.

During the same eleven-year period, the eight largest dealers accounted for more than 80 percent of total transactions, the five largest accounted for over 60 percent, and the three largest for over 40 percent. The composition of the three groups of dealers changed during the period, however. The degree of dealer specialization is highest in certificates and lowest in bills. Specialization in certificates is heightened by increased Treasury reliance upon them during periods of tight money, while specialization in bonds is lessened because of the broad interest in long-terms during periods of monetary ease. Six firms appear to dominate the market—they are active throughout the entire maturity range, have large sales staffs, and numerous branch offices. But their share of the total market decreased during the 1948–1958 period.[63]

Gross profits of dealer firms are derived primarily from speculative activity, nonspeculative trading, and interest on a long position. Speculative profits[64] may be gotten from a long position when securities prices rise or from a short position when securities prices fall. Nonspeculative trading profit stems from the spread between bid and asked quotations at a given level of securities prices. Finally, dealers receive

[63] *Ibid.*, pp. 67–68.

[64] M. A. Gilmartin, Jr., has identified the following types of speculative trading:

> *Trend Trading* I would define as any purchase and/or sale made for subsequent reversal, predicated solely upon one's judgment or guess of future market levels; *Spread Trading* as any simultaneous purchase and sale, or the converse, made with or without anticipation of a subsequent reversal, to procure an existing advantage or favorable disparity in price, in yield, or in maturity. *Arbitrage*—The term as used commercially is a misnomer when applied to traffic in Government securities. In Government securities transactions the term means the simultaneous purchase and sale, or the converse, for subsequent reversal of obligations *definitely* comparable in standing and to the calculated maturity; the exchange involved to be initiated at such price or yield differential as essential experience tables or charts indicate with reasonable probability will permit an ultimate reversal gain.

This quotation is taken from "Exploring Management Problems of U.S. Government Securities Portfolio," *Savings Bank Journal,* April, 1940, vol. 21, no. 2, p. 46.

interest on their long position. The latter concept is straightforward in the case of coupon instruments, since it consists simply of coupon interest. In the case of discount instruments, a change in the basis introduces a speculative element. In either case the separation of nonspeculative trading profit from speculative profit is conceptually difficult because of fluctuations in the level of the market.[65] Moreover, the available data do not correspond to these ideal concepts.

Gross earnings reported for the 1948–1958 period consist of trading profit, interest received, and other earnings. Trading profit occurs whenever a sale is made at a price exceeding the cost of purchase. Thus the concept of trading profit includes both the spread and a speculative element. In 1953, 1957, and 1958, trading profit constituted the largest single source of gross earnings.[66] In each of the remaining eight years of the 1948–1958 period, interest received was the largest source.[67]

As related to sales, trading profits peaked in 1949, 1953, 1957, and 1958. Gross earnings, consisting primarily of trading profits and interest received, were relatively high in 1949, 1953, 1954, 1957, and 1958. (See Table 3-6.) These were periods of comparative ease in the money market. The relative prosperity enjoyed by the dealers stemmed from speculative return on relatively high net long positions. (See Table 3-5.) In addition, there was a noticeable increase in spreads after the Treasury–Federal Reserve Accord of March, 1951.[68]

A rough measure[69] of the financial burden entailed in holding a long position is given by subtracting interest paid from interest re-

[65] Suppose, for example, that a security is purchased when the quotation is 99.28–par. Later the same day, the same issue is sold when quoted 99.29–99.31. Has the dealer suffered a capital loss of 1/32, enjoyed a profit from the spread of 1/32, or something else depending upon the terms on which he acquired his position in this issue? Or suppose the spread remains the same, the market is down, but a block is still sold at a profit. The resulting net profit is the algebraic sum of a capital loss and a quotation spread.

[66] Trading profit includes a relatively small item, profit from investment accounts.

[67] See Meltzer and von der Linde, *A Study of the Dealer Market for Federal Government Securities,* table VII-1, p. 108.

[68] See Dudley G. Luckett, " 'Bills Only,': A Critical Appraisal," *Review of Economics and Statistics,* vol. 42, no. 3, part 1, August, 1960, chart 1, p. 302.

[69] The suggested measure is inaccurate, since interest paid includes interest on borrowed securities, and interest received includes interest on long positions held as a hedge or for the purpose of reducing the financing cost of a short position.

TABLE 3-6   Dealer earnings and expenses[1]

	1948	1949	1950	1951	1952	1953	1954	1955	1956	1957	1958
Total trading profit	60.65	153.11	46.40	104.15	112.06	213.99	152.58	71.48	117.22	370.04	353.46
Interest received	121.86	231.22	109.06	103.93	130.32	152.48	161.55	147.76	151.07	196.04	165.16
Other earnings	4.11	4.27	3.98	4.90	7.76	6.33	6.41	9.14	11.47	13.92	7.36
Gross earnings	186.62	388.60	159.44	212.98	250.14	372.80	320.54	228.38	279.76	580.00	525.98
Interest paid	78.94	172.54	89.92	102.87	119.07	138.31	125.97	137.71	160.86	261.00	186.20
Salaries	48.71	59.84	34.12	44.30	45.78	50.33	44.23	46.13	51.20	60.90	58.91
Other current expenses	39.56	45.47	36.51	44.51	47.53	53.31	50.64	57.55	60.99	62.64	62.59
Local taxes and statistical discrepancy	2.61	4.66	1.76	1.71	2.24	2.23	1.62	1.61	1.95	3.48	4.73
Net income before special charges and income taxes	16.80	106.09	−2.87	19.59	35.52	128.62	98.08	−14.62	4.76	191.98	213.55
Number of dealers reporting	8	10	11	12	12	13	13	13	13	13	13

[1] SOURCE: Allan H Meltzer and Gert von der Linde, A Study of the Dealer Market for Federal Government Securities, materials prepared for the Joint Economic Committee, 86th Congress, 2d Session, Washington, D.C.: Government Printing Office, 1960, table VII-4, p. 114. Amounts are in dollars per million dollars of sales.

ceived. (See Table 3-7.) The dealers enjoyed an over-all positive carry during the 1948–1955 period. They suffered an over-all negative carry in 1956, 1957, and 1958. This record highlights the increasing difficulty confronting the dealer in his search for the means of financing a long position. This development also provided a major share of the impetus

TABLE 3-7   Position carry[1]

Year	Interest received	Interest paid	Interest differential
1948	121.86	78.94	42.92
1949	231.22	172.54	58.68
1950	109.06	89.92	19.14
1951	103.93	102.87	1.06
1952	130.32	119.07	11.25
1953	152.48	138.31	24.17
1954	161.55	125.97	35.58
1955	147.76	137.71	10.05
1956	151.07	160.86	− 9.79
1957	196.04	261.00	−64.96
1958	165.16	186.20	−21.04

[1] SOURCE: Allan H. Meltzer and Gert von der Linde, A Study of the Dealer Market for Federal Government Securities, materials prepared for the Joint Economic Committee, 86th Congress, 2d Session, Washington, D.C.: Government Printing Office, 1960, table VII-7, p. 120. Amounts are in dollars per million dollars of sales.

given to the perfection of the repurchase technique. The dealer has been compressed by the turn of the screw as the disappearance of the wartime excess in liquidity has driven up call-money rates at the same time that the maturity of dealer inventories has shrunk.

THE BANK DEALER

The dealer department of a commercial bank is something of an enigma. On the one hand, it absorbs funds that might be used by the loan department. On the other hand, it may generate income directly from its own operations and indirectly by attracting new deposits. The value of the public relations role is understandably difficult to assess. That there is no clear-cut conception of the cost of the dealer operation is evident from the wide variety of practices employed by dealer banks. The dealer department may not be assessed a charge for the funds it uses. It may, on the other hand, be charged a rate of interest equal to the discount rate, the Federal funds rate, the Treasury bill rate, the dealer-loan rate, or perhaps the customer-loan rate. A rational allocation of funds is, of course, not easy to attain. But it is unlikely that all of these methods could be rational at one and the same time. Many of the larger banks have refused to establish dealer departments, perhaps reflecting the difficulty of determining their value to the over-all commercial banking operation.[70]

The position policy of the bank dealer tends to be more conservative than that of the large nonbank dealer. This conservatism is reflected in a desire to avoid short sales and in a tendency to concentrate on shorter maturities. The latter policy is, of course, consistent with the commercial-loan theory of bank assets, according to which it is improper for a commercial bank to make long-term commitments. It is true, on the other hand, that bank dealers will sell bills short if they are in need of reserves and the bill rate is below the funds market.

For tax purposes, the position of the dealer department of a commercial bank must be kept strictly segregated from the bank's investment account. The investment department is also morally bound to maintain strict secrecy regarding its transactions with nonbank dealers, especially in the case of borrowed securities.

[70] In one instance, the bank does not wish to be put in the position of being accused of pushing the Government market around in the event it has a large block of business to do.

There is some evidence that the bank dealers enjoy a competitive advantage over the nonbank dealers from the point of view of costs. During the 1948–1958 period, the rate paid for funds by dealer departments appears to have been lower in most years than the rate paid by nonbank dealers. If all interest received and paid by dealer departments of commercial banks were excluded from the totals described above, a negative interest differential would appear in 1951, 1952, and 1955, as well as in 1956, 1957, and 1958.[71] (See Table 3-7.)

THE VALUE OF A TAX AND LOAN ACCOUNT DEPOSIT

The Treasury may reduce the interest cost of a new issue by permitting commercial bank depositaries to pay for their subscriptions through credits to the Treasury's Tax and Loan (T and L) Account.[72] Nonbank dealers sit on the sidelines during these financings because of the superior competitive position of the commercial banks. However, the research departments of nonbank as well as bank dealers are actively engaged in computing the value of a tax and loan account deposit. This is a service provided commercial bank customers.

Treasury depositaries enjoy a competitive advantage because of the potential profitability of acquiring Governments through T and L account credits. This profit potential is based upon the lower-than-average velocity of tax and loan account deposits. If, for example, an individual bank has excess reserves of $1 million, that bank can either make loans of $1 million[73] or, assuming a 20 percent reserve requirement, buy $5 million in Governments with T and L account credit. The bank can acquire a multiple amount of securities in the latter case because the T and L account is normally not subject to immediate call. Or the bank can sell the Governments thus acquired and make higher-yielding loans of $5 million for the period prior to the call.[74]

---

[71] See Meltzer and von der Linde, *A Study of the Dealer Market for Federal Government Securities,* pp. 121–122, 130.

[72] This practice is normally restricted to cash offerings of tax bills or certificates. See appendix for a bibliography on Treasury Tax and Loan Accounts.

[73] At a particular point in time, a single bank can lend an amount equal to excess reserves. It cannot lend more because of the expected loss of the reserves as a result of the lending process. Over time, a bank may make loans in excess of its initial excess reserves because of the existence of derivative deposits.

[74] Of course, the banking system as a whole could not sell these Govern-

If all T and L account deposits were subject to immediate call. their velocity would not be less than deposits derived from making the usual loan. Hence the operation would not be profitable. However, suppose that, though T and L account deposits are not normally subject to immediate call, the Treasury decides to offer the banks a single issue for T and L account credit with immediate call. In this case, it would still be profitable for the individual bank to subscribe. This is due to the fact that each depositary is subject to call anyway, regardless of its participation in this particular financing. Consequently, in order to maintain the level of its slow-moving deposits and corresponding assets, the bank must subscribe.

When the Treasury does call the deposits corresponding to the new acquisition, the banking system as a whole cannot, assuming zero excess reserves, meet the call simply by selling the newly acquired Governments, though sales to nonbanks will release a fractional amount of the needed reserves. The remainder will have to be obtained at the discount window, or the Federal Reserve will have to see to it that the necessary reserves are provided by one means or another.

The profitability of the T and L account may be measured in terms of the basis-point loss that can be sustained when the securities acquired are sold to obtain the funds required to meet the Treasury call.[75] To illustrate the method of computation, suppose 1 million 270-day tax bills are won at a price of 98.312500, that is, on a 2.25 basis.[76] To pay for the bills, the bank credits the Treasury T and L account $983,125.

Next, an estimate must be made of the period of time that the funds will be left with the bank. In arriving at this figure, the bank considers the Treasury's cash position, nearness to a tax date, and its own experience with Treasury calls.

An experience factor may be calculated as follows. Suppose the

---

ments and gain $5 million in new reserves. However, the individual bank is certain of increasing its assets by $5 million with the T and L account acquisition. Should it decide to sell the Governments in order to gain reserves with which to make loans, its assets will still be greater than otherwise so long as the customers of other banks purchase more Governments from it than its customers purchase from other banks in a similar position. This will be the case even though the banking system as a whole cannot gain new reserves.

[75] As pointed out earlier, the level of T and L account deposits is protected even though the securities are sold at or below the break-even point.

[76] For the mechanics of bill-yield and -price computation, see Chap. 1.

total T and L account balance after the tax-bill acquisition is $1,966,-250. After six days, assume the Treasury issues a 2 percent call. Then $(0.02)(\$1,966,250)(983,125/1,966,250) = \$19,662.50$ is the amount of the call coming out of that portion of the T and L account due to the TABs. This leaves a balance of $\$983,125 - \$19,662.50 = \$963,462.50$ due to the TABs. The $983,125 was held six days, giving 5,898,750 dollar-days. This procedure is followed through successive calls until the remainder due to the TABs reaches a negligible magnitude. Then, the sum of dollar-days is divided by the initial $983,125 to give the average number of days the funds were available.

Alternatively, an actual forecast of the Treasury's cash flows may be used as a basis for estimating calls on the T and L account. Whatever the method used, suppose that the funds will be left with the bank for twenty days. If the bills are then sold at the same price they were acquired at, the basis will be 2.43. Thus, a loss of 18 basis points may be sustained and still break even.[77]

If the bank does not have excess reserves, it may go to the discount window. If the reserve requirement is 20 percent, the discount rate is 2 percent, and the funds are repaid in 20 days, the break-even basis would be 2.40. That is, $(0.20)(0.02)(98.3125)(20/360) = 0.0218472$, the cost of the required reserves on the basis of 100. The addition of 0.0218472 to 98.3125 gives 98.3343472, the higher price which must now be obtained to break even. The discount then becomes 1.6656528, and $r = (360/250)(0.016656528) = .02398540032$.

The value of a T and L account balance may also be computed on the assumption that the tax bills are sold immediately,[78] a portion of the new funds set aside for the additional required reserves, and the remainder lent in the funds or bill market.[79] The dollar return to this investment can then be divided by the appropriate dollar value of an .01 to give the value of the T and L account in basis points.

[77] Since the bills were bought on a 2.25 basis, a sale at 2.43 involves a loss of 18 basis points.

[78] In these calculations, it is assumed that the bills are sold at their acquisition price, an unrealistic assumption. The nonbank market is generally lower because it cannot subscribe with T and L account credits.

[79] For no less than eighteen different rates used by various commercial banks in computing the earning value of their T and L account balance, see *Report on Treasury Tax and Loan Accounts, Services Rendered by Banks for the Federal Government, and Other Related Matters,* Treasury Department Fiscal Service, June 15, 1960, p. 7.

chapter 4

A THEORY OF
THE DETERMINATION
OF DEALER POSITIONS

This chapter is theoretical in content. The first section is devoted to the question of defining dealer performance in making a market—which, it is found, is reflected in dealer position policy—and to identifying the factors that determine a dealer's willingness to make a market, that is, to take a position in the market. In the second section, an abstract model of dealer position policy is constructed.

THE MARKET PERFORMANCE
OF THE GOVERNMENT SECURITIES DEALERS

A willingness to commit capital-at-risk in taking the positions involved in making a market is the essence of the dealer function. The exercise of this function generates place, time, and form utility. The location of the market to which investors may have recourse is widely publicized and generally known in the financial community. In maintaining this market, therefore, it may be said that the dealers are creating place utility. In addition, a time gap is bridged between the desire of one investor to buy and that of another to sell. The dealer bridges this gap through shifts in his position and thereby produces what may be called time utility. Finally, investors may require earning assets which do not correspond to the maturity dates of outstanding issues. Dealers create form utility by standing ready to buy outstanding securities

118

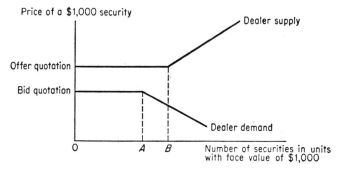

Figure 4-1.

when investors wish to disinvest. They also create form utility through
the medium of a repurchase agreement. By this means, a dealer creates
special maturities and removes market risk for the investor. In the performance of the function of making a market, the dealer incurs costs
and bears the risk of capital loss. In compensation, he hopes to extract
from the market a trading profit—the spread between bid and asked
quotations.

The Government securities dealers form the apex of the market;
they do not, on the other hand, comprise the total market. The market
is composed of all of the myriad private investors in Government
securities, along with the Treasury, the Federal Reserve System, and
other governmental units or agencies. It is the composite of changes in
supply and demand emanating from all of these sources that dominates
the rise and decline in the level of interest rates and shifts in their
maturity structure. Consequently, dealer performance cannot be inferred from the historical pattern of interest rates. Rather, the quality
of the market which dealers make must be judged by the pattern of
their operations.

Further insight into the nature of dealer performance may be had
by referring to Figure 4-1. Here an individual dealer's supply of, and
demand for, a particular security are depicted.[1] *OA* shows the quantity
of securities for which the bid quotation represents a firm commitment. *OB* represents the number of securities for which the offer quota-

[1] There is a highly efficient communication system in the dealer market,
so that dealer quotes tend to be the same throughout the market. This eliminates one of the problems of aggregation. Aggregate schedules would, nevertheless, be stepped, because different dealers would undertake commitments
of different magnitudes at various prices.

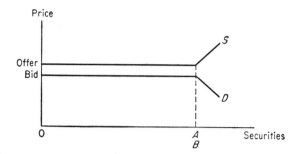

Figure 4-2.

tion is good. For larger quantities, a dealer's supply and demand become less than perfectly elastic.[2]

The quality of the dealer's market, then, is measured by the quantity of securities for which the bid and offer quotations are firm and by the narrowness of the spread between these quotations. Typically, these characteristics of good market behavior will appear simultaneously. For a dealer will narrow his spreads in order to compete more effectively.[3] Hence a willingness to undertake larger commitments is implied by, and accompanies, a narrowing of spreads. A good market appears in Figure 4-2. Here spreads are narrow, and commitments are large and the same on both sides of the market.

A thin market is illustrated in Figure 4-3. The dealer has backed away from the market by widening his spread. Quotations are nominal, and commitments will be made only at sharply scaled prices.[4] In a

[2] In Figure 4-1, $OB > OA$, indicating that the dealer is making a better market on the offer side. This relationship might be reversed, or the segments might be equal.

[3] In order to get a new customer, a dealer might even offer at the bid price or buy at the offer quotation.

[4] The fact that there is variation in the quantity for which a particular quotation represents a firm commitment makes difficult the interpretation of published quotations and yield patterns. For example, during a particular period there may be substantial sales of intermediate-term Governments by commercial banks, accompanied by relatively little activity in the long-term sector on the part of insurance companies. A humped yield pattern might result. If such a term structure of interest rates were accepted at face value, it might be concluded that insurance company portfolios were in equilibrium at the indicated long-term yields. In fact, these portfolios are in equilibrium only at the higher yields which would be effective were the securities actually sold. Thus, to be realistic, a yield pattern would have to be adjusted so that the amount for which each quotation was good would be the same throughout the list.

badly demoralized market, characterized by great uncertainty, the supply and demand schedules might vanish altogether. The dealer would accept orders only on a work-out basis.[5] That is, he would cease to be a dealer and would be performing only a brokerage function.

In a disorderly market, characterized by a rapid upward or downward movement in the level of interest rates, one side of the market may vanish. Such a condition would be represented by Figure 4-2 with one of the schedules removed. The remaining schedule would be perfectly elastic over a wide range, reflecting the dealer's desire to achieve a rapid shift in his position.

In addition to making markets for the purpose of gaining a trading profit, dealers also speculate. Their speculative transactions will accelerate the rate of change of securities prices if, when prices are falling, dealers increase their rate of sales or decrease their rate of purchases or if, when prices are rising, they increase their rate of purchases or decrease their rate of sales. Dealers, therefore, may accelerate as well as retard the movement of securities prices.

In other markets, the effects of such speculative activities might be deplored. The Government securities market is unique, however, in that changes in the level and structure of interest rates, which may be objectives of economic policy, are involved. If, in other words, speculative transactions are undertaken as a result of a shift in monetary or debt-management policy, these dealer actions promote the attainment of a policy objective.

Whatever the cause, however, of the shifting structure of the basic

[5] Even under stable market conditions, an extremely large order will be accepted only on this basis.

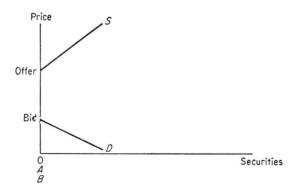

Figure 4-3.

conditions of supply and demand, it would be fatuous to suppose that dealers could, even if they would, buck a market trend. For were they to attempt to do so, they would face certain bankruptcy; and the existing market mechanism would be destroyed. A market trend could not be halted or reversed by the limited resources of the dealers. Such an objective could be achieved only through intervention by monetary authorities with unlimited power to create or destroy money.

Nevertheless, barring an underlying change in market conditions, it is desirable to have dealers behave in a manner that results in a retardation of interest-rate movements. It is not desirable to have a rapid movement in interest rates occur whenever an investor wishes to execute a portfolio shift. The market should absorb such adjustments easily.

It is true that market improvement of this variety tends to make Government securities more liquid. Hence if dealers' expectations are in error, with their operations tending to be contrary to the tenor of economic policy, good market performance provides a limited "escape" from a restrictive monetary or debt-management policy. Thus market improvement would make it easier for banks and other financial institutions to substitute loans for Government securities, offsetting to some extent the effects of a restrictive policy by facilitating an increase in expenditures and, therefore, monetary velocity.[6] All that is required from the viewpoint of economic policy, however, is a more energetic execution of the policy in question. But the market would still perform better in that erratic fluctuations in interest rates bearing no relationship to a fundamental change in economic conditions or economic policy would be limited. The objective of improved performance in the Government securities market, therefore, deserves the attention of those who seek a smoothly functioning capital market.[7]

[6] See, e.g., Assar Lindbeck, The "New" Theory of Credit Control in the United States, Stockholm Economic Studies, Pamphlet Series no. 1 (2d ed.), Stockholm: University of Stockholm, 1962, p. 49.

[7] On the role of the capital market, see Norman Macrae, The London Capital Market, London: Staples Press, 1955, pp. 11–12, quoted by Maurice A. Gilmartin, Jr., in testimony for Chas. E. Quincey and Co., Employment, Growth, and Price Levels, Hearings before the Joint Economic Committee, 86th Congress, 1st Session, part 6C: The Government's Management of Its Monetary, Fiscal, and Debt Operations, Washington, D.C.: Government Printing Office, 1959, p. 1828.

It has been shown that the performance of a dealer may be identified with his willingness to commit himself at narrow spreads. Since dealer policy with respect to commitments and spreads reflects a particular position objective, performance can also be depicted in terms of position policy.

Moreover, looking toward an eventual empirical evaluation, it must be recognized that the content of commitment and spread policy defies detection. Commitments will vary within the same market day as a result of changes in the dealer's position. That is, so long as a difference between the actual and desired position exists, commitments will be relatively large or small according to the relationship between the position objective and the customer's side of the market. Once a position proximate to that desired is achieved, commitments will tend to be more nearly the same size. These variations in commitment policy are not subject to empirical verification, since no published data on the subject are available.

Comparable difficulties arise in the case of spread policy. Actual transactions regularly occur at inside spreads. These true spreads are narrower than those reflected in the published quotations, and they vary more frequently than quoted spreads in response to fluctuations in market conditions. Unfortunately, only published quotations are available.[8] An empirical evaluation of dealer performance must look, then, to dealer positions.

Since investor offers and bids tend to be imperfectly synchronized, dealer positions tend to be larger when spreads are narrow and commitments are large.[9] Hence the quality of the market[10] ordinarily varies with the magnitude of gross positions. A large long position reflects the willingness of a dealer to risk his capital in the outright ownership of securities. A large short position involves a similar capital risk

[8] Dudley G. Luckett found significant variations in monthly averages of daily quoted spreads. Weekly averages, on the other hand, were relatively insensitive to weekly variations in market conditions. See his " 'Bills only': A Critical Appraisal," *Review of Economic Statistics,* vol. 42, no. 3, part 1, August, 1960, pp. 302–303.

[9] It is true that a prolonged one-way movement in interest rates would be characterized by extremely poor synchronization, wide spreads, and one-sided commitments. Nevertheless, some lack of synchronization is a necessary condition for the existence of a dealer function.

[10] As measured by spreads and commitments.

that results from supplying securities which the dealer does not own.[11]

It might appear to be ideal if the dealer always held a long position in each outstanding issue in order to be able to satisfy bids for any security. However, financing costs and the risk of capital loss may inhibit such a policy. Despite this fact, market performance need not be affected adversely so long as the dealer is willing to short the security in question. Nevertheless, these possible patterns of dealer behavior make it difficult to judge market performance by reference solely to positions.

In general, however, a small net position in combination with small gross positions will be accompanied by large spreads. This will provide prima-facie evidence of dealer withdrawal from the market. A large net position associated with a large short *or* long position will usually indicate that the dealer has been actively engaged in moving with the market trend. Such a movement tends to be accompanied by wide spreads. A small net position accompanied by large gross positions, on the other hand, will usually be accompanied by narrow spreads and will reflect good market performance.

The determinants of position policy may be classified in two categories, those affecting the expected return and those affecting the variance of that return. The former category encompasses all of those factors which, in turn, determine interest-rate expectations. The crucial role of interest-rate expectations is accounted for by the fact that, at least for the larger, more aggressive dealers, speculative profits and losses constitute the chief sources of changes in net worth.[12] The tenor of interest-rate expectations is the outcome of the whole complex of factors that affect the forecast of economic activity, economic policy, and conditions in the money and capital markets. Thus an expectation of lower interest rates will be associated with an increase in long positions and a decrease in short positions, an expectation of an up-

[11] Cf. the following view: "Thus, it is to be expected that when dealers are doing their job in making markets, their positions will be relatively large, will turn over rapidly, and will usually include gross long and gross short holdings considerably larger in the aggregate than the net position." *Treasury–Federal Reserve Study of the Government Securities Market,* Washington, D.C.: Treasury Department and Board of Governors, Federal Reserve System, February, 1960, part 3, p. 11.

[12] Smaller dealers who restrict themselves largely to a merchandising operation in bills are not affected as much by interest-rate expectations.

ward movement with a reduction in long positions and an expansion in short positions.

The effect of interest-rate expectations upon dealer positions, though clear-cut in direction, is subject to certain asymmetries. The impact of the factors involved combines to inhibit the ability of the dealer to make a profit when interest rates are rising as readily as when they are declining.[13] The rationale of this apparent fact is not easy to construct.[14] However, certain important considerations can be identified. One concerns financing arrangements. Net financing charges may be positive or negative with either a long or short position. With a long position, the net financing rate is equal to:

the holding-period yield of the securities

less

the opportunity cost, in yield terms, of the capital tied up in margining the securities and in accrued interest.[15]

less

the interest rate charged on the loan or repurchase agreement by which the position is financed.

On a short position, the net financing rate is equal to:

the holding-period yield of securities bought with the proceeds of the short sale and put up as collateral for the borrowed securities

less

---

[13] It has been suggested that the duration of cycle phases explains this asymmetry. However, in twenty-five cycles during the 1854–1958 period, the duration of expansions exceeded that of contractions in sixteen cases. This was true of all of the postwar cycles of the 1945–1958 period. See *The National Bureau's Research on Indicators of Cyclical Revivals and Recessions,* New York: National Bureau of Economic Research, August, 1960, table 1, p. 5.

An alternative hypothesis, but one of restricted applicability, is that a dealer bank would not want it known that it had built up its short position and then raised the prime rate.

[14] Its existence is vividly described but hardly explained in the following quotation: "On a rising market there is always one big seller able to supply stock at a price. In a falling market there is not even one big buyer." See *The Economist,* July 6, 1957, p. 53.

[15] The dealer is reimbursed for outlays on accrued interest when coupons are cashed or when the securities are sold.

the coupon on the securities borrowed plus $\frac{1}{2}$ of 1 percent

less

the opportunity cost, in terms of yield, of the capital used to margin the borrowed securities.[16]

Though it is not clear that the balance of financing costs favors the long position, the conventional premium on borrowed securities tends to make it so.[17]

A more important consideration is the difficulty of finding the securities to sell short. The financial officers of some institutions are not permitted by their governing bodies to lend securities. Moreover, and particularly in the case of small issues, it may be difficult to locate holdings of the desired issue in institutions that will lend securities.

A related factor of great importance is the uncertainty attached to the borrowing commitment. It is true that the market may become thin on either the upside or the downside. But a dealer does not have to unwind his long position on the upside. Although financing costs may be against him, he can usually finance a long position at some price. The lender of securities, on the other hand, may call his loan and force the dealer to cover his short position at an inopportune moment.

Moreover, it may be more difficult in terms of price movements to cover a short position than to liquidate a long one. That is, in unwind-

---

[16] If accrued interest is paid the lending institution, the dealer recoups the same when the borrowed securities are delivered to the buyer.

[17] Characteristically, a dealer would consider the carry, a simpler concept of net financing charges than that described above. Long-position carry is defined as the coupon on the securities owned less the interest rate charged on the collateral loan or RP. With a short position, carry consists of the coupon on the securities used as collateral less the sum of the coupon on the borrowed securities and $\frac{1}{2}$ of 1 percent.

A concept that is at an intermediate level of sophistication with respect to carry and holding-period yield is stock yield. This differs from carry when, e.g., a security is sold short at a price below par. The stock-yield computation would then take account of the fact that the dealer is paying interest for the use of the proceeds of a short sale that amounts to *less* than $1,000 per bond.

Stock yield and coupon are both carry concepts and both reflect more faithfully a dealer's manner of thinking about his commitment. I.e., he takes on a speculative position and then considers financing costs separately from the question of capital gains or losses. Hence, holding-period yield, which includes changes in capital value, is inappropriate.

ing a long position, dealer supply shifts to the right and faces a relatively elastic demand in a buoyant market. In covering a short position, dealer demand increases in the face of relatively inelastic supply. The latter lock-in effect stems from institutional irrational constraints which limit the realization of capital losses.[18] For these reasons, an expected decline in securities prices will not evoke the same response in gross and net positions as an expected movement in the opposite direction.

Thus the first factor affecting expected return is the direction of the movement of interest rates. A second factor related to expected return is the cost of available financing accommodation. It has just been observed that the balance of financing costs may have an unequal impact upon long and short positions. However, asymmetries aside, the net return from a dealer's position is necessarily affected by deductions for the cost of financing, regardless of the side of the market the dealer is on. Since borrowed funds account for the bulk of a dealer's financing, the relative cost of financing would seem to be an important determinant of dealer position policy.

As noted before, dealers finance their positions chiefly through call loans from money-market banks and repurchase agreements with out-of-town commercial banks, nonfinancial corporations, and other institutional lenders.[19] The call-loan rate is a preferential rate to dealers on loans collateralized by Governments. However, it regularly exceeds other money-market rates and normally imposes a negative carry. Moreover, even at these levels, the dealers cannot always rely upon the New York banks.[20]

The onerous level of call-loan rates has given the dealers an incentive to cultivate other financing sources, chiefly in the form of repurchase-money accommodation. Given the same interest charge, dealers would prefer to borrow from the money-market banks. These

[18] To some extent the lock-in effect is offset by commercial bank tax switching. Commercial banks, as has been noted earlier, are permitted to write off net capital losses against ordinary income. On the other hand, it must be remembered that tax switching consists of the sale of one security plus its replacement by a similar security. It does not consist simply of sloughing Governments for the purpose of expanding the loan portfolio.

[19] See appendix for a bibliography on dealer financing.

[20] There are a few exceptional banks which play the role of lenders of last resort to the dealers. The relationship is much like the Bank of England's relationship to the London discount houses.

loans do not involve a search for funds, nor do they require tailoring of terms to suit the lender. But out-of-town borrowing costs have usually been less. To a large extent, dealers finance their bill portfolios and other short-term paper with repurchase agreements, relying more heavily upon the New York banks for funds to carry long-term holdings. The cost of carrying a short position is regularly reduced by the return from a corresponding long position in short maturities. This is not necessarily a hedging operation. Rather, it may simply be a matter of getting some return from the proceeds of the short sale.

Finally, in promoting the objectives of monetary policy, the Federal Reserve Bank of New York sometimes lends to the dealers under repurchase agreement.

The impact of financing terms upon position taking varies with maturity, since the longer the term of the security, the greater the importance of the trend in interest rates as far as capital values are concerned. In so far as the cost of accommodation is measured by posted rates, these costs tend to lag behind movements in open-market rates. To some extent, therefore, the asymmetry of position policy is softened by this relationship. That is, during periods of rising interest rates, financing relationships, for a time at least, tend to be favorable, particularly as short-term market rates flex rapidly upward. The reverse is true of the downswing. Whatever the relationship may be, however, financing costs necessarily play an important role because of the low margin of equity capital.

The remaining factors affecting position policy operate through their impact upon the variance of the expected return, that is, the degree of certainty with which the expected return is expected.

An increase in the degree of uncertainty regarding future interest-rate movements may evoke either of two kinds of reactions from the dealers with regard to position policy. On the one hand, the dealer may reduce his gross position. On the other, he may maintain his gross position and counteract the increased uncertainty by hedging his existing gross position through an offsetting position on the opposite side of the market. For example, if, in order to take care of a customer, a dealer reluctantly takes a security into long position, he may do one of two things. He may get even by selling out, or he may sell something else short. In the latter case, he will try, of course, to short an issue which he feels is high-priced relative to the one he owns.

On the other hand, if the dealer is a reluctant seller, he may cover immediately. Or he may hedge through taking a similar maturity into long position. Even if the dealer does not hedge, he will typically invest the proceeds of a short sale in bills simply as a matter of reducing financing costs. This practice in part explains the fact that a dealer never shows an over-all net short position.

More specifically, the possible reactions to an increase in uncertainty may be delineated as follows. First, an increase in uncertainty may lead to a reduction in gross long *and* gross short positions. Second, the result may be a relatively constant long position accompanied by an increase in short sales. The latter reaction will be forthcoming if the benefit derived from the reduction in uncertainty due to hedging exceeds the benefit given up as a result of the loss that may stem from the short position.

With reference to gross short position, the above dichotomy implies a decrease in Case 1 and an increase in Case 2. With regard to net position, the second case obviously implies a decrease. The first case also implies a decrease in net position. This is true because of the bias in favor of a long position as dealer commitments expand. There seems to be a bias in this direction for several reasons. First, as explained earlier, dealers will tend to offset a short position by a long position in something in order to reduce financing costs regardless of hedging considerations. Second, dealers will prefer to be long in order to have the goods on the shelf, as it were, when demand appears. Finally, as noted before, there are numerous factors contributing an asymmetry to position policy against the short side. In particular, the dealer may encounter difficulty in borrowing securities; and even if he is successful, he is never certain as to when the lender will call his securities, forcing the dealer to cover his short position, perhaps prematurely.

Of the two possible reactions described above, the first seems the more plausible. One might suppose that a dealer who is confronted by greater uncertainty could still maintain large gross positions by means of hedging. Several considerations may prevent such a policy, however. First, the balance of hedged costs may not give a positive carry. Second, the prices of the securities involved may not move together in the same direction. Finally, there are the asymmetries involved in a short position that are not offset by a corresponding long position.[21]

[21] When differing maturities are considered, two kinds of hedges may be distinguished. A bull hedge consists of hedging a short sale of shorts by going

An important determinant of the degree of uncertainty, and hence of dealer performance, is the volume of transactions at a given level of securities prices. When confronted by increased activity on both sides of the market, a dealer is willing to raise his bid prices and increase his long position because he can readily sell whatever he buys. Similarly, he is willing to lower his offer prices and decrease his long position or increase his short position because he knows he can easily buy what he sells. In other words, greater volume means reduced uncertainty concerning the dealer's ability to sell what he has bought and buy what he has sold. Hence greater volume reduces the uncertainty of the return which the dealer may expect from his position. Increased activity on both sides of the market, therefore, will lead to larger gross long and short positions. It will also tend to result in a larger positive net position because of the bias toward the long side of the market.[22]

A marked expansion in activity on one side of the market will, of course, result in wider spreads and a tendency for gross positions to move with the market rather than in a compensatory fashion.

An important determinant of volume and the degree of uncertainty is the size of the issue held outside the Federal Reserve System and Treasury-managed trust funds.[23] A larger issue will tend to be held more widely. Thus there will tend to be more buy and sell orders, and these orders will tend to be of a more random character.

A small issue, on the other hand, tends to be tucked away in investment portfolios and is difficult to buy. Thus dealers are reluctant to short the issue for fear of being whipsawed by the market in attempting

---

long longs. This is designated a bull hedge because the price of the longs is expected to rise more than the price of the shorts. A bear hedge consists of hedging a short sale of longs by going long shorts. In this case, it is expected that prices will decline but that the decline in the price of the longs will be greater than the decline in the price of the shorts.

[22] Cf. *Stock Market Volume and Price Trends,* Bernstein-Macaulay, Inc., New York, Jan. 2, 1963.

[23] The market value of outstanding corporate bonds has been used as a measure of their marketability. See Lawrence Fisher, "Determinants of Risk Premiums on Corporate Bonds," *Journal of Political Economy,* vol. 67, no. 3, June, 1959, p. 225.

In an unpublished study of activity in Treasury securities, Morris Mendelson and Sally J. Altman found a *negative* relationship between size of issue and changes in institutional holdings as reported in the Treasury Survey of Ownership for 1951–1958. They explained the negative correlation by a lumpiness factor. That is, there tends to be a minimum-size block for doing business.

to cover their short position. Similarly, a long position may be difficult to unwind because the issue is not well known and therefore not in demand.

Another important determinant of volume is Treasury financing operations. Investor interest in particular issues is clearly sparked by the imminence of a Treasury financing, and volume and position reflect this factor. Following the closing of the books on a cash offering and before the payment date, sales on a when-issued basis will be in evidence. Transactions in rights will expand prior to an exchange offering; and when the terms of the exchange offering are announced, trading in the new security begins on a when-issued basis. Depending, of course, upon their "success" in the weekly bill auction, dealers' bill inventories rise and fall as the new bill is taken in and then distributed.

A trend factor has also been operating on volume since the advent of flexible interest rates in 1951. This has been the growth of tax switching by commercial banks. As noted earlier, these institutions are permitted, under certain circumstances, to offset current taxable income with long-term capital losses.[24] They can thereby reduce their tax liabilities by selling one security at a loss and replacing it with another security that is dissimilar for tax purposes but similar enough for purposes of maintaining the desired position.

The volatility of interest rates also affects the degree of uncertainty and, consequently, a dealer's position policy. A great deal of up-and-down price movement will be accompanied by greater uncertainty with regard to the future trend of interest rates. In these circumstances, dealers tend to compensate for the increased uncertainty by making poorer markets, which are reflected in wider spreads and smaller gross positions.

Finally, an important factor affecting dealer performance is the maturity of the issue involved. *Ceteris paribus,* near-term securities will be positioned more readily for the simple, arithmetical reason that given changes in interest rates have a lesser impact upon their prices.[25] Hence the risk of loss tends to be less than in the case of longer-dated securities.[26]

---

[24] See the discussion of tax switching in Chap. 2.

[25] See the discussion of the relationship between maturity and liquidity in Chap. 1.

[26] The greater range of short-term interest-rate movements does not appear to offset this factor completely.

AN ABSTRACT MODEL OF DEALER POSITION POLICY[27]

This section is devoted to the construction of a theory of the determination of dealer positions. The theory will be based upon the expected-utility hypothesis,[28] according to which the decision maker is assumed to maximize utility, which, in turn, depends upon a subjective evaluation of the function's moments. The theoretical model that is constructed will summarize the factors affecting dealer positions delineated in the preceding section. The model will also serve as a rudimentary basis for an empirical evaluation of the importance of these factors.

Let Y represent the change in wealth, a random variable, and let utility depend on Y in the following way:

$$U(Y) = \alpha Y - \beta Y^2$$

where $\alpha > 0$ and $\beta > 0$.

Thus it is assumed that utility varies positively with the first moment of the income distribution and negatively with the second moment.[29]

Let Y be defined as follows:

$$Y = X_L y_L$$

where X_L represents the number of $1,000 (face value) bonds (issued on a discount basis) held in long position, and

$$y_L = u_L - p_L$$

where u_L is the future price, p_L the present price of the security, and y_L the difference between these two prices.

[27] The author is indebted to the editors of *Rivista Internazionale di Scienze Economiche e Commerciali* for permission to base this section on Ira O. Scott, Jr., "An Abstract Model of Dealer Position Policy," *Rivista Internazionale di Scienze Economiche e Commerciali,* anno 9, n. 9, 1962, pp. 3-8.

[28] This hypothesis serves the author's present purposes. However, many doubt its validity as a description of human behavior. See, e.g., G. L. S. Shackle, *Expectations in Economics,* New York: Cambridge University Press, 1952; C. F. Carter, G. P. Meredith, and G. L. S. Shackle, *Uncertainty and Business Decisions,* Liverpool: Liverpool University Press, 1957; and James W. Angell, "Uncertainty, Likelihoods and Investment Decisions," *Quarterly Journal of Economics,* vol. 74, no. 1, February, 1960, pp. 1–28.

[29] For a discussion of the relationship between moments and degree in a utility function, see Harry M. Markowitz, *Portfolio Selection,* New York: John Wiley & Sons, Inc., 1959, pp. 286–287; and Marcel K. Richter, "Cardinal Utility, Portfolio Selection and Taxation," *Review of Economic Studies,* vol. 27 (3), no. 74, June, 1960, p. 153.

Next, suppose that u_L is a random variable and that $\overline{u}_L$ is its expected value. Then $\overline{y}_L = \overline{u}_L - p_L$, with $\overline{u}_L > p_L$; therefore $\overline{y}_L > 0$.
Expected income, therefore, is defined as

$$E(Y) = X_L \overline{y}_L \tag{1}$$

while the variance of income is

$$V(Y) = X_L{}^2 \sigma_L{}^2 \tag{2}$$

where σ_L is the variance of y_L.[30]
Expected utility then becomes

$$E(U) = \alpha E(Y) - \beta [E(Y)]^2 - \beta V(Y) \quad \text{[31]}$$
$$= \alpha X_L \overline{y}_L - \beta X_L{}^2 \overline{y}_L{}^2 - \beta X_L{}^2 \sigma_L{}^2$$

Assuming that the dealer maximizes $E(U)$,[32] $\delta E(U)/\delta X_L = 0$, or

$$X_L = \frac{\alpha \overline{y}_L}{2\beta(\overline{y}_L{}^2 + \sigma_L{}^2)} \tag{3}$$

Finally, there is the budget equation:

$$\frac{1}{r_L}(b - M) = X_L p_L \tag{4}$$

where r_L represents the margin requirement for borrowing with X_L as collateral, b stands for the beginning cash position, and M is the ending cash position. Therefore, $M \geq 0$.[33]

There are, consequently, four equations, four variables [$E(Y)$, $V(Y)$, X_L, and M], and eight parameters (α, β, r_L, b, $\overline{u}_L$, p_L, $\overline{y}_L$, and σ_L).

[30] Thus y is determined by factors affecting interest-rate expectations and financing costs. Factors such as volume, the size of the issue, maturity, and interest-rate volatility—which affect the degree of uncertainty with respect to y—determine σ.

[31] Hence the condition that $\delta E(U)/\delta E(Y) > 0$ implies $\alpha/\beta > 2\ E(Y)$.

[32] Alternatively, it might be assumed that the long-run value of wealth is maximized. This goal may be approached by choosing that portfolio with the highest geometric mean of returns weighted by their respective probabilities. See Henry Allen Latané, "Criteria for Choice among Risky Ventures," *Journal of Political Economy*, vol. 67, no. 2, April, 1959, pp. 144–155; and Markowitz, *Portfolio Selection*, chap. 7.

[33] The cash position does not enter the utility function. Therefore, X_L is independent of b, and M is determined residually. If the desired portfolio exceeds the capacity of b, the actual portfolio will exhaust b, leaving $M = 0$. M cannot be negative, since the dealer cannot commit more than his total capital, b, to his position in securities. Equilibrium X_L is, therefore, the smaller of the results obtained by solving (3) and (4) with $M = 0$.

Next, the relationship between the long position, X_L, and the crucial parameters, $\bar{y}_L$ and σ_L, may be investigated.

From (3) it may be determined that $\delta Y_L / \delta \bar{y}_L > 0$ when $\sigma_L{}^2 > \bar{y}_L{}^2$.[34] This means that, given the indicated constraint upon the relationship between σ^2 and $\bar{y}_L{}^2$, the magnitude of the long position will vary directly with the expected income from maintaining that long position.

Similarly, it may be shown that $\delta X_L / \delta \sigma_L{}^2 < 0$ so long as $\bar{y}_L > 0$. The latter condition is true by assumption. Thus, the size of the long position will vary inversely with the variance of expected income.

Next, the characteristics of a short-position model will be investigated. In this case, income is defined as $Y = X_s y_s$, where X_s represents the number of bonds held in short position. Hence $X_s < 0$ when an actual short position is being carried. Also $y_s = u_s - p_s$, where u_s represents the expected future price *plus* financing costs; and $\bar{y}_s = \bar{u}_s - p_s$ with $\bar{u}_s < p_s$, so that $\bar{y}_s < 0$.

Expected income is therefore

$$E(Y) = X_s \bar{y}_s \tag{5}$$

The variance of income is

$$V(Y) = X_s{}^2 \sigma_s{}^2 \tag{6}$$

Maximizing expected utility gives

$$X_s = \frac{\alpha \bar{y}_s}{2\beta(\bar{y}_s{}^2 + \sigma_s{}^2)} \tag{7}$$

Finally, the relevant budget equation is

$$\frac{1}{r_s}(b - M) = -X_s p_s \quad [35] \tag{8}$$

where M must now be interpreted as unencumbered, ending cash.[36] Equations (5) through (8) thus determine the system.

It can be shown that $\delta X_s / \delta \bar{y}_s > 0$ so long as $\sigma_s{}^2 > \bar{y}_s{}^2$. Thus, given

[34] This result apparently follows from the hypothetical utility function and reflects the danger of too much income! Thus the utility function is only useful within a certain range. For an alternative approach, see Jack Hirschleifer, "Efficient Allocation in an Uncertain World," *American Economic Review, Papers and Proceedings*, vol. 54, no. 3, May, 1964, pp. 77–85.

[35] Since X_s represents bonds borrowed, a liability, the negative sign is appropriate.

[36] That is, the cash proceeds of the short sale plus that portion of b which is equal to $r_s (- X_s p_s)$ will be required as collateral for the borrowed securities.

this condition, the absolute size of the short position will vary positively with the absolute size of the expected return from a short sale.

It can also be shown that $\delta X_s / \delta \sigma_s^2 > 0$ as long as $\bar{y}_s < 0$. The latter condition is true by assumption. In other words, the short position decreases in size (becomes more positive) as the variance of the expected return increases.

Finally, the two models which have been constructed may be combined in order to examine the properties of a hedged position. In this model $E(Y)$ will be a resultant of the combined positions.

$$E(Y) = X_L \bar{y}_L + X_s \bar{y}_s \qquad (9)$$

The variance of income is

$$V(Y) = X_L^2 \sigma_L^2 + 2 X_L X_s \rho \sigma_L \sigma_s + X_s^2 \sigma_s^2 \qquad (10)$$

where ρ is the coefficient of correlation between y_L and y_s. To maximize $E(U)$, set $\delta E(U)/\delta X_L = \delta E(U)/\delta X_s = 0$, giving

$$X_L = \frac{(\alpha \bar{y}_L / 2\beta) - X_s(\bar{y}_L \bar{y}_s + \rho \sigma_L \sigma_s)}{\bar{y}_L^2 + \sigma_L^2} \qquad (11)$$

and

$$X_s = \frac{(\alpha \bar{y}_s / 2\beta) - X_L(\bar{y}_L \bar{y}_s + \rho \sigma_L \sigma_s)}{\bar{y}_s^2 + \sigma_s^2} \qquad (12)$$

The budget equation for the combined model may take either of two forms. If the short position is less than fully hedged, equation (8), the budget equation for the simple short-position model, is applicable.

$$\frac{1}{r_s}(b - M) = -X_s p_s \qquad (8)$$

where b represents cash holdings after the long position has been acquired and M is again interpreted as unencumbered, ending cash. If the short position is fully hedged, M, ending cash, is given by the following expression:

$$X_L p_L = -X_s p_s(1 + r_s) + \frac{1}{r_L}[b - (-r_s X_s p_s) - M] \qquad (13)$$

Equations (8) through (12), or (9) through (13), determine the values of $E(Y)$, $V(Y)$, X_L, X_s, and M.

Consider equation (10). Suppose, to begin with, that $X_L = 0$. $V(Y)$ then depends entirely upon X_s. Now increase X_L. With $X_s < 0$ and

$\rho > 0$, $V(Y)$ is likely to decrease.[37] In other words, if returns from the two types of securities are positively correlated, taking on a long position in one security may serve as a hedge for the short position in the sense that the variance of the portfolio may be reduced.[38]

Next, let $X_s = -1$ and let k represent the number of units of X_L per unit of X_s which will minimize $V(Y)$. Substituting for X_L and X_s in (10), $V(Y) = k^2\sigma_L^2 + 2k\rho\sigma_L\sigma_s + \sigma_s^2$. Setting $\delta V(Y)/\delta k = 0$,[39] $k = -\dfrac{\rho\sigma_s}{\sigma_L}$. Since $k = X_L/X_s$, $X_s = -(\sigma_L/\rho\sigma_s) X_L$. Substituting for X_s in (11), it can be shown that $\delta X_L/\delta \sigma_s > 0$.[40] That is, an increase in the riskiness of the short position results in a larger hedge.

It seems more plausible, on the other hand, to suppose that the dealer maximizes utility subject to no constraint upon the variance of the portfolio. In this case, equations (11) and (12) must be solved for X_L in order to find $\delta X_L/\delta\sigma_s$. Assume an initial equilibrium is disturbed by an increase in σ_s. As far as his long position is concerned, the dealer may react in either one of two ways. On the one hand, he may simply reduce his long position and hold more cash.[41] Alternatively, the dealer may increase his long position.[42] The latter policy will be

---

[37] $\delta V(Y)/\delta X_L < 0$ when $X_L\sigma_L^2 < -X_s\rho\sigma_L\sigma_s$.

[38] If $\rho < 0$, $V(Y)$ is likely to increase. This condition would be characteristic of an arbitrage operation or an expected shift in debt-management policy. In these instances, the simultaneous short and long positions would both be speculative, a hedge would not be involved, and therefore both would contribute to variance.

[39] For a similar treatment of hedging in the commodity market, see Leland L. Johnson, "The Theory of Hedging and Speculation in Commodity Futures," *Review of Economic Studies*, vol. 27 (3), no. 74, June, 1960, pp. 139–151.

[40] $\dfrac{\delta X_L}{\delta\sigma_s} = -\dfrac{\alpha \bar{y}_L^2 \bar{y}_s \sigma_L}{2\beta\rho\sigma_s[\bar{y}_L^2 - (\sigma_L/\rho\sigma_s)\bar{y}_L\bar{y}_s]^2} > 0$

[41] $\delta X_L/\delta\sigma_s < 0$.

[42] $\delta X_L/\delta\sigma_s > 0$. With $\bar{y}_L < 0$ and $\bar{y}_s < 0$, this derivative will be positive (1) if

$$(1 - \rho^2)\left(\frac{\sigma_L}{\bar{y}_L}\right)^2 > 0$$

and

$$0 < \sigma_s < \sigma_L\left(\frac{\bar{y}_s}{\bar{y}_L}\right)\frac{1 - \sqrt{1 - \rho^2}\sqrt{1 + \rho^2(\sigma_L/\bar{y}_L)^2}}{\rho[1 - (1 - \rho^2)(\sigma_L/\bar{y}_L)^2]}$$

or (2) if

followed whenever the gain in utility due to the decrease in variance resulting from the larger hedge exceeds the loss in utility due to decrease in the expected return to the portfolio which also results from the greater hedge.[43]

$$0 < (1 - \rho^2) \left(\frac{\sigma_L}{\bar{y}_L} \right)^2 < 1$$

and

$$0 < \sigma_s < \sigma_L \left(\frac{\bar{y}_s}{\bar{y}_L} \right) \frac{1 - \sqrt{1 - \rho^2} \sqrt{1 + \rho^2 (\sigma_L/\bar{y}_L)^2}}{\rho [1 - (1 - \rho^2)(\sigma_L/\bar{y}_L)^2]}$$

or

$$\sigma_s > \sigma_L \left(\frac{\bar{y}_s}{\bar{y}_L} \right) \frac{1 + \sqrt{1 - \rho^2} \sqrt{1 + \rho^2 (\sigma_L/\bar{y}_L)^2}}{\rho [1 - (1 - \rho^2)(\sigma_L/\bar{y}_L)^2]}$$

For this derivation, the author is indebted to Frederick J. Ernst.

[43] An investor may hedge an interest-rate forecast by holding both long-term and short-term securities, so that a capital loss may be offset by an interest-rate gain, or vice versa. See James Tobin, "An Essay on Principles of Debt Management," in *Fiscal and Debt Management Policies*, Commission on Money and Credit, Englewood Cliffs, N.J.: Prentice-Hall, Inc., 1963, p. 165.

chapter 5

AN EMPIRICAL EVALUATION OF THE DETERMINATION OF DEALER POSITION POLICY

In attempting an empirical evaluation of the determinants of dealer position policy, a literal application of the abstract model constructed in the preceding chapter might have been undertaken. Thus estimates of the parameters relating expected return and variance to the dependent variables might have been made directly. Such an approach, however, would have required a distribution of dealer expectations, which was not available.[1] Consequently, a model has been constructed consisting of variables which, it is hoped, are effective surrogates for those in the theory. The results of this approach comprise the present chapter.

THE ECONOMIC SETTING

The first data on dealer positions made available to the public by the Federal Open Market Committee cover a fourteen-month period beginning on October 30, 1957. Fortunately, the fourteen months covered by these time series encompass a substantial decline, as well as a

---

[1] A distribution of dealer expectations, to be used with position data currently being collected for publication, might be constructed through periodic interviews of the officers or partners of several Government bond houses.

marked recovery, in economic activity.[2] A cyclical decline began in the third quarter of 1957. It was the combined effect of an inventory liquidation, a contraction in business outlays on plant and equipment, a cutback in defense outlays and Government contract awards, a drop in purchases of consumer durables, and a decrease in exports.

Dramatic effect was given to the arrival of the new recession on November 18, 1957, when the discount rate was reduced by $\frac{1}{2}$ of 1 percentage point. Immediately after the announcement, the Treasury offered a $3\frac{1}{8}$ percent bond maturing in 1974. This long-term instrument encouraged speculative participation on the basis of the rapid run-up in bond prices recorded in 1953 and 1954. These expectations were soon confirmed; and the $3\frac{1}{8}$s, well as the 4 percent issue offered prior to the discount-rate change, moved quickly to substantial premiums. Speculative interest thus received a further stimulus.

After the turn of the year, a number of factors contributed to the continued increase in the prices of fixed-interest-bearing securities. Current statistical measures of business activity, credit demands, and bank reserve positions indicated that the recession and easy money might persist for some time. Initially, market interest was confined largely to professionals—dealers, a few institutions, and some brokerage houses—plus a small number of knowledgeable individuals. Commercial banks, although aware of the opportunities then available in the bond market, initially lacked the excess reserves and the portfolio liquidity to participate actively. With the freeing of more reserves, however, the banks became active buyers of intermediate-term Treasury securities, helping to push prices higher despite a large volume of new intermediate- and long-term offerings. As a result, price increases of two new Treasury bonds issued in the February refunding provided striking evidence of the profit opportunities in Treasury bond offerings during a recession. Anticipation of continued advances in bond prices led investors to bid aggressively for new intermediate-term issues offered for cash in February and April, and the secondary-market performance of these issues further confirmed bullish expectations. Also, lags in the timing of Federal Reserve countercyclical actions in open-market operations, discount rates, and reserve requirements tended to generate expectational rumors that additional System actions to ease credit might be taken. An additional factor was that many of the investors

[2] See appendix for a bibliography on the historical, economic background of the 1958 break in the Government bond market.

who were buying Government bonds hoped to obtain the tax advantage of long-term gains. Consequently, it was expected that a large share of the new securities that would be acquired would not be resold in the market until after the six-month holding period required for the favorable tax treatment of capital gains. Moreover, some of the investors who bought bonds on margin early in the period of market advance subsequently used the appreciated value of these bonds as margin for credit purchases of new Treasury offerings, thus pyramiding the use of credit in the market.

In June, 1958, the Treasury offered a $3\frac{1}{4}$ percent twenty-seven-year bond for cash and, in exchange for a note and two bonds maturing June 15, offered an eleven-month certificate at $1\frac{1}{4}$ percent and a $6\frac{2}{3}$-year bond at $2\frac{5}{8}$ percent. The market consensus prior to the announcement of these terms was that bond prices would continue to rise and that the Treasury would offer a long-term bond as one option in the exchange. Reflecting this consensus, June "rights" moved to premiums. In addition to the general economic and credit outlook, several specific factors reinforced investor confidence in the expectation of rising bond prices. One factor was the Treasury's call of two optional bonds for refunding in September. Another was a Presidential press-conference statement suggesting that economic conditions justified lower long-term interest rates. Since the spread between short- and long-term interest rates was unusually wide at the time and since corporate bond offerings were expected to slacken, this indication of official concern over long rates added support to the expectation then prevalent that they would fall further.

The $2\frac{5}{8}$ percent bond appealed to both banks and nonfinancial corporations because it was expected to carry a higher secondary-market premium than the $1\frac{1}{4}$ percent certificate, the other exchange offering in the June refunding. Many holders of rights, therefore, were encouraged to exchange into the bond, even though they ultimately wanted a liquidity instrument, on the assumption that they could immediately and profitably swap into the certificate in the secondary market.

The extreme liquidity of lenders combined with the very low yields on short-term Treasuries provided a powerful incentive for lenders to seek better-yielding alternatives for short-term money. Since rates obtainable on repurchase agreements against rights approximated the $2\frac{5}{8}$ to $2\frac{7}{8}$ percent coupons on maturing securities, in contrast to a yield of about $\frac{5}{8}$ of 1 percent on ninety-one-day bills, repurchase agreements on rights presented an attractive medium for placing short-term funds. Borrowers, meanwhile, were able to carry speculative positions by putting up a premium of 7/32 to 15/32 in cash while financing the remainder on credit with a zero net interest cost. A major role in the speculative movement was played by money brokers. These firms adapted the repurchase contract to the financing of speculative purchases for individuals by capitalizing on the knowledge which banks and corporations had developed in making repurchase agreements with Government securities dealers, as well as by utilizing their own contacts made in regular Federal funds trading.

The bond-market decline consisted of two phases. Initially, there was an apparent technical[3] reaction to the refunding. Later, this gave way to a more fundamental decline in Government securities prices. Although an active speculative interest in rights had been observed prior to the June refunding period, announcement of the size of the exchange into $2\frac{5}{8}$ percent bonds represented a distinct surprise to the market. This news posed the question whether the market might be faced with a serious technical problem in absorbing the large volume of intermediate securities. Moreover, questioning of the technical situation deepened as the market became aware that corporate repurchase agreements in these and other securities would have to be refinanced to the extent that they represented the temporary investment of accumulated reserves for payment of June tax liabilities. Additional market pressure stemmed from the need to make a cash payment for the new $3\frac{1}{4}$ percent long-term bonds on June 18.

In the eyes of some, these technical difficulties could have been successfully taken in stride had there been no change in the general outlook for interest rates. In fact, however, some uncertainty had already begun to develop before the refunding. Statistical evidence began to appear which suggested that the business downswing was bottoming out. Lower weekly figures on free reserves in early June were also raising questions as to whether the Federal Reserve might have shifted the emphasis of its policies.

These developing market uncertainties were highlighted by several press reports concerning the business outlook and the prospects for Federal Reserve policy. Even before mid-June, bond prices turned

---

[3] This term is used generally in the market to describe temporary aberrations in market conditions which for a short period offset to some degree the pervasive influence of more persistent, underlying forces.

down slightly, reflecting some selling pressure generated when speculative positions in rights that had been financed temporarily and without margin on corporate repurchase agreements had to be refinanced and margins supplied. Following the press reports, downward price pressures became stronger.

In the initial phase of the decline, there was considerable market uncertainty as to whether bond-price changes reflected a basic shift in the direction of interest-rate movements or merely a temporary technical reaction following the refunding. In this period, selling came largely from weak positions—speculators who had bought on margin and investors who wanted a shorter-term security but had taken $2\frac{5}{8}$ percent bonds merely to capture a quick gain. Selling in this period was absorbed largely by commercial banks, which continued to buy bonds at declining prices, and by the Treasury, which near the end of June initiated a program of open-market purchases of the $2\frac{5}{8}$s.

As price declines persisted, evidence began to accumulate that the movement was more than a mere technical reaction. Banks became less willing buyers and in some cases more active sellers. Appearance of bank liquidation set off further selling by those holding securities on margin; and the weight of this more general selling, in turn, caused some liquidation by institutional investors. Among those selling in the late summer were investors who revised earlier plans for holding securities for six months in order to establish long-term capital gains and now hoped to avoid or minimize losses. Other factors helped project the decline beyond the dimensions of a technical adjustment. First, there was growing realization that the turning point of the recession had occurred. Second, there was mounting evidence that the budget deficit in fiscal 1959 would be large and result in pressure on the Government securities market. Finally, the international crisis in the Near East, which involved the landing of American troops in Lebanon, produced the threat of war, with the implication of further pressure upon capital-market resources. By the end of July, the Treasury and the Federal Reserve combined had bought more than $1.8 billion of rights and when-issued securities in an attempt to prevent panic conditions in the bond market.

The mainsprings of the economic revival were fourfold: Government outlays on goods and services, consumption expenditures on nondurables and on services, housing construction, and a cessation in inventory liquidation. The revival of economic activity introduced one of the most difficult periods ever faced by the Treasury. In addition to the usual problems of refinancing in a declining bond market, it was necessary to raise $18.5 billion in new cash to meet a $12.5 billion deficit during fiscal 1959 and a $6 billion seasonal deficit during the first half of fiscal 1960. Moreover, the debt managers were forced to struggle against these overwhelming odds while they were burdened with two serious handicaps, the interest-rate ceiling and the public-debt limit.

Such, in brief compass, was the economic environment of the period in which dealer behavior has been studied.

THE VARIABLES SELECTED FOR STUDY

Twelve dependent variables have been used. These are aggregate long position, short position, and net position of the seventeen dealer firms existing at the time, in each of four maturity classes: bills; certificates, and notes and bonds due within one year; notes and bonds due in one to five years; and bonds due in five years or more.[4] Observations are for Wednesdays, from November 1, 1957, through December 31, 1958. Position figures include commitments to repurchase securities under long-term repurchase agreements (RPs).[5] Position data also include securities held in investment accounts,[6] new commitments originating under trading arrangements for regular (next-day) delivery, and commitments in securities on a when-issued basis. Thus, long positions include not only securities physically owned but also commitments to purchase at a future date. Short positions include delivery commitments as well as commitments to return borrowed securities.

[4] Source: *Treasury–Federal Reserve Study of the Government Securities Market,* Washington, D.C.: Treasury Department and Board of Governors, Federal Reserve System, 1960, part 2, pp. 135–139, 148. Maturity classes are according to final maturity rather than to date of first call.

[5] These data, therefore, reflect more than current inventory available for immediate sale. That is, RPs running for a period in excess of fifteen days are essentially investment transactions from the viewpoint of the dealer's customer; and the securities involved are not for sale during the term of the agreement, though substitutions may be made if both parties agree. These relatively long-term contracts account for a substantial portion of total RPs and also an important share of dealers' commitments in short-term securities, especially Treasury bills.

[6] Securities held for long-term capital gains purposes are segregated from the trading account.

Since the dependent variables are classified according to maturity, discontinuities are introduced as issues move from one maturity class to another. For example, $6,755,000,000 in 2½s of 1963 moved from the greater-than-five-year class to the one-to-five-year class in August, 1958. This fact doubtless gives an upward bias to the rate at which dealers were shaving their bond portfolios at that time. Such discrete movements occur only sporadically, however, and thus have a limited effect upon the statistical fit.[7]

In addition to the effect of the passage of time, debt-management operations also affected the magnitude of outstanding debt in each maturity class. Treasury bills, of course, were affected only by debt-management policy. They amounted to $26,659,000,000 in October, 1957. After rising to $27,260,000,000 in January, they fell to $22,401,-000,000 by August, 1958. Then they rose to $29,748,000,000 by year-end. This pattern of outstandings would tend to reduce the goodness of statistical fit. Certificates, and notes and bonds due within one year, were better behaved in that they tended to increase in the first part and diminish in the latter part of the period. But they fluctuated over an extremely narrow range, varying from a low of $50,662,000,000 to a high of $53,597,000,000. Notes and bonds due in one to five years varied over a wider range—$39,401,000,000 to $50,013,000,000—but much more erratically. Bonds due in more than five years behaved in a favorable manner, since they increased fairly steadily from $38,149,-000,000 in October, 1957, to $54,224,000,000 in June, 1958, then declined to $47,234,000,000 at year-end. In any case it was felt that these fluctuations in outstandings were not of a magnitude which would warrant introducing the variable explicitly.

Turning to the independent variables, a search was next made for suitable variables to represent expected return. It was decided, first of all, to use a measure of the past rate of change of interest rates as a proxy variable for interest-rate expectations. The use of this variable is implied by the assumption that traders project past trends into the future. The vulnerability of week-to-week changes to erratic, technical pressures led to the use of a fitted trend in yields.[8] More specifi-

[7] For an adjustment to eliminate the effect of such abrupt changes in maturity categories, see Joseph W. Conard, *Introduction to the Theory of Interest*, Berkeley: University of California Press, 1959, pp. 340–343.

[8] Yields used with the four classes of dependent variables were, respectively, Wednesday figures for the new three-month bill, and averages of daily figures

cally, each observation consisted of the ratio of the slope of the trend in yields for the five previous time periods to the mean level of yields during the same period.[9]

The trend in yields was also introduced by means of a dummy variable. This was designed to reflect the announcement effect of the reversal in outlook. As noted earlier, the advent of recession was heralded by the reduction of the discount rate on November 18, 1957. This was represented by a −1 in the first period. The return to prosperity was signaled by the break in the bond market occurring in the latter part of June of the following summer. This definite reversal was identified by a +1 in the thirty-third period.

Next it was decided to introduce the level of free reserves as a proxy variable for expected interest-rate levels. This decision was made only after much hesitation, since the difficulties of employing this statistic for this purpose are numerous.[10] To cite a few obstacles, the relationship between the level of free reserves and conditions in the money market varies as a function of the discount rate relative to other money-market rates, the geographical distribution of free reserves, the liquidity characteristics of bank portfolios, bankers' attitudes toward borrowing, and their conception of the desired level of excess reserves. In addition, free reserves will fluctuate as a result of mistaken forecasts of factors affecting member bank reserves, such as a float, thus limiting their usefulness as an indicator of Federal Reserve intentions.

Despite these shortcomings, it was felt that free reserves were among the best available indicators on a weekly basis. Perhaps no other statistic is given as much attention by money-market analysts. Restricting its use to the relatively short period under consideration limits the effect of slowly changing behavior patterns and relationships. And its use reflects the tendency to project the recent past or present

---

for the week ending Wednesday of nine- to twelve-month issues, three- to five-year issues, and bonds maturing or callable in ten years or more. Source: *Federal Reserve Bulletin.*

[9] This construction incorporates Keynes's theory of the normal rate, since, given the slope, a higher mean implies lower expected rates.

The use of the forecast implicit in the time structure of interest rates was rejected on the ground that though the yield pattern may reflect expectations, it does not explain them. The explanation itself is, of course, the proper source of the desired variable.

[10] See appendix for a bibliography on bank reserves and monetary expansion.

into the future. A five-week moving average centered in the fifth week was used in order to minimize the effect of erratic fluctuations.[11]

Finally, expected yield was represented in the empirical investigation by a financing variable, yield less the rate charged for borrowed funds.[12] Thus an attempt was made to introduce relevant financing costs. Many lenders extending RP accommodation are restricted to maturities up to eighteen months. Consequently, RP rates were used with the two shorter-maturity categories.[13] The call-loan rate to dealers on Governments was used with the two longer-maturity categories.[14]

Two problems arise with the use of this variable. First, there is some evidence of a cyclical shift between these two financing sources. When money is very easy, New York money-market banks may be favored as a source of loan funds. When money becomes tight, the dealers scour the countryside for repurchase money. But then, when money becomes very tight, there is some tendency to return to the New York money-market banks for something akin to lender-of-last-resort accommodation. A second difficulty arises from the fact that the financing variable measures the cost of financing a long position. The design of a variable which would measure with any degree of accuracy the cost of financing a short position would be difficult to achieve. This is true for two reasons. First, there is a variety of issues which the dealer may purchase with proceeds of a short sale. Second, the yield of the issues purchased will depend upon their maturity and the term structure of interest rates at the time of purchase. In addition, the $\frac{1}{2}$ of 1 percent borrowing charge must be introduced into the calculation.

The variance of expected return was represented empirically by several variables. First, yield-uncertainty variables were constructed. For Treasury bills, this variable consisted of the average of accepted bids less the lowest accepted bid at the preceding Monday's auction.[15]

---

[11] This method is actually used by one astute money-market observer as a means of gauging the tenor of Federal Reserve policy. Source of data on free reserves: *Federal Reserve Bulletin.*

[12] A more realistic representation would have consisted of a weighted average of coupons less a weighted average of borrowing rates.

[13] Data were based on a sample of rates received by selected nonfinancial corporations.

[14] Sources for these data were the *New York Times* and the *American Banker.*

[15] Source: *Treasury Bulletin.* The lowest price accepted was used, rather than the lowest bid received, in order to eliminate throwaway bids. Use of the

The degree of uncertainty varies directly with the size of this difference. For the other maturity classes, uncertainty variables were constructed by computing the ratio of the algebraic sum of daily price changes during the preceding week to the absolute sum of the same changes.[16] The absolute values of these ratios were used. The degree of uncertainty varies inversely with these absolute values.

Next, the uncertainty of expected return was represented by the volume of dealer trading in each maturity class during the preceding week.[17] As discussed earlier, the use of volume as a proxy variable in this instance may be justified on the ground that unless the dealer is drastically shifting his position in a single direction, higher volume indicates greater ease in getting out of a particular existing position. That is, the greater the amount of activity on both sides of the market, the smaller the amount of price movement entailed in unwinding a long position or covering a short position.

An attempt was made to eliminate the effect of debt-management operations upon dealer volume by introducing an offering effect. In Treasury offerings, there are three important dates: the offering date, when the books are open; the allotment date, in the case of cash offerings only; and the issue date. In a cash offering, commitments enter the position figures at the time of allotment. In an exchange, commitments enter on a when-issued basis at the time of the offering. It was decided to introduce the amount of allotments to dealers and brokers on the observation date following the day the books were open.[18] If the two dates coincided, a one-week lag was used unless the position seemed markedly affected on the offering date. The offering-effect variable was then reduced by one-half in the first week, reduced by one-quarter in the second week, and eliminated entirely in the third week. This procedure was designed to reflect the gradual distribution of a new issue.

---

average eliminates the effect of the highest bid. Though accepted, this bid may reflect a lack of knowledge of the market rather than uncertainty of interest-rate expectations.

[16] The data were based on quotations provided by Salomon Brothers, Hutzler.

[17] Source: *Treasury–Federal Reserve Study of the Government Securities Market,* part 2, pp. 135–137, 140–141, 149. These data consist of the sum of gross purchases and sales by dealers. Purchases include allotments and awards of new Treasury issues. RP transactions are excluded.

[18] Source: *Treasury Bulletin.*

The offering-effect variable, of course, is relevant only in connection with long and net positions.

STATISTICAL METHODS AND RESULTS

Multiple linear regression equations relating the above variables were computed by the least-squares method. Residuals from the multiple regression equations were then related to the dependent variables in a test for nonlinearity. Significant second-order terms appeared. Consequently, it was decided to fit multiple linear regression equations to the logarithms of the values of the variables.

Since logarithms cannot be taken of negative numbers, it was necessary to make certain adjustments. First, net position was taken to be the ratio of the long position to the absolute sum of long and short positions. This ratio was substituted for the algebraic sum of long and short positions. Instead of using the difference between the yield and the rate on borrowed funds, the financing variable was computed by taking the ratio of the borrowing rate to yield.[19] As noted earlier, the sign of the uncertainty variable was ignored. Since the trend-of-yields variable was already in ratio form, logarithms of this variable were not used. In the case of free reserves, which may be negative, the variable used was the log of the quantity: free reserves plus twice the absolute value of the mean of free reserves over the time period used for each observation. All of the remaining variables took on only positive values.

The results of the empirical investigation are presented in Tables 5-1 to 5-6. In each table appear the multiple coefficients of determination measuring the relationship between the dependent and the independent variables $(\bar{R}^2)$; partial regression coefficients (b_{yj}); partial

---

[19] Since, in the case of coupon instruments, dealers look to the *difference* between *coupon* and financing rate, this variable appears less than ideal on two counts. However, during the cyclical upswing occurring in the latter part of the period studied, yields in the two longer-term categories actually moved up absolutely more, but not proportionately more, than financing rates. Therefore, the use of the ratio method compensates to some extent for the lack of rigidity in yields that would characterize the behavior of coupons. In the case of bills, of course, yield is the proper variable. In the less-than-one-year category, the yield is more rigid than the financing rate, so that the substitution of yield for coupon is admissible. Moreover, in both of the two shorter-term categories, the ratio moves generally in the same direction as the difference.

"t" ratios (t_{yj});[20] and measures of collinearity in the system, multiple coefficients of determination reflecting the relationship among the independent variables $(\bar{R}^2)$. These tables, then, present the statistical parameters generated by regressions on the following independent variables: rate of change of yield, announcement effect, free reserves, financing costs, uncertainty, volume, and offering effect.

Tables 5-1 and 5-2 provide statistical parameters for long positions in each maturity class. In Table 5-2, distribution parameters have been corrected for first-order serial correlation.[21] The "t" statistics have some meaning in this instance. This is not so in the case of the uncorrected parameters, presented in Table 5-1. The uncorrected regression coefficients, or elasticities, are, on the other hand, meaningful in a historical sense, even though the observations of the variables are serially correlated. Consequently, primary attention will be given to regression coefficients found for the uncorrected data.

The rate of change of yield shows the correct sign and relatively high elasticities in the second and fourth maturity classes. In any event, one would not expect a strong expectations effect in the case of bills. The announcement-effect variable shows up effectively only in the third maturity class.[22]

Free reserves have an impressive elasticity only in the fourth ma-

---

[20] The following is a table of significance levels for "t" ratios corrected for degrees of freedom:

Significance level	"t" ratio (approximate)
.2500	.7
.2000	.9
.1000	1.3
.0500	1.7
.0250	2.0
.0100	2.4
.0005	3.5

[21] The procedure used was that suggested by Theil and Nagar. See H. Theil and A. L. Nagar, "Testing the Independence of Regression Disturbances," *Journal of the American Statistical Association*, vol. 56, no. 296, December, 1961, pp. 793–806.

[22] A primary reason for this result is undoubtedly the lack of variance in the dummy variable itself.

TABLE 5-1   The determination of long positions: uncorrected parameters

Maturity class:	$\overline{R}^2$		Rate of change of yield	Announcement effect	Free reserves	Financing costs	Uncertainty	Volume	Offering effect
(1) Bills:	.3562	b_{yi}	.435	−.224	.0534	−.800	.0413	.262	.000301
		t_{yi}	.86	−.97	.59	−4.85	1.00	1.36	.060
		R^2	.375	.0828	.299	.498	.206	.254	.206
(2) Securities less than 1 year other than bills:	.4987	b_{yi}	−3.066	−.0245	−.0377	−.826	.114	.227	−.0000484
		t_{yi}	−2.55	−.062	−.26	−3.22	.65	1.51	−.072
		R^2	.489	.0769	.180	.419	.0301	.468	.364
(3) Notes and bonds, 1–5 years:	.7528	b_{yi}	.558	.340	.0869	−.747	.0109	.699	−.000457
		t_{yi}	.24	1.19	.68	−4.36	.082	7.19	−.64
		R^2	.594	.0326	.433	.486	.0979	.523	.0908
(4) Bonds over 5 years:	.7840	b_{yi}	−2.871	.0795	.398	.118	.182	.417	.000711
		t_{yi}	−.63	.32	2.98	.85	1.64	4.79	3.42
		R^2	.447	.0703	.618	.539	.0876	.639	.363

TABLE 5-2   The determination of long positions: corrected parameters

Maturity class:	$\bar{R}^2$		Rate of change of yield	Announcement effect	Free reserves	Financing costs	Uncertainty	Volume	Offering effect
(1) Bills:	.0589	b_{yj}	.060	−.251	.124	−.355	−.0025	.147	.003
		t_{yj}	−.10	−1.63	.98	−2.33	−.08	.95	.89
		R^2	.312	.051	.155	.348	.11	.166	.104
(2) Securities less than 1 year other than bills:	.0590	b_{yj}	−3.099	−.040	.030	−.221	.079	.053	−.0002
		t_{yj}	−2.20	−.16	.14	−.94	.74	.51	−.39
		R^2	.243	.064	.084	.257	.064	.336	.342
(3) Notes and bonds, 1–5 years:	.4540	b_{yj}	−1.960	.140	.127	−.679	−.012	.419	.0002
		t_{yj}	−.67	.74	.80	−3.25	−.14	4.71	.31
		R^2	.325	.022	.104	.272	.077	.193	.090
(4) Bonds over 5 years:	.6414	b_{yj}	−1.398	−.039	.091	−.023	.181	.447	.0008
		t_{yj}	−.22	−.26	.60	−.14	2.52	5.72	3.44
		R^2	.138	.042	.227	.211	.156	.421	.295

turity class. This is consistent, however, with the thesis that speculative activities are greatest at the long end. Moreover, a special problem arises in relating free reserves to long positions in bills. When free reserves are used as a proxy variable for interest-rate expectations, one would expect to find bill positions increasing with free reserves. However, it is precisely at such a time that the banks enjoy a surfeit of cash and, as a result, the dealers are denuded of bills. In addition, free reserves will not always coincide nicely with dealer expectations. For example, in November and December, 1957, net borrowed reserves were brought down slowly, yet dealers rapidly built up their positions on the basis of the expected decline in interest rates. Also, because of the demoralized state of the market, the Fed was slow to bring free reserves down in the late summer and fall of 1958, though dealers shaved their inventories rapidly.

Financing costs show up rather well. They have relatively high elasticities for the first three maturity groups. The fact that financing charges are relatively unimportant for long-terms may be taken as indirect evidence of the dominance of speculative tendencies at this level.

The uncertainty variable is relatively stronger in the second and fourth maturity classes. With regard to bills, where the regression coefficient is small and its sign is wrong, the following difficulty arises. When uncertainty pervades the bill auction, dealers tend to scale their bids. As a consequence, if other buyers do not do so or if they tend to withdraw from the market, the dealers may end up winning a large quantity of bills precisely at the time of great uncertainty.[23]

Volume is a relatively important variable, and particularly in the longer-maturity groups. This result is consistent with the role of volume as a certainty factor and the greater importance of certainty considerations in the longer maturities. In the case of bills, positions may rise precisely at the time of low volume as dealers get stuck with their awards. When volume is good, they get rid of their bills soon after the auction.

The contribution of the offering effect is practically nil.

---

[23] In the bill auction, in other words, there is an instantaneous price adjustment to compensate for uncertainty. The lower price is the payment exacted by the market for the greater uncertainty.

This view of dealer behavior could be verified if access could be had to dealer allotments to see if they vary with the dispersion of bids.

Correction for serial correlation has a noticeable effect upon the explanatory value of the independent variables, but especially in the two shorter-maturity classes. The $\bar{R}^2$s for the two longer maturities sustain the test remarkably well, especially in view of the fact that the underlying data consist of weekly observations.

The correction has a favorable effect upon the rate-of-change-of-yield relationship in that the sign of the regression coefficient changes for the third maturity class. The strength of the announcement effect remains about as before. The effect on free reserves as an explanatory variable is somewhat favorable in the first and third maturity classes but damaging at the long end. The effect upon financing costs is apparent, but they generally come through very well. Moreover, the sign changes in the fourth maturity group. The correction has an adverse effect upon the uncertainty relationship except in the longest maturity. Volume remains as one of the most important variables, while the offering effect continues to exert a negligible influence upon the outcome.

To summarize, yield trend, financing costs, and volume appear to be the most important determinants of dealer long positions. The over-all explanatory value of the independent variables tends to increase with the maturity of the dependent variable. This result may reflect a tendency on the part of the dealers to think of their investment in shorter-term inventories as something of a merchandising operation, while speculative elements dominate the opposite end of the maturity spectrum.

Tables 5-3 and 5-4 present corresponding parameters for short positions. The rate of change of yield is most impressive and increasingly so as a function of maturity. This result, combined with the less impressive showing for long position, supports the thesis that there tends to be a bias toward long positions regardless of the trend and that position policy on the short side is profoundly affected by expectations.

The announcement effect is relatively weak, though the signs are correct in three of the four maturity categories.

The behavior of free reserves tends to support the above conclusion regarding the trend in yields. Their strength improves as maturity advances in the two longer-maturity classes.

Financing costs are relatively strong but of positive sign. Since this variable was designed to measure the cost of financing a long position,

TABLE 5-3   The determination of short positions: uncorrected parameters

Maturity class:	$\bar{R}^2$		Rate of change of yield	Announcement effect	Free reserves	Financing costs	Uncertainty	Volume	Offering effect
(1) Bills:	.2229	b_{yj}	2.409	−.193	−.0493	.750	.187	−.0952	−.0172
		t_{yj}	1.87	−.33	−.21	1.77	1.78	−.19	−1.34
		R^2	.375	.0828	.299	.498	.206	.254	.206
(2) Securities less than 1 year other than bills:	.3925	b_{yj}	6.374	−.584	.346	1.317	−.442	.252	.000771
		t_{yj}	2.59	−.72	1.16	2.51	−1.23	.82	.56
		R^2	.489	.0769	.180	.419	.0301	.468	.364
(4) Notes and bonds, 1-5 years:	.3886	b_{yj}	9.243	.0298	−.337	.258	−.0922	.0261	.00106
		t_{yj}	3.44	.091	−2.28	1.31	−.60	.23	1.29
		R^2	.594	.0326	.433	.486	.0979	.523	.0908
(4) Bonds over 5 years:	.7572	b_{yj}	26.157	−.258	−.802	1.245	−.372	−.229	−.0000647
		t_{yj}	4.41	−.80	−4.64	6.94	−2.58	−2.03	−.24
		R^2	.447	.0703	.618	.539	.0876	.639	.363

TABLE 5-4   The determination of short positions: corrected parameters

Maturity class:	$\bar{R}^2$		Rate of change of yield	Announcement effect	Free reserves	Financing costs	Uncertainty	Volume	Offering effect
(1) Bills:	.0231	b_{yj}	1.230	.158	−.318	.461	.189	−.508	−.007
		t_{yj}	.75	.37	−.92	1.10	2.14	−1.18	−.65
		R^2	.312	.052	.160	.351	.114	.168	.106
(2) Securities less than 1 year other than bills	.0997	b_{yj}	5.449	−.395	.153	.817	−.078	.059	.0008
		t_{yj}	1.79	−.62	.34	1.44	−.28	.22	.56
		R^2	.318	.063	.113	.305	.057	.358	.344
(3) Notes and bonds, 1–5 years:	.2496	b_{yj}	9.059	.076	−.286	.215	−.096	−.013	.0017
		t_{yj}	2.76	.25	−1.52	.89	−.66	−.10	1.97
		R^2	.491	.020	.322	.420	.069	.422	.083
(4) Bonds over 5 years:	.7616	b_{yj}	25.099	−.258	−.955	1.275	−.323	−.164	−.0002
		t_{yj}	4.19	−.81	−5.10	6.87	−2.24	−1.51	−.45
		R^2	.430	.093	.638	.576	.096	.634	.348

interpretation of these results is difficult.[24] To some extent, however, they may indicate that periods of relatively high financing costs coincide with those in which other conditions are appropriate for short positions, including speculative factors and the use of short positions as a means of financing long positions.

Uncertainty is relatively impressive in all but the third category.[25]

Volume is of some importance only for the longest-maturity class, where it is negative. Since this variable fails to distinguish between long- and short-position transactions, this result appears to indicate that low volume is characteristic of periods in which short positions are appropriate.

The offering effect is insignificant, as would be expected.

Corrected parameters are shown in Table 5-4, where no dramatic changes in the elasticities have been induced. The correction procedure markedly reduces $\bar{R}^2$ in the first two maturity classes and somewhat reduces it in the third class, but in fact increases it in the longest-maturity sector.

In summary, yield trend is outstanding as an explanatory variable. The financing-cost relationship is strong but more difficult to evaluate.

Tables 5-5 and 5-6 present similar parameters for net positions. The rate of change of yield shows up quite well, with increasing elasticities as maturities increase.

The impact of the announcement effect was negligible.

Free reserves are very weak. To a degree, the longest-maturity level is an exception.

Financing costs are relatively strong at all levels. As noted before, the presence of short positions clouds the interpretation of this result. On the other hand, the negative signs may represent the dominance of long positions in the net inventory statistic.

Uncertainty is relatively impressive only at the long end. Earlier findings plus the fact that the present relationship is positive, revealing a decrease in net positions with an increase in uncertainty, indicate

---

[24] As noted earlier, financing costs are determined by the combination of maturities involved, the yield pattern, and the fixed borrowing fee.

[25] One might expect to find an increase in uncertainty associated with an upward trend in interest rates. However, splitting the data into two periods failed to reveal a significant difference in the relationship between uncertainty and yield trend. The fact that such a difference failed to appear may, of course, reflect a deficiency in the construction of the uncertainty variable.

TABLE 5-5 The determination of net positions: uncorrected parameters

Maturity class: $\overline{R}^2$		Rate of change of yield	Announcement effect	Free reserves	Financing costs	Uncertainty	Volume	Offering effect
(1) Bills: .3037	b_{yj}	−.162	.00746	.0155	−.126	−.00879	.0429	.00189
	t_{yj}	−1.36	.14	.72	−3.22	−.90	.94	1.60
	R^2	.375	.0828	.299	.498	.206	.254	.206
(2) Securities less than 1 year other than bills: .2825	b_{yj}	−1.448	−.00828	.000799	−.139	.0755	.0186	−.0000813
	t_{yj}	−2.80	−.048	.013	−1.26	1.00	.29	−.28
	R^2	.489	.0769	.180	.419	.0301	.468	.364
(3) Notes and bonds, 1–5 years: .6767	b_{yj}	−2.454	.0913	.0976	−.212	−.00680	.159	−.000280
	t_{yj}	−2.51	.76	1.81	−2.96	−.12	3.89	−.94
	R^2	.594	.0326	.433	.486	.0979	.523	.0908
(4) Bonds over 5 years: .7812	b_{yj}	−7.472	.0670	.266	−.251	.130	.152	.0000714
	t_{yj}	−4.08	.67	4.99	−4.52	2.92	4.36	.86
	R^2	.447	.0703	.618	.539	.0876	.639	.363

TABLE 5-6   The determination of net positions: corrected parameters

Maturity class:		$\bar{R}^2$	Rate of change of yield	Announcement effect	Free reserves	Financing costs	Uncertainty	Volume	Offering effect
(1) Bills:	b_{yj}	.1462	-.127	-.0057	.055	-.084	-.012	.085	.001
	t_{yj}		-.87	-.13	1.81	-2.05	-1.37	1.94	1.19
	R^2		.322	.057	.230	.391	.128	.128	.129
(2) Securities less than 1 year other than bills:	b_{yj}	.0	-.946	-.0236	-.021	-.022	.061	.069	-.003
	t_{yj}		-1.42	-.20	-.21	-.28	1.20	1.39	-1.13
	R^2		.251	.063	.087	.262	.063	.338	.342
(3) Notes and bonds, 1–5 years:	b_{yj}	.3298	-2.598	.0080	.098	-.178	-.009	.113	-.0004
	t_{yj}		-1.96	.09	1.36	-1.88	-.22	2.74	-1.25
	R^2		.346	.021	.123	.290	.076	.214	.089
(4) Bonds over 5 years:	b_{yj}	.7455	-7.249	.0495	.283	-.241	.117	.140	.0001
	t_{yj}		-3.54	.50	4.50	-3.85	2.64	3.86	1.11
	R^2		.404	.074	.611	.549	.101	.618	.333

that dealers react to increased uncertainty by reducing long positions *and* increasing short commitments.[26] The alternative explanation, namely, that the observed phenomenon may be the result of dealers reacting to uncertainty by decreasing their short commitments relatively less than they decrease long positions, is precluded by the negative relationship between uncertainty and long positions, on the one hand, and the positive relationship between uncertainty and short positions, on the other.

Volume is relatively strong for the two longer-maturity categories. This probably reflects mainly the relationship of this variable to long positions.

The offering effect is of no importance.

As in the case of short positions, correction for serial correlation has little effect upon the regression coefficients. The $\bar{R}^2$s are reduced; but again the longer maturities, and especially the longest, withstand the test exceedingly well.

Since the same explanatory variables are used for a particular maturity level regardless of position, the pattern of the multiple coefficient of determination among the independent variables is the same for each type of position. In general, multicollinearity appears strongest among rate of change of yield, free reserves, financing costs, and volume; and there appears to be some tendency for it to increase as a function of maturity.

Considering these empirical results as a whole, the following conclusions may be drawn. First, dealers are strongly affected by interest-rate expectations, especially in the case of the longer maturities where speculative gains and losses count for so much of a dealer's success or failure. Next, financing costs appear to influence a dealer's position policy. Finally, volume, as an indicator of uncertainty, may play an important role.

[26] Cf. the discussion of possible dealer reactions to increased uncertainty in Chap. 4.

chapter 6

SOME PUBLIC-POLICY ISSUES

This study of the United States Government debt and its dealers will be concluded with a brief discussion of some related policy issues. Where relevant, the empirical findings of the preceding chapter will be brought to bear upon the conclusions drawn. Throughout, the market-performance criterion will be featured, so that the impact of the policy in question upon the dealer mechanism will receive especial attention.

THE BILLS-ONLY POLICY[1]

With the announcement of the Treasury–Federal Reserve Accord on March 4, 1951, the Federal Open Market Committee (FOMC) moved rapidly toward freeing the Government bond market. Flexible monetary policy had lain dormant during World War II and its aftermath. The FOMC was understandably concerned about the operational aspects of flexible open-market policy. Consequently, at its meeting on May 17, 1951, the FOMC authorized an *ad hoc* subcommittee to study the effect of its operations upon the functioning of the Government securities market. The subcommittee was organized during April and May, 1952. Beginning on June 9, 1952, the subcommittee con-

[1] See appendix for a bibliography on the bills-only policy. The author is indebted to the University of Chicago Press for permission to base parts of this discussion on David I. Fand and Ira O. Scott, Jr., "The Federal Reserve System's 'Bills Only' Policy: A Suggested Interpretation," *Journal of Business,* vol. 31, no. 1, January, 1958, pp. 12–18.

ducted secret hearings with various Government securities dealers as witnesses. On November 12, 1952, the *ad hoc* group presented its report. The principal recommendations of the subcommittee were adopted by the FOMC at the March 4–5, 1953, meeting. The new ground rules were rescinded on June 11, 1953, but were reinstated by the FOMC on September 24, 1953. Among the procedural reforms suggested by the *ad hoc* subcommittee was the recommendation that the FOMC cease operating regularly at all maturity levels. That is, except in correcting disorderly markets, System account operations in the open market should be confined to short-term securities. This was the origin of the so-called bills-only policy.

One of the avowed objectives of the new policy was to promote the making of better markets by the Government securities dealers. In general, as noted earlier, a dealer's market performance, or receptivity to an offer of securities or an order for securities, is measured by the width of the spread between his bid and offer quotations. A narrow spread reflects the dealer's willingness to invest or take a position in the securities being demanded and offered.

The central bank may wish to generate uncertainty in the Government securities market as a deliberate matter of policy. As a general rule, however, it is desirable to have a smoothly functioning market, and bills-only contributes to an improved bond market through a reduction in uncertainty. Suppose, for example, a dealer considers moving into a short position in bonds in order to accommodate customer demand. Assume that the System is not committed to a bills-only policy. It is thus possible that the Open Market Account will buy bonds in order to adjust bank reserves or prevent an "undue" decline in bond prices at precisely the same time the dealer is attempting to cover his short position. In these circumstances, the dealer would compensate for this uncertainty by adding a few thirty-seconds to the offering side of the short sale. In other words, in going short, the dealer must borrow the bonds which he sells. Eventually, he must actually buy bonds to return to the lender of the borrowed bonds. If, because of FOMC buying operations, bond prices rise in the meantime, the dealer will suffer a loss. He would protect himself against such a loss by raising his offer price.

Consider, on the other hand, a decision to position bonds in order to meet a customer's need for a buyer. If the System is not committed to a bills-only policy, the dealer will be confronted by the possibility of open-market sales of bonds. This uncertainty will lead to the subtraction of several thirty-seconds from the bid side of the market as the dealer accommodates customer supply.

Greater uncertainty, therefore, results in higher asked and lower bid quotations—a widening of the dealer's spread, a lessening of the dealer's willingness to do business, a poorer market performance. The reduction in this kind of uncertainty provided by a bills-only policy narrows the spread and thus improves the market.[2]

Open-market operations in short-term securities do not affect the market adversely because of the relatively narrow range of price fluctuations at the short end of the maturity structure. Demand for short-term securities is relatively elastic with respect to changes in price. Short-term securities are thus ideal for the probing of the money market so necessary in the everyday execution of monetary policy. Shorter maturities can be bought and sold by the Open Market Account without causing gyrations in interest rates. Demand for longer maturities, however, is characteristically inelastic. Open-market operations at the long end, as in the case of any purchase or sale of a large block of long-term securities, would cause sharp changes in bond prices. The sledgehammer approach of using long-term securities would disturb the market unnecessarily. Dealers would find these fluctuations in bond prices to be intolerable. They could not afford to bear the risks involved in taking positions except at much wider spreads. Consequently, bills-only contributes to narrower spreads and to better dealer performance in the long-term sector.

It has been suggested that dealers may gain as well as lose as a consequence of open-market operations. However, the dealers themselves do not seem to think so.[3] And their attitude may be rationalized with the following simple model. Let X_B represent the number of

[2] It is, of course, true that the Fed could completely eliminate uncertainty by going to the opposite extreme, i.e., by pegging a rate pattern or by severely limiting fluctuations in interest rates by direct intervention in the market. The present discussion of uncertainty must be considered in the context of a relatively free capital-market environment.

[3] See their testimony in *Employment, Growth, and Price Levels, Hearings before the Joint Economic Committee,* 86th Congress, 1st Session, part 6C; The Government's Management of Its Monetary, Fiscal, and Debt Operations, Washington, D.C.: Government Printing Office, 1959, pp. 1861–1874, 1939–1957.

bonds held by the dealer and X_b the number of bills. Then $X_B +$ $X_b = a$, the total number of securities in, say, long position. In situation 1, assume a *bonds*-only policy, $X_b = 0$, and P_1, P_2, and P_3 as three possible prices at which the bonds may sell as a result of open-market operations. Let $P_1 < P_2 = 1 < P_3$. If the probability of each price is the same, utility $U_1 = \frac{1}{3} u(P_1 a) + \frac{1}{3} u(P_2 a) + \frac{1}{3} u(P_3 a)$. In situation 2, assume a *bills*-only policy, $X_B = 0$, and p_1, p_2, and p_3 as the relevant prices, with $p_1 < p_2 = 1 < p_3$. Then utility $U_2 = \frac{1}{3} u(p_1 a) + \frac{1}{3} u(p_2 a) + \frac{1}{3} u(p_3 a)$. Given these utility functions, assuming that the utility function of wealth is concave—that is, marginal utility is a diminishing function of wealth—and with $P_3 > p_3$ and $P_1 < p_1$, it follows that $U_1 < U_2$. The conditions $P_3 > p_3$ and $P_1 < p_1$ are implied by the fact that Federal Reserve policy, whether directed toward changing bank reserves or interest rates, will generate greater price changes in the long-term sector than in the short-term sector.

The thinness of the bond market since the Treasury–Federal Reserve Accord has been cited as evidence of the failure of bills-only to engender improved market performance. This view fails to comprehend the scope of the various determinants of dealer position policy. FOMC policy with respect to the maturity at which it operates is not the only, nor even the primary, determinant of market performance. Hearsay evidence and the empirical findings of this study indicate that a dealer's position policy is determined importantly by interest-rate expectations. During periods when interest rates are expected to rise, dealers cannot be expected to undertake long positions in bonds, regardless of FOMC trading practices. The crucial point is that, *given* interest-rate expectations, a dealer will be more likely to enter the market on *either* side under the aegis of a bills-only policy.[4]

Perhaps the most severe criticism of bills-only has been made by those who feel that the central bank should, as a matter of public policy, regularly determine the interest-rate structure to a greater de-

---

[4] It has been maintained in some quarters that an elimination of bills-only would increase the willingness of the dealers to undertake arbitrage operations by moving from one maturity to another when the difference in yields seemed to be out of line with what is thought to be the normal pattern. But FOMC operations at all maturity levels would in effect determine the yield pattern in advance and thus eliminate the need and, for that matter, the opportunity for such operations on the part of professional traders.

gree than that entailed by a bills-only policy.[5] This is a plausible and feasible public-policy objective, the merits of which will not be debated here. It should be observed, however, that in adopting such a policy, there may be certain costs in terms of market performance that should be weighed in the balance.

For the most part, critics of bills-only have emphasized the limitation which the policy places upon the Federal Reserve System's ability to give direct support to the long-term sector of the capital market during periods of business recession. And much has been written about the stickiness of the long-term rate. It is not clear how this stickiness is to be measured, for the behavior of long-term interest rates is quite consistent with either an institutional or an expectations approach to the theory of the structure of rates.[6] Indeed, it is precisely when the economy is moving into a recession that the expectation effect manifests itself through strong speculative movements, and there is little need for Federal Reserve support.[7] Be this as it may, there need be no ill effects with regard to market performance so long as FOMC action is in the same direction as interest-rate expectations, that is, so long as it reinforces the market impact of dealer position policy. Such a departure from bills-only, so long as it does not generate disorderly market conditions, is quite.consistent with the objective of improved performance.

[5] E.g., in Great Britain, monetary policy has traditionally been more directly oriented toward interest rates than toward the level of bank reserves, as in the United States.

[6] See appendix for a bibliography on the term structure of interest rates.

[7] It has been shown that the long-term rate responds about as well to operations in the short-term sector as it does to operations in the long-term sector. This is apparently due to the support provided by speculative activities. See Arthur M. Okun, "Monetary Policy, Debt Management and Interest Rates: Quantitative Appraisal," in *Stabilization Policies,* Commission on Money and Credit, Englewood Cliffs, N.J.: Prentice-Hall, Inc., 1963, pp. 331–380.

The fact that the impact of open-market operations in bills may spread promptly to other maturities has been cited in support of the view that the risk incurred by dealers is about the same regardless of the maturities used by the FOMC. This view, however, ignores the potential role of the dealer in the arbitrage process. If the Fed deals in shorts, the dealer can pass the effect along to the long-term sector, and performance will not be impaired. I.e., the result depends upon who is holding the long-term securities when their prices change. If it is the dealers' reactions that bring about the price changes, the dealers will not be affected adversely.

On February 20, 1961, the Federal Reserve System announced that it was terminating the bills-only policy.[8] Such a move had been recommended as a means of solving simultaneously the problems presented by the recession and the balance of payments.[9] Again, social priorities may warrant the subordination of the market-performance objective. However, it is conceivable that the twin objectives of meeting recovery and balance-of-payments needs, on the one hand, and desirable market performance, on the other, can be achieved simultaneously. This feat may be accomplished by having the Treasury flatten the yield curve through its debt-management operations while leaving the Federal Reserve free to maintain a bills-only policy.

In other words, it is an oversimplification to fail to distinguish be-

[8] *New York Times,* Feb. 21, 1961. The statement, issued in New York on February 20, 1961, by the Board of Governors of the Federal Reserve System, was as follows:

> At the direction of the Chairman of the Open Market Committee of the Federal Reserve System, the following announcement was made today by the Manager of the System Open Market Account for the information of the public and all participants in the market for government securities:
>
> "The System Open Market Account is purchasing in the open market U.S. Government notes and bonds of varying maturities, some of which will exceed 5 years.
>
> "Price quotations and offerings are being requested of all primary dealers in U.S. Government securities. Determination as to which offerings to purchase is being governed by the prices that appear most advantageous, *i.e.,* the lowest prices. Net amounts of all transactions for System Account will be shown as usual in the condition statements issued every Thursday.
>
> "During recent years transactions for the System Account, except in correction of disorderly markets, have been made in short-term U.S. Government securities. Authority for transactions in securities of longer maturity has been granted by the Open Market Committee of the Federal Reserve System in the light of conditions that have developed in the domestic economy and in the U.S. balance of payments with other countries."

See also *The Federal Reserve System, Purposes and Functions,* 4th ed., 2d printing, Washington, D.C.: Board of Governors of the Federal Reserve System, April, 1961, pp. 35–41.

[9] Cf. Paul A. Samuelson, "Prospects and Policies for the 1961 American Economy," a report submitted to President-elect Kennedy, Jan. 6, 1961; and Roy Blough, Paul W. McCracken, and Allan Sproul, "The Economic Situation and the Balance of Payments," a report submitted to President Kennedy, Jan. 18, 1961.

tween debt-management operations by the Treasury and open-market operations by the central bank. As presently conducted, Treasury financings are announced in advance, and dealers can readily adjust their portfolios prior to the offerings. FOMC operations, on the other hand, are conducted without warning.[10] Hence the two kinds of operations have a different bearing upon the dealer market. The suggested compromise, therefore, would seem to possess some merit.[11]

POSITION FINANCING AND BORROWING SECURITIES[12]

Among the factors which determine a dealer's expected return and hence his willingness to take a position are the cost and availability of borrowed funds. As noted earlier, dealers operate on an exceedingly low margin of equity capital. This accounts for the dealer's sensitivity to the availability of borrowed capital and the terms according to which it may be obtained.

It will be recalled that there are two principal sources of borrowed funds. First, there are the New York money-market banks, from which the dealers borrow funds using their holdings of Governments as collateral. Second, there is the group of sundry institutions, including commercial banks outside New York City, nonfinancial corporations, the Federal Home Loan Bank System, the states and their political subdivisions, and foreign agency banks, with which the dealers typically engage in repurchase agreements. The ability of a dealer to obtain financial accommodation on terms which permit a positive carry contributes favorably to a dealer's willingness to position securities, whereas a negative carry acts as a deterrent.

During periods of easy money, dealers can normally obtain funds from the New York money-market banks. During these periods, loan

[10] The crucial distinction here, of course, is the nature of the operating technique, not the institution involved. I.e., the Fed could announce its operations in long-term securities in advance, after the Treasury pattern. Such a procedure would, however, presumably be inconsistent with the apparent preference of the central bank for limiting "open-mouth" policy to a minimum and letting its actions speak for themselves.

[11] Since the System account might encounter a shortage of bills, authority could be given the Treasury and Federal Reserve to engage in maturity-exchange operations with each other. Alternatively, the central bank might be given the authority to create its own obligations for sale in the open market.

[12] See appendix for a bibliography on dealer financing.

demand is slack, and these banks are willing to extend call-loan privileges to the dealers at relatively advantageous rates. During periods of tight money, however, call-loan rates are raised sharply to levels which preclude a positive carry. Thus precisely at the time when markets are thin anyway because of rising interest rates, the cost and availability of local accommodation further discourage the dealer from holding Government securities.

The inadequacy and relative cost of money-market collateral loan financing promoted the cultivation of repurchase-money sources. However, reliance upon these sources entails certain costs, such as additional handling and clearance charges, greater inflexibility regarding maturities and the substitution of collateral, and the time and expense involved in scouring the country for funds.[13]

It is for these reasons that attention has been given to the possible need for additional dealer-financing facilities. First, it has been suggested that the money-market banks be persuaded to provide the non-bank dealers loan capital continuously at a positive carry. One might suppose the banks would be willing to do this in any case, particularly with short-term securities as collateral. That is, a call loan is more liquid than its collateral, and such loans could be treated as a part of the banks' essential stock of liquidity. In fact, however, it appears that neither the banks nor the dealers treat these loans in the impersonal way which was characteristic of the old call-loan market. Rather, they are treated more or less as customer loans. Consequently, they are actually not as liquid as one would expect a call loan to be; and they must, therefore, compete with customer-loan rates.

As has been suggested in some quarters, the money-market banks could afford to provide such accommodation were they permitted to borrow from the Federal Reserve System a corresponding amount not subject to criticism. It would appear, however, that if the Federal Reserve System is going to provide the financial accommodation in any event, it should do so directly. This method would be more susceptible to maintaining central bank control over the amount and allocation of such funds.

The FOMC may, of course, provide the dealers with direct financial

[13] Moreover, there are indirect costs to the dealers. Repurchase money may make a net contribution to the dealer's financing needs, but there are offsets. A nonfinancial corporation which puts out its money on RPs is temporarily out of the bill market.

assistance.[14] During periods of particular stress in the money market, the Securities Department of the Federal Reserve Bank of New York will enter into repurchase contracts with the nonbank dealers. These are normally done at the discount rate, but they are undertaken at the initiative of the Federal Reserve rather than at the initiative of the dealer. In contrast, discount-window accommodation is at the initiative of the member bank rather than the Federal Reserve.

Several arguments have been raised against giving dealers access to Federal Reserve funds at their own initiative. On the one hand, it is said that such accommodation would inhibit the effectiveness of monetary policy. If, for example, the FOMC was conducting selling operations in order to enforce a policy of restraint, the dealers could request repurchase agreements. The Federal Reserve would thus be injecting reserves with one hand while taking them out of the market with the other. This is true. But to the extent that banks are willing borrowers from the Fed, it is also true of discount-window accommodation. When the FOMC sells, member banks may regain the lost reserves through the discount window. Presumably, so long as the Federal Reserve does not set penalty rates, some form of credit rationing would be needed in the case of dealers as is now true in the case of the banks. Nevertheless, in both cases, discount-window accommodation would serve as something of an escape valve and consequently contribute to better market performance.

Thus, given the dealers' desire for a positive carry, some improvement in market performance should be gained through the provision of additional financing facilities. The variable representing financing costs, it will be recalled, was one of the most influential determinants of dealer positions. On balance, it would appear that such additional accommodation as might be provided should be administered directly by the FOMC because of the close relationship between the dealer operation and the execution of monetary policy. The extension of discount-window privileges to the nonbank dealers, even though they are not member banks, seems warranted by the crucial role they play in our system of monetary controls.

The dealers not only borrow cash; they also borrow bonds. The completion of a short sale requires delivery of securities which must

[14] For a reference to the favorable inventory effect of RP accommodation, see Stephen H. Axilrod and Janice Krummack, "Federal Reserve Security Transactions, 1954–63," *Federal Reserve Bulletin,* July, 1964, p. 828.

be borrowed from some investor's portfolio. The quality of market performance on the supply side is affected adversely by the difficulty which a dealer may experience in locating the securities he has sold short.[15] Moreover, some institutional portfolio managers are not permitted to lend securities.

Facilitating the search for securities to borrow could take several forms. First, financial institutions could be encouraged through official appeals to adopt a more lenient policy. Second, the Treasury, through its Survey of Ownership, or dealers, through a trade association of their own, might collect data on the location of specific issues and make this information available to each dealer firm. Third, the FOMC and the Treasury-managed trust funds could make securities available on a loan basis to meet this dealer need.

As has been noted earlier, there are numerous sources of asymmetry in doing a short position. Facilitating the borrowing of securities would tend to reduce the influence of one of these sources and contribute to the improvement of market performance on the supply side.

THE REGULATION OF MARGIN REQUIREMENTS

It has been suggested that margin requirements be employed as a means of curbing speculation in the Government securities market. Speculation is usually defined as taking a position in a commodity or a security with the expectation that a profit can be gained as a result of the anticipated change in the price of the commodity or security. To some extent, speculation in any market should be encouraged. The possibility of speculative profits provides an added incentive for risk bearing, and desirable trading activity may be promoted. The increase in activity, or volume, due to the operations of speculators may reduce uncertainty and improve the market's performance. That is, an increase in buying and selling tends to increase the willingness of dealers to take positions and hence provide a better market by raising their bid prices and lowering their offer prices.

Speculation may accelerate movements of prices or it may dampen these movements. Speculative activities cause a deceleration of a price

[15] For a reference to the related problem of covering a short sale in the municipals market, see Roland I. Robinson, *Postwar Market for State and Local Government Securities,* Princeton, N.J.: Princeton University Press, 1960, p. 141.

movement if speculators increase their long positions or decrease their rate of reducing these positions when prices are falling. Contrariwise, speculators accentuate a price change if they sell or reduce their rate of purchases when prices are falling.

The acceleration of a price movement in the Government securities market may be desirable if it reinforces a trend in interest rates desired by the monetary authorities. On the other hand, speculative activity may be undesirable if, say, a rise in prices is carried so far that they are out of line with underlying market conditions. When the discrepancy becomes apparent, in this case, securities held on small margins must be liquidated, and a collapse of securities prices ensues. The associated gyration in interest rates serves no useful economic purpose.

Present-day concern regarding speculation in the Government securities market has its origin in the rapid advance in interest rates which accompanied the turnaround in economic activity in June, 1958.[16] The sharp movement in bond prices occurring at that time led to demands for controls on speculative activity through the institution of margin requirements.

The regulation of margins on the extension of credit to purchase or carry Government securities may serve either of two purposes. First, margin requirements may be set at a level which assures the soundness of the loan from a credit point of view. Second, margins may be set much higher with the objective of curtailing purchases by temporary holders.

As a matter of their own protection, lenders usually require margins which are sufficient to assure the credit soundness of each loan made with Government securities as collateral. These margins are normally related to the range of possible price declines. The New York Stock Exchange, for example, requires its member firms to obtain a margin of at least 5 percent of the principal amount of all Government securities financed for their customers. Exceptions to this rule are made by special permission, however, in the case of short-dated instruments.

In April, 1960, the Comptroller of the Currency directed national banks to require, as a general rule, a 5 percent margin on their loans against Government securities. Dealers in Government securities are

[16] See Chap. 5 for a description of this break in the Government bond market.

exempt from the ruling. Also, national bank examiners are allowed a fair amount of discretion in deciding when the 5 percent requirement should apply. For example, lesser margins may be permitted if short-term securities are held as collateral, since the prices of shorter maturities tend to fluctuate less than those of longer-term issues.[17]

No such uniform minimum standards exist, however, for other banks, brokers and dealers not members of the New York Stock Exchange, nonfinancial corporations, or other lenders. It has been suggested that nonregulated lenders should be required to impose minimum margin requirements on loans to purchase Governments.[18] Relatively small margins, such as the 5 percent requirement in the case of New York Stock Exchange member firms and national banks, would not prevent all credit extensions without adequate margins, since Government securities prices might fall by more than 5 percent. However, such margin requirements would make an important contribution to a sounder credit structure. It must, on the other hand, be recognized that these margins are maintenance margins, in the sense that they must be continuously maintained. If the price of the pledged security declines, the lender issues a margin call. Consequently, maintenance margins do not protect the market from forced selling in the event the borrower is unable to put up additional cash.

Alternatively, high initial margin requirements, in excess of what might be sufficient to cover any likely decline in securities prices, may be employed to limit more effectively the amount of speculation and to provide high enough margins so that a price decline will not immediately result in margin calls and forced liquidation.

Two approaches to the provision of high initial margins have been suggested. On the one hand, margin requirements might be administered along the lines of Regulations T and U by the Federal Reserve System. On the other hand, if it appeared that speculation in new issues was in greatest need of regulation, the Treasury might require

[17] See letter by Ray M. Gidney, Comptroller of the Currency, to all District Chief National Bank Examiners, Apr. 6, 1960; Edwin L. Dale, Jr., *New York Times,* Apr. 14, 1960; and *Business Week,* Apr. 23, 1960.
[18] See *Treasury–Federal Reserve Study of the Government Securities Market,* Washington, D.C.: Treasury Department and Board of Governors, Federal Reserve System, 1960, part 3, pp. 47–66; and *Employment, Growth, and Price Levels,* Report no. 1043, Joint Economic Committee, 86th Congress, 2d Session, Washington, D.C.: Government Printing Office, 1960, pp. 40–41.

high cash deposits with subscriptions for cash offerings and evidence of a corresponding amount of equity in the rights to an exchange issue.

It would appear at first that a general formula similar to Regulations T and U would provide the best vehicle for broad and effective control. However, the analogy between the stock market and the Government securities market should not be pressed too hard. Regulations T and U are relied upon to prevent excessive speculation in stocks which usually takes place during periods of business expansion. That is, strong bull markets in stocks tend to occur during periods of prosperity when inflation is threatening and expenditures need to be restrained. In other words, an inflation of stock values increases the monetary value of an investor's holdings and hence may induce an increase in consumption expenditures. The rise in stock values also decreases the cost of equity financing and consequently may lead to a rise in investment outlays. Speculation in the bond market, on the contrary, tends to occur during periods of business recession. This is precisely the time when the object of public policy is to promote recovery by getting bond prices up and interest rates down. In addition, stock prices fluctuate over a relatively wide range, as compared with the prices of bonds. And a persistent, upward trend in stock prices would, in the absence of margin requirements, give rise to possibilities of pyramiding credit.

Lending against stock-market collateral also differs in other important respects. First, in the field of stock speculation, regulations concerning only credits extended by banks and brokers and dealers have been generally adequate. Brokers are prohibited by the Securities and Exchange Act from borrowing on listed stocks from nonbank lenders. However, nonbank lenders have been active in the government securities market. In addition, loans against Governments tend to be larger than against stocks, since bonds are normally in larger dollar denominations than stocks. Therefore, loans against Governments have greater appeal for large institutional lenders. Moreover, loans to finance the purchase of Governments are often made under repurchase agreements. These arrangements are comparable to other investment commitments, since prime-quality securities are in effect being purchased, while lending to purchasers of stock would provide an investment outlet markedly different in quality.

A second approach to regulation would be through the control of speculation in new issues. These securities, when issued on a fixed-price basis, may give unusual opportunities for speculation because of possible discrepancies between their yields and those on outstanding issues. The Treasury, in effect, already imposes margin requirements on cash offerings by insisting that subscriptions be accompanied by a down payment in cash. In the case of exchange offerings, the Treasury might require certification that the subscriber had a minimum equity in the maturing securities he was presenting for exchange. Alternatively, the Treasury could cease offering preemptive rights to holders of maturing issues which it proposed to refund. All new issues could be offered for cash and the Treasury could control speculation in the new issues by controlling down payments and allotments.[19]

Treasury-administered controls have a narrower coverage because they apply only to new issues. Therefore, they could be administered more flexibly. New legislation would be unnecessary. Requirements could be changed by administrative action as market conditions warranted. On the other hand, such control techniques might be inadequate to the task of effectively curbing speculation, since they would not cover purchases in the secondary market.

The wisdom of regulating speculation in Government securities may be questioned on several grounds. First, it must be reiterated that speculation may play a useful role. Margin requirements high enough to control speculation effectively would discourage initial subscriptions to new issues and, consequently, would increase the interest cost of floating new issues. In addition and, as noted earlier, in contrast with speculation in stocks, most speculative activity in debt instruments occurs during periods of business recession. This is precisely the time when lower interest rates are desired for economic-stabilization purposes. Money-market ease promotes short-term credit availability. The use of this credit for purposes of speculating in the long-term market in turn transmits conditions of ease throughout the maturity structure.

Second, a sell-off of the sort that occurred in 1958 would to some extent accompany the troughs of future business cycles regardless of the existence of margin requirements. When the business outlook turns

[19] On Treasury moves in this direction, see Joseph R. Slevin, *New York Herald Tribune,* Apr. 4, 1960; *First National City Bank Monthly Letter, Business and Economic Conditions,* June, 1960, pp. 66–68; and Robert Van Cleave, *C. F. Childs and Company Review,* no. 339, July 11, 1960.

from one of pessimism to one of optimism, investors in Government securities tend to unload their positions and build up their holdings of equities.

➤ Third, although high initial margins are undesirable, maintenance margins promote sound credit conditions from the point of view of both borrower and lender. However, it is desirable to have flexible loan administration on the part of the lender. The pattern set by the New York Stock Exchange and national bank supervisors should be applied to other lenders, including nonfinancial corporations.

Finally, it must be emphasized that dealers in Government securities should in all cases be exempt from margin requirements. As has been observed before, there is even at present a need for improvement in dealer-financing facilities. If margin requirements were increased through regulation, the potential return on capital invested in the dealer operation would be reduced. Given the amount of capital invested, the potential magnitude of dealer gross positions would be reduced. Thus the imposition of margin requirements would be detrimental to market performance. As far as the soundness of the credit structure in the Government securities market is concerned, the FOMC can be relied upon to impose sufficiently rigorous standards of financial adequacy upon the dealer firms.

DEBT-MANAGEMENT POLICY

For reasons that will be delineated later, Treasury and central bank officials have a continuing interest in bringing about a more regularly spaced maturity distribution of the marketable debt. From the point of view of the dealer market, regularized spacing combined with a reduction in the number of issues outstanding would contribute to improved performance through a reduction of uncertainty. Greater regularization of maturities would enable investors to match Treasury maturities more easily with periodic needs for cash. Hence the volume of transactions would tend to increase and become more regular, and the volatility of interest rates would tend to be dampened. An increase in the size of each issue through a reduction in the number of issues outstanding would improve the market on both sides. The better known the issue and the wider its distribution, the more it would tend to be in demand, thus evoking higher bids from the dealers. On the other hand, relative ease of borrowing the security would promote lower offering prices.[20]

There are many conceivable maturity distributions of the debt that would meet these broad requirements. And the Treasury has made substantial progress toward regularizing the short-term sector. Treasury bills are now offered on a regular basis. Continued progress in this direction could be achieved by increasing the maturity of issues offered to investors in this manner. Certificates, notes, and bonds as well might eventually be given specific niches on the debt-management calendar. Regularity of offerings need not imply an undue proliferation of maturities. Consolidation—a reduction in the number and an increase in the size of outstanding issues—could be achieved through periodic offerings of outstanding maturities.

Regular offerings of longer-term securities would serve to maintain more realistic market quotations on these instruments. That is, quotations in the new-issue market tend to be more accurate than those for outstandings, since they are bought and sold infrequently. In addition, a program of spacing and consolidation would engender better market performance in numerous ways. As emphasized earlier, the Government securities dealers would be able to make better markets. Other participants in the market would benefit from the proposal for this and other reasons.

From the point of view of the Treasury, the number of outstanding issues of varying initial maturity would be reduced. Refundings would eventually be evenly spaced on the calendar so as to avoid market congestion. The Treasury could price exchange offerings more efficiently because of the more realistic guide in the prices of outstanding issues. Regularization of Treasury offerings would encourage the systematic allocation of funds for new Treasury issues by individual as well as by institutional investors, thus broadening the market. By reducing uncertainty about the timing and maturity of new issues, such a program should broaden the secondary market as well as stimulate more interest in new issues. Thus the absorptive capacity of the market would be expanded. At the same time, other borrowers would be in a better position to plan their trips to the market so as to avoid conflicting with Treasury operations.

Investors would benefit in numerous ways. Greater foreknowledge

[20] See appendix for a bibliography on debt spacing and consolidation.

of Treasury financing plans would permit more efficient portfolio planing and fund allocation. Spacing would permit better portfolio balance. A more realistic yield curve would prove a better basis for the evaluation of market conditions.

The monetary authorities would benefit because the market would become better accustomed to Treasury operations. Consequently, Federal Reserve policy would not be interrupted as formerly because of debt-management needs. Moreover, a well-spaced debt with no major gaps in the maturity distribution would provide an effective conduit for the communication of monetary policy to all maturity sectors of the capital market.

The nature of the ideal distribution of the debt is one about which reasonable people hold different opinions. And there is a wide range of debt distributions that could make a substantial contribution to improved market performance through a regularization program. An aggressive countercyclical debt-management policy could, for example, be readily executed within the framework of such a program. When business activity slackened, offerings of longer-term issues could be reduced. When inflation threatened, the debt could be lengthened. In the case of either debt shortening or lengthening for stabilization purposes, attention may still be given to considerations of spacing and balance in the maturity sectors involved.

During the recent period, the Treasury has actively pursued a program of lengthening the maturity distribution of the debt by means of the leapfrog, or advance-refunding, technique.[21] Such a policy has perhaps been warranted as a stopgap method of preventing an excessively rapid shortening in the debt due solely to the passage of time. However, once a better balance in the distribution of the debt has been achieved, this technique should be used sparingly. The use of this funding procedure has an adverse effect upon the dealer market for the simple reason that it tends to bypass that market. That is, it is a technique which is specifically designed to effect an exchange of issues directly between the Treasury and the ultimate investor. As a consequence, dealer volume is reduced, and accordingly, market performance is affected adversely.[22]

[21] See appendix for bibliography on advance refunding.

[22] The welter of possible exchanges and implied investor yields typically associated with an advance refunding is a self-defeating feature of this debt-management technique. See David I. Fand, "An Analysis of Advance Refund-

Within the framework of a balanced, consolidated debt, any of a number of offering techniques may be employed. Conversion issues may be planned. Cash offerings may be made on a fixed-price basis. Or new issues may be offered for cash on an auction basis.[23]

A major argument of Treasury officials against the use of the auction method is that this type of offering is susceptible to undesirable speculative activity. In the case of a fixed-price issue, on the other hand, awards can be made according to official discretion. But speculative activity may actually redound to the Treasury's advantage. During a period in which the pace of business activity is quickening, for example, Treasury officials may oppose the use of the auction technique on the ground that speculative movements in the securities market would force the Treasury to pay an unduly high rate of interest. In fact, however, the auction reveals the realities of market conditions. To refuse to face these realities is to invite a financing failure— unduly high attrition. During a cyclical decline, on the other hand, the Treasury may fear that speculators are bidding up the prices of Government securities to dangerously high levels. But again market forces cannot readily be contained. Moreover, the Treasury's position is surely more tenable if the securities are actually issued at these higher prices than if the issue prices are actually below the market and the initial holders enjoy an unusual speculative gain. In any case, both the Treasury and the central bank may be relied upon to dampen market gyrations should they appear to be excessive.

The point is often made in defense of the fixed-price offering that the Treasury reduces uncertainty and creates a market consensus simply by stating a price. This argument, however, ignores the uncertainty associated with respect to the size of the allotment in a fixed-price offering. Ascertaining the allotment percentage, as noted earlier, has been called the biggest guessing game in Wall Street. And it must be noted that overestimating this proportion has much in common with bidding a price that is too low in an auction system. Underestimating the allotment percentage is much like overbidding the market.

Even though they agree to the advisability of employing the auction technique, some would substitute the Dutch Market procedure for

---

ing," paper presented to Cleveland meetings of the Econometric Society, Sept. 5, 1963.

[23] See appendix for a bibliography on auctioning Treasury securities.

present Treasury practice in the bill auction. Thus awards would be made at the stop-out, rather than the prices actually bid. This debate involves such imponderables as the effect on issue prices of giving up investor "surplus" versus the effect on these prices of increased market participation inspired by eliminating the danger of bidding too high. The crucial argument in favor of present procedures, however, is that dealers and other specialists are rewarded for their role in submitting "underwriting" bids below the to-be-sure level. To substitute the Dutch Market technique would be to eliminate the possibility of receiving such returns, dampen the dealer incentive for risk taking, and, therefore, reduce the level of market performance.

BIBLIOGRAPHIC APPENDIX

ADVANCE REFUNDING

Staff Report on Employment, Growth, and Price Level, Prepared for consideration by the Joint Economic Committee, Congress of the United States, 86th Congress, 1st Session, Dec. 24, 1959, Washington, D.C.: Government Printing Office, 1959, pp. 426–427.

"Manager of the National Debt," *Business Week,* June 18, 1960.

Debt Management and Advance Refunding, Washington, D.C.: U.S. Treasury Department, September, 1960.

"New Approach to Debt Stretching," *Morgan-Guaranty Survey,* October, 1960.

"A Gift to Bondholders?" *First National City Bank Monthly Letter, Business and Economic Conditions,* October, 1960.

"Remarks by Under Secretary of the Treasury Baird, October 15, at the Annual Meeting of the Stockholders of the Federal Reserve Bank of Boston, Boston, Massachusetts," *Annual Report of the Secretary of the Treasury on the State of the Finances for the Fiscal Year Ended June 30, 1960,* Washington, D.C.: Government Printing Office, 1961, pp. 296–301.

"The Longer She Stands the Shorter She Grows," *Federal Reserve Bank of Richmond Monthly Review,* April, 1961.

Money and Credit: Their Influence on Jobs, Prices, and Growth, Report of the Commission on Money and Credit, Englewood Cliffs, N.J.: Prentice-Hall, Inc., 1961, pp. 111–114.

"Advance Refunding: A Technique of Debt Management," *Federal Reserve Bank of New York Monthly Review,* December, 1962.

David I. Fand, *An Analysis of Advance Refunding,* paper presented to Cleveland Meetings of the Econometric Society, Sept. 5, 1963.

179

AUCTIONING TREASURY SECURITIES

Testimony by Robert B. Anderson in *Employment, Growth, and Price Levels, Hearings before the Joint Economic Committee,* 86th Congress, 1st Session, July 24, 28, 29, and 30, 1959, Washington, D.C.: Government Printing Office, 1959, part 6A, pp. 1150–1153.

Testimony by Milton Friedman in *Employment, Growth, and Price Levels, Hearings before the Joint Economic Committee,* 86th Congress, 1st Session, Oct. 26, 27, 28, 29, and 30, 1959, Washington, D.C.: Government Printing Office, 1959, part 9A, pp. 3023–3026.

Milton Friedman, "Debt Management and Banking Reform," *A Program for Monetary Stability,* New York: Fordham University Press, 1960, pp. 52–76.

Henry Goldstein, "The Friedman Proposal for Auctioning Treasury Bills," *Journal of Political Economy,* vol. 70, no. 4, August, 1962, pp. 386–392.

Henry N. Goldstein, "Should the Treasury Auction Long-term Securities?" *Journal of Finance,* vol. 17, no. 3, September, 1962, pp. 444–464.

"Treasury Eyes Competitive Bidding," *Business Week,* Oct. 13, 1962.

Michael Rieber, "Collusion in the Auction Market for Treasury Bills," *Journal of Political Economy,* vol. 72, no. 5, October, 1964, pp. 509–512.

Milton Friedman, "Comment on 'Collusion in the Auction Market for Treasury Bills,'" *Journal of Political Economy,* vol. 72, no. 5, October, 1964, pp. 513–514.

Michael Rieber, "Collusion in the Auction Market for Treasury Bills: Rejoinder," *Journal of Political Economy,* vol. 72, no. 5, October, 1964, p. 513.

BANK RESERVES AND MONETARY EXPANSION

George Horwich, "Element of Timing and Response in the Balance Sheet of Banking, 1953–1955," *Journal of Finance,* vol. 12, no. 2, May, 1957, pp. 238–255.

"The Significance and Limitations of Free Reserves," *Federal Reserve Bank of New York Monthly Review,* vol. 40, no. 11, November, 1958.

Hobart C. Carr, "Why and How to Read the Federal Reserve Statement," *Journal of Finance,* vol. 14, no. 4, December, 1959, pp. 504–519.

Richard E. Mooney, *New York Times,* June 20, 1960.

Business Scope, vol. 4, no. 7, Aug. 13, 1960.

A. J. Meigs, "Free Reserve and the Money Supply," Ph.D. thesis, University of Chicago, Chicago, 1960.

Colin D. Campbell, *The Federal Reserve and the Business Cycle,* Tuck Bulletin 26, Graduate School of Business Administration, Dartmouth College, Hanover, N.H., January, 1961.

Milton Friedman, "Vault Cash and Free Reserve," *Journal of Political Economy,* vol. 69, no. 2, April, 1961, pp. 181–182.

"The Vault Cash Provision: Has It Changed the Way Banks Manage Their Reserves," *Federal Reserve Bank of Philadelphia Monthly Review,* September, 1961.

"Free Reserve and Bank Reserve Management," *Federal Reserve Bank of Kansas City Monthly Review,* November, 1961.

Jack C. Rothwell, "Vault Cash and Free Reserve: Some Evidence," *Journal of Political Economy,* vol. 70, no. 2, April, 1962, pp. 187–188.

William G. Dewald, "Free Reserves, Total Reserves, and Monetary Control," *Journal of Political Economy,* vol. 71, no. 2, April, 1963, pp. 141–153.

Eugene M. Lerner, "A Schizoid Money Market," *Business Scope,* vol. 7, no. 4, May 25, 1963.

"Controlling Reserves: The Heart of Federal Reserve Policy," *Federal Reserve Bank of Atlanta Monthly Review,* September, 1963.

Albert H. Cox, Jr., and Ralph E. Leach, "Settlement Periods of Member Banks," *Journal of Finance,* vol. 19, no. 1, March, 1964, pp. 76–93.

Peter D. Sternlight, "Reserve Settlement Periods of Member Banks: Comment," *Journal of Finance,* vol. 19, no. 1, March, 1964, pp. 94–98.

Paul S. Nadler, "What Do 'Free Reserves' Predict?" *Banking Journal of the American Bankers Association,* April, 1964, pp. 43–44.

Allan H. Meltzer and Karl Brunner, *The Federal Reserve's Attachment to the Free Reserve Concept,* staff analysis, Subcommittee on Domestic Finance, Committee on Banking and Currency, House of Representatives, 88th Congress, 2d Session, May 7, 1964, Washington, D.C.: Government Printing Office, 1964.

Stephen H. Axilrod and Janice Krummack, "Federal Reserve Security Transactions 1954–63," *Federal Reserve Bulletin,* July, 1964.

Federal Reserve Bank of Atlanta, "Federal Reserve Policy-making and Its Problems," *Readings in Southern Finance,* no. 7, July, 1964.

Irving Auerbach, "New Series on Federal Funds," *Federal Reserve Bulletin,* August, 1964, pp. 944–964.

Warren L. Smith, "The Instruments of General Monetary Control" (Unpublished ms.).

James Tobin, "The Monetary Mechanism" (Unpublished ms.).

BILLS-ONLY POLICY

"Federal Open Market Committee Report of Ad Hoc Subcommittee on the Government Securities Market, Nov. 12, 1952," in *U.S. Monetary Policy: Recent Thinking and Experience, Hearings before the Subcommittee on Economic Stabilization of the Joint Committee on the Economic Report,* 83d Congress, 2d Session, Dec. 6, 7, 1954, Washington, D.C.: Government Printing Office, 1954, pp. 257–286.

Paul A. Samuelson, "Recent American Monetary Controversy," *Three Banks Review,* March, 1956, pp. 3–21.

Louise Freeman, "The 'Bill-only' Policy: An Aspect of the Federal Reserve's Relationship to the United States Government Securities Market," M.A. thesis, Columbia University, New York, March, 1957.

Deane Carson, "Federal Reserve Support of Treasury Refunding Operations," *Journal of Finance,* vol. 12, no. 1, March, 1957, pp. 51–63.

David I. Fand and Ira O. Scott, Jr., "The Federal Reserve System's 'Bill-only' Policy: A Suggested Interpretation," *Journal of Business,* vol. 31, no. 1, January, 1958, pp. 12–18.

"Fed Shift Saves Sinking Bonds," *Business Week,* July 26, 1958.

" 'Bills Only' Policy Is Out—or Is It?", *C. F. Childs and Company Review,* no. 298, Aug. 4, 1958.

"Open Market Operations in Long-term Securities," *Federal Reserve Bulletin,* November, 1958.

"Why Doesn't the Fed Do Something about Government Bond Prices?" *Federal Reserve Bank of Philadelphia Business Review,* July, 1959.

Robert Haney Scott, "Treasury Bills Only? A Compromise," *Current Economic Comment,* Bureau of Economic and Business Research, University of Illinois, vol. 21, no. 1, February, 1959, pp. 13–20.

Sidney Weintraub, "The Theory of Open Market Operations: A Comment," *Review of Economics and Statistics,* vol. 41, no. 3, August, 1959, pp. 308–312.

Dudley G. Luckett, " 'Bill-only': A Critical Appraisal," *Review of Economics and Statistics,* vol. 42, no. 1, part I, August, 1960, pp. 301–306.

Ralph A. Young and Charles A. Yager, "The Economics of 'Bills Preferably,' " *Quarterly Journal of Economics,* vol. 74, no. 3, August, 1960, pp. 341–373.

Ralph F. Leach, *Reflections of a Portfolio Manager,* Excerpts from a talk at the New York State Bankers Association Investment Seminar, Sept. 30, 1960.

"Bills Usually, Bonds Sometimes?", *C. F. Childs and Company Review,* no. 346, Nov. 7, 1960.

"The Fed Decides to Intervene," *Business Week,* Nov. 12, 1960.

Employment, Growth, and Price Levels, Hearings before the Joint Economic Committee, 86th Congress, 1st Session, Washington, D.C.: Government Printing Office, 1960, part 10, p. 3340.

Goldsmith–Nagan Washington Service, *United States Government Securities,* Feb. 18, 1961.

Money and Credit: Their Influence on Jobs, Prices and Growth, Report of the Commission on Money and Credit, Englewood Cliffs, N.J.: Prentice-Hall, Inc., 1961, pp. 62–64.

Karl R. Bopp, "The Tradition to Adapt," *Federal Reserve Bank of Philadelphia Business Review,* June, 1961.

"Looking Ahead," *C. F. Childs and Company Review,* no. 374, Jan. 2, 1962.

Goldsmith–Nagan Washington Service, *United States Government Securities,* Feb. 17, 1962.

Sidney Weintraub, "Interest Rates on the New Frontier: A Small Pinch after the Slight Nudge," *Business Scope,* vol. 5, no. 13, Feb. 24, 1962.

"A Footnote to 'Nudge,' " *C. F. Childs and Company Review,* no. 381, Apr. 9, 1962.

James R. Schlesinger, "The Sequel to Bills Only," *Review of Economics and Statistics,* vol. 44, no. 2, May, 1962.

"Hurricane Season," *C. F. Childs and Company Review,* no. 391, Sept. 4, 1962.

"What Price Long-term Bonds?" *C. F. Childs and Company Review,* no. 415, September 13, 1963.

The Townsend Letter for Savings and Loan Executives, Aug. 22, 1963.

Arthur M. Okun, "Monetary Policy, Debt Management and Interest Rates: A Quantitative Appraisal," in *Stabilization Policies,* Commission on Money and Credit, Englewood Cliffs, N.J.: Prentice-Hall, Inc., 1963, pp. 331–380.

Albert H. Cox, Jr., and Ralph F. Leach, "Settlement Periods of Member Banks," *Journal of Finance,* vol. 19, no. 1, March, 1964, pp. 76–93.

Peter D. Sternlight, "Reserve Settlement Periods of Member Banks: Comment," *Journal of Finance,* vol. 19, no. 1, March, 1964, pp. 94–95.

Stephen H. Axilrod and Janice Krummack, "Federal Reserve Security Transactions, 1954–63," *Federal Reserve Bulletin,* July, 1964.

COMMERCIAL BANKS

Pearson Hunt, *Portfolio Policies of Commercial Banks in the United States, 1920–1939,* Business Research Studies, no. 24, Boston: Graduate School of Business Administration, Harvard University, January, 1940.

Charles R. Whittlesey, *Bank Liquidity and the War,* Occasional Paper 22, New York: National Bureau of Economic Research, May, 1945.

Office of Commissioner of Internal Revenue, *Reserve Method of Accounting for Bad Debts in the Case of Banks,* Com.-Mimeograph Coll., no. 6209, Washington, D.C.: Treasury Department, Dec. 8, 1947.

Herbert V. Prochnow, *Term Loans and Theories of Bank Liquidity,* Englewood Cliffs, N.J.: Prentice-Hall, Inc., 1949.

Roland I. Robinson, *The Administration of Bank Funds,* New York: McGraw-Hill Book Company, 1951.

Lawrence H. Seltzer, *The Nature and Tax Treatment of Capital Gains and Losses,* New York: National Bureau of Economic Research, 1951.

George W. Coleman, "Lending and Investment Practices of Commercial Banks," *Law and Contemporary Problems,* vol. 17, no. 1, Winter, 1952, pp. 108–127.

L. J. Pritchard, "Bank Capital and Lending Ability of Commercial Banks," *American Economic Review,* vol. 43, no. 3, June, 1953, pp. 362–365.

Internal Revenue Service, *Reserve Method of Accounting for Bad Debts in the Case of Banks,* IR-Mimeograph No. 54–55, Washington, D.C.: Treasury Department, Apr. 8, 1954.

"Member Bank Loans Move Higher and Raise Some Important Questions," *Federal Reserve Bank of Richmond Monthly Review,* September, 1956.

"Liquid Assets and Bank Liquidity," *Federal Reserve Bank of Chicago Business Conditions,* December, 1956.

Raymond H. McEvoy, "Variation in Bank Asset Portfolios," *Journal of Finance,* vol. 11, no. 4, December, 1956, pp. 463–473.

Benjamin Haggott Beckhart, "Business Loans of American Commercial Banks and Inflation," *Three Banks Review,* no. 33, March, 1957.

"Deposits on the Move," *Federal Reserve Bank of Philadelphia Business Review,* March, 1957.

Ira O. Scott, "The Changing Significance of Treasury Obligations in Commercial Bank Portfolios," *Journal of Finance,* vol. 12, no. 2, May, 1957, pp. 213–222.

J. S. G. Wilson, "America's Changing Banking Scene. II. The Commercial Banks," *The Banker,* vol. 107, no. 376, May, 1957, pp. 322–328.

Lawrence S. Ritter, *Commercial Bank Liquidity and Medium and Longer Term Loans in the United States,* V Reunion de Tecnicos de Los Bancos Centrales del Continente Americano, Bogotá, Colombia, June, 1957.

John T. Masten, *Bank Management: Some Principles and Cases,* Lexington: Kentucky School of Banking, University of Kentucky, July, 1957.

"Liquidity of Eight District Banks," *Federal Reserve Bank of St. Louis Monthly Review,* vol. 39, no. 7, July, 1957.

"Deposit Instability at Individual Banks," *Federal Reserve Bank of Kansas City Monthly Review,* September, 1957.

L. W. Seidman, "Proper Handling of Bond Account Can Yield Better Income for Banks through Lower Tax," *American Banker,* Nov. 22, 1957.

"The Problem of Bank Liquidity," *Banking,* November, 1957.

The Problem of Commercial Bank Liquidity, New York: American Bankers Association, 1957.

"Reserve Adjustment of City Banks," *Federal Reserve Bank of Kansas City Monthly Review,* February, 1958.

"Loss from Wash Sales of Stock or Securities," *Internal Revenue Bulletin,* no. 1958–19, May 12, 1958, pp. 23–33.

Robert H. Parks, "Income and Tax Aspects of Commercial Bank Portfolio Operations in Treasury Securities," *National Tax Journal,* vol. 11, no. 1, March, 1958, pp. 21–34.

Raymond Rodgers, "Another Decline in Banking Rates Seen," *American Banker,* vol. 123, no. 97, May 19, 1958.

"Term Loans Gain in Importance," *Federal Reserve Bank of Atlanta Monthly Review,* July, 1958.

"How Liquid Are the Banks?" *Federal Reserve Bank of Philadelphia Business Review,* October, 1958.

Robert H. Parks, "Portfolio Operations of Commercial Banks and the Level of Treasury Security Prices," *Journal of Finance,* vol. 14, no. 1, March, 1959, pp. 52–66.

"Commercial Bank Investments in Recession and Expansion," *Federal Reserve Bank of Kansas City Monthly Review,* March, 1959.

"Bank Liquidity and Rising Business," *Federal Reserve Bank of Chicago Business Conditions,* June, 1959.

"Losses of Securities Cut into Bank Profits," *Federal Reserve Bank of Minneapolis Monthly Review,* August, 1959.

New York State Bankers Association, *Proceedings of the Tenth Annual Investment Seminar,* Sept. 18, 1959, pp. 49–51.

"Banks Loaned Up?" *Federal Reserve Bank of Chicago Business Conditions,* October, 1959.

National Bank Amendments, 1959, Hearing before the Committee on Banking and Currency, Senate, 86th Congress, 1st Session, Aug. 14, 1959, Washington, D.C.: Government Printing Office, 1959.

Benjamin Haggott Beckhart, *Business Loans of American Commercial Banks,* New York: The Ronald Press Company, 1959.

"Potential Problems for Monetary Policy," *Federal Reserve Bank of Cleveland Annual Report,* 1959.

"Capital Gains Taxation," in *The Federal Revenue System Facts and Problems, 1959,* Joint Economic Committee, 86th Congress, 1st Session, Washington, D.C.: Government Printing Office, 1959, pp. 45–46.

"A Look at the Liquidity Concept," *Federal Reserve Bank of Minneapolis Monthly Review,* vol. 15, no. 2, Feb. 29, 1960.

"Recent Development in District Bank Liquidity," *Federal Reserve Bank of Kansas City Monthly Review,* May, 1960.

Donald R. Hodgman, "Credit Risk and Credit Rationing," *Quarterly Journal of Economics,* vol. 74, no. 2, May, 1960, pp. 258–278.

"Bank Reactions to Security Losses," *Federal Reserve Bank of Kansas City Monthly Review,* June, 1960.

"Commercial Bank Liquidity," *Federal Reserve Bank of St. Louis Monthly Review,* vol. 42, no. 8, August, 1960.

The Commercial Bank and Economic Growth, New York University, Graduate School of Business Administration, C. J. Devine Institute of Finance, Bulletin no. 1, December, 1960.

"Taxes and the Term Structure of Yields," *Federal Reserve Bank of Kansas City Monthly Review,* December, 1960.

Roger A. Lyon, *Investment Portfolio Management in the Commercial Bank,* New Brunswick, N.J.: Rutgers University Press, 1960.

Internal Revenue Code of 1954, as Amended and in Force on Jan. 3, 1961, Washington, D.C.: Government Printing Office, 1961, sec. 11, 582, 1201, 1091, 1211, 1222.

"Term Lending by New York City Banks," *Federal Reserve Bank of New York Monthly Review,* vol. 43, no. 2, February, 1961.

"Liquidity of Business Loans," *Federal Reserve Bank of Chicago Business Conditions,* March, 1961.

Donald D. Hestor, *An Empirical Examination of a Commercial Bank Loan Offer Function,* Cowles Foundation Discussion Paper no. III, Apr. 20, 1961.

Paul S. Nadler, "Commercial Banking in the Sixties," *Journal of Finance,* vol. 16, no. 2, May, 1961, pp. 226–240.

Paul H. Cootner, "Common Elements in Future Markets for Commodities and Bonds," *American Economic Review, Papers and Proceedings,* vol. 51, no. 2, May, 1961, pp. 173–183.

Sam B. Chase, Jr., "Credit Risk and Credit Rationing: Comment," *Quarterly Journal of Economics,* vol. 75, no. 2, May, 1961, pp. 319–329.

Donald R. Hodgman, "Reply," *ibid.,* pp. 327–329.

Daniel Orr and W. G. Mellon, "Stochastic Reserve Losses and Expansion of Bank Credit," *American Economic Review,* vol. 51, no. 4, September, 1961, pp. 614–623.

"Recent Developments in Bank Liquidity," *Federal Reserve Bank of New York Monthly Review,* November, 1961.

"Bank Loans and Liquid Assets," *Federal Reserve Bank of Chicago Business Conditions,* December, 1961.

Jules I. Bogen, *The Changing Composition of Bank Assets,* New York: Graduate School of Business Administration, New York University, 1961.

Albert J. Wojnilower, "Changes in the Quality of Business Loans of Commercial Banks," Ph.D. thesis, Columbia University, New York, 1961.

Richard C. Porter, *A Model of Bank Portfolio Selection,* Cowles Foundation Paper no. 168, reprinted in *Yale Economic Essays,* vol. 1, no. 2, 1961.

"Corporate Income Taxes and the Banking System," *Federal Reserve Bank of New York Monthly Review,* January, 1962.

Andrew F. Brimmer, "Foreign Banking Institutions in the United States Money Market," *Review of Economics and Statistics,* vol. 44, no. 1, February, 1962.

Dudley G. Luckett, "Compensatory Cyclical Bank Asset Adjustments," *Journal of Finance,* vol. 17, no. 1, March, 1962, pp. 53–62.

Douglas A. Hayes, "Bank Liquidity and Loan Demand," *Michigan Business Review,* vol. 14, no. 3, May, 1962, pp. 23–29.

"The Long and the Short of It: Bankers Are Reaching Out for Longer-term Securities Again," *Federal Reserve Bank of Philadelphia Business Review,* April, 1962.

D. R. Cawthorne, Sam B. Chase, Jr., and Lyle E. Gramley, *Essays on Commercial Banking*, Federal Reserve Bank of Kansas City, August, 1962.

"Banks in the Bond Market," *C. F. Childs and Company Review*, Sept. 17, 1962.

Lyle E. Gramley, "A Study of Scale Economies in Banking," *Federal Reserve Bank of Kansas City Monthly Review*, November, 1962.

Kalman J. Cohen and Donald R. Hodgman, "A Macro-econometric Model of the Commercial Banking Sector," Carnegie Institute of Technology and University of Illinois, Dec. 6, 1962 (Unpublished ms.)

Howard D. Crosse, *Management Policies for Commercial Banks*, Englewood Cliffs, N.J.: Prentice-Hall, Inc., 1962.

American Bankers Association, *The Commercial Banking Industry*, Commission on Money and Credit, Englewood Cliffs, N.J.: Prentice-Hall, Inc., 1962.

Roland I. Robinson, *The Management of Bank Funds*, New York: McGraw-Hill Book Company, 1962.

"Commercial Banks as Suppliers of Capital Funds to Business," *Federal Reserve Bank of New York Monthly Review*, December, 1963.

Ronald R. Hodgman, *Commercial Bank Loan and Investment Policy*, Urbana, Ill.: Bureau of Economic and Business Research, University of Illinois, 1963.

Deane Carson (ed.), *Banking and Monetary Studies in Commemoration of the Centennial of the National Banking System*, Homewood, Ill.: Richard D. Irwin, Inc., 1963.

Edward W. Reed, *Commercial Bank Management*, New York: Harper & Row, Publishers, Incorporated, 1963.

John A. Galbraith, *The Economics of Banking Operations*, Montreal: McGill University Press, 1963.

Deane Carson and Ira O. Scott, Jr., "Commercial Bank Attributes and Aversion to Risk," in *Banking and Monetary Studies*, Deane Carson (ed.), Homewood, Ill.: Richard D. Irwin, Inc., 1963, pp. 420–433.

"Banks, Governments, and Cycles," *Federal Reserve Bank of San Francisco Monthly Review*, April, 1964, pp. 81–87.

"District Bank Liquidity," *Federal Reserve Bank of Dallas Business Review*, May, 1964, pp. 3–10.

William R. Russell, "Commercial Bank Portfolio Adjustments," *American Economic Review, Papers and Proceedings*, vol. 54, no. 3, May, 1964, pp. 544–553.

"A Microeconomic Model to Explain Bank Behavior," *Business Review,* University of Washington, College of Business Administration, vol. 23, nos. 4–5, April–June. 1964, pp. 26–36.

"Techniques of Member Bank Borrowing at the Federal Reserve," *Federal Reserve Bank of New York Monthly Review,* vol. 46, no. 4, April, 1964, pp. 66–68.

CORPORATE CASH MANAGEMENT

Avram Kisselgoff, "Liquidity Preference of Large Manufacturing Corporations (1921–1939)," *Econometrica,* vol. 13, no. 4, October, 1945, pp. 334–344.

Acheson J. Duncan, " 'Free Money' of Large Manufacturing Corporations and the Rate of Interest," *Econometrica,* vol. 14, no. 3, July, 1946, pp. 251–253.

W. W. Cooper, "Revisions to the Theory of the Firm," *American Economic Review,* vol. 39, no. 6, December, 1949, pp. 1204–1222.

John S. Sprowls, "Short Term Investment Practices of Large Non-Financial Corporations," MBA thesis, University of Pittsburgh, Pittsburgh, Pa., 1953.

Charles E. Silberman, "The Big Corporate Lenders," *Fortune,* August, 1956.

Sally S. Ronk, "The Acceleration of Corporate Income Tax Payments," *Journal of Finance,* vol. 11, no. 4, December, 1956, pp. 474–481.

George Hanc, "How Corporate Measurers Select Their Depositories," *Banking,* March, 1957.

George Katona, *Business Looks at Banks,* Ann Arbor, Mich.: The University of Michigan Press, 1957.

Colin D. Campbell, "Investments in United States Government Securities by Nonfinancial Corporations, 1952–56: Comment," *Quarterly Journal of Economics,* vol. 73, no. 287, May, 1958, pp. 292–297.

William J. Frazer, Jr., "Large Manufacturing Corporations as Suppliers of Funds to the United States Government Securities Market," *Journal of Finance,* vol. 8, no. 4, December, 1958, pp. 499–509.

"The Repurchase Agreement," *Treasury–Federal Reserve Study of the Government Securities Market,* Washington, February, 1960, part 3, pp. 67–94.

"Interest Rates," *Townsend Letter for Savings and Loan Executives,* June 24, 1960.

John J. McCall, "Difference between the Personal Demand for Money and the Business Demand for Money," *Journal of Political Economy,* vol. 68, no. 4, August, 1960, pp. 358–368.

Sidney M. Robbins, "Getting More Mileage out of Cash," *National Association of Accountants Bulletin,* vol. 42, no. 1, September, 1960, pp. 65–74.

"Corporate Participation in the Government Securities Market," *Federal Reserve Bank of Kansas City Monthly Review,* December, 1960.

"Financing the Government Securities Market," in *A Study of the Dealer Market for Federal Government Securities,* materials prepared for the Joint Economic Committee, 86th Congress, 2d Session, Washington, D.C.: Government Printing Office, 1960, pp. 71–96.

"Managing the Corporate 'Money' Position," *Federal Reserve Bank of Philadelphia Business Review,* March, 1961.

"Profits on Commercial Bank Time Deposits," *Federal Reserve Bank of New York Monthly Review,* September, 1961.

Ernest Bloch, "Corporate Liquidity Preference," Ph.D. thesis, New School for Social Research, New York, 1961.

Alan Heston, "Corporate Cash and Securities Holdings: An Empirical Study of Cash, Securities and Other Current Accounts of Large Corporations," Ph.D. thesis, Yale University, New Haven, Conn., 1962.

Harold Bierman, Jr., and A. K. McAdams, *Management Decisions for Cash and Marketable Securities,* Cornell Studies in Policy and Administration, Graduate School of Business and Public Administration, Cornell University, Ithaca, N.Y., 1962.

"Cash Flows and Corporate Investment," *Federal Reserve Bank of San Francisco Monthly Review,* February, 1963.

"Living Higher on the Hog," *Business Week,* Oct. 19, 1963, pp. 166–178.

Ernest Bloch, "Corporate Demand for Government Securities," *American Economic Review,* vol. 53, no. 3, December, 1963, pp. 1058–1077.

William J. Frazer, Jr., "The Financial Structure of Manufacturing Corporations and the Demand for Money: Some Empirical Findings," *Journal of Political Economy,* vol. 72, no. 2, 1964.

Lawrence E. Thompson, "Income Velocity, Liquid Assets of Households and Non-financial Corporations, and Monetary Policy" (Unpublished ms.).

DEALER FINANCING

Stabilization, Hearings before the Committee on Banking and Currency, House of Representatives, 69th Congress, 1st Session, Apr. 20, 21, 22, 27, 30; May 3, 4, 5, 6; June 10, 1926; and February 4, 1927; Washington, D.C.: Government Printing Office, 1927, part 2, pp. 930, 982–1005.

Bernice C. Turner, *Federal Funds Market,* Englewood Cliffs, N.J.: Prentice-Hall, Inc., 1931, pp. 34–35.

Operation of the National and Federal Reserve Banking Systems, Hearings before a Subcommittee of the Committee on Banking and Currency, Senate, 71st Congress, 3d Session, Washington, D.C.: Government Printing Office, 1931, Appendix, part 6, p. 797.

Stanley L. Miller, "Financing Security Brokers and Dealers," in *Money Market Essays,* Federal Reserve Bank of New York, March, 1952, pp. 27–33.

Edward C. Simmons, "Sales of Government Securities to Federal Reserve Banks under Repurchase Agreements," *Journal of Finance,* vol. 9, no. 1, March, 1954.

Lester V. Chandler, *Benjamin Strong, Central Banker,* Washington, D.C.: The Brookings Institution, 1958, p. 115.

Federal Funds Market, Washington, D.C.: Board of Governors of the Federal Reserve System, May, 1959, pp. 45–49, 54–56.

"Repurchase Agreements," in *National Bank Amendments, 1959, Hearings before the Committee on Banking and Currency,* Senate, 86th Congress, 1st Session, Aug. 14, 1959, Washington, D.C.: Government Printing Office, 1959, pp. 31–55.

Testimony by Girard L. Spencer in *Employment, Growth, and Price Levels, Hearings before the Joint Economic Committee,* 86th Congress, 1st Session, Aug. 5, 6, 7, 1959, Washington, D.C.: Government Printing Office, 1959, part 6B, pp. 1558–1559.

"The Repurchase Agreement," in *Treasury–Federal Reserve Study of the Government Securities Market,* Washington, D.C., Feb. 1, 1960, part 3, pp. 67–94.

"Financing the Government Securities Market," in *A Study of the Dealer Market for Federal Government Securities,* materials prepared for the Joint Economic Committee, 86th Congress, 2d Session, Washington, D.C.: Government Printing Office, 1960, pp. 71–96; Table III-2, p. 37; Table VI-5, p. 103; Table VI-2, p. 103.

Jules I. Bogen and Herman E. Krooss, *Security Credit; Its Economic Role and Regulation,* Englewood Cliffs, N.J.: Prentice-Hall, Inc., 1960.

"Bank Loans Secured by Stocks and Bonds," *Federal Reserve Bulletin,* July, 1963, pp. 904–921.

"Repurchase Agreements," *Federal Reserve Bank of Cleveland Economic Review,* May, 1964, pp. 2–13.

"The Financing of Government Securities Dealers," *Federal Reserve Bank of New York Monthly Review,* June, 1964, pp. 107–115.

"New Series on Federal Funds," *Federal Reserve Bulletin,* August, 1964, pp. 947–948.

DEBT AND INTEREST-RATE CEILINGS

H. J. Cooke and M. Katzen, "The Public Debt Limit," *Journal of Finance,* vol. 9, no. 3, September, 1954, pp. 298–303.

Testimony by Secretary of the Treasury Robert B. Anderson in *Debt Ceiling Increase, Hearings before the Committee on Finance,* Senate, 85th Congress, 2d Session, Jan. 27, 28, Feb. 4, 7, 1958, Washington, D.C.: Government Printing Office, 1958, pp. 3–5.

Following papers appearing in the *1958 Proceedings of the Fifty-first Annual Conference on Taxation* held under the auspices of the National Tax Association: B. U. Ratchford, "State and Local Debt Limitations," pp. 215–229; Harley F. Lutz, "Case for a Federal Debt Limit," pp. 230–245; Walter W. Heller, "Why a Federal Debt Limit?" pp. 246–256.

A Public Debt Ceiling and Interest Rate Ceiling on Bonds, Hearings before the Committee on Ways and Means, House of Representatives, 86th Congress, 1st Session, June 10, 11, 12, 1959, Washington, D.C.: Government Printing Office, 1959, pp. 14–26.

Debt Ceiling Increase, Hearing before the Committee on Finance, Senate, 86th Congress, 1st Session, June 25, 1959, Washington, D.C.: Government Printing Office, 1959, pp. 2–6.

The Money Market and the Position of the Treasury, Graduate School of Business Administration, New York University, Bulletin no. 5, September, 1959, pp. 9–10.

"Congress Looks at Ceilings," *Federal Reserve Bank of Richmond Monthly Review,* October, 1959.

"The Interest Rate Ceiling on the Federal Debt," *Federal Reserve Bank of St. Louis Monthly Review,* vol. 41, no. 10, October, 1959.

"Debt Management," in *Staff Report on Employment Growth, and Price Levels,* Joint Economic Committee, 86th Congress, 1st Session, Washington, D.C.: Government Printing Office, Dec. 24, 1959, pp. 427–428.

Ira O. Scott, Jr., "Some Overripe Problems in Federal Debt Management," *Commercial and Financial Chronicle,* Dec. 31, 1959.

Marshall A. Robinson, *The National Debt Ceiling,* Washington, D.C.: The Brookings Institution, 1959.

Charls E. Walker, "Should the Interest Rate Ceiling Be Removed?" *Tax Review,* vol. 21, no. 5, May, 1960, pp. 17–20.

Warren L. Smith, *Debt Management in the United States,* Study Paper no. 19, materials prepared in connection with the study of employment, growth, and price levels, Joint Economic Committee, 86th Congress, 2d Session, Washington, D.C.: Government Printing Office, 1960, pp. 153–154.

William C. Freund and Murray G. Lee, *Investment Fundamentals*, New York: American Bankers Association, 1960, p. 45.

"Treasury Advance Refunding Cleared of Technical Obstacles by Attorney General," Treasury Department Press Release, Apr. 27, 1961.

Goldsmith–Nagan Washington Service, *United States Government Securities*, Bulletin no. 629, Apr. 29, 1961.

Review of Report of the Commission on Money and Credit, Hearings before the Joint Economic Committee, 87th Congress, 1st Session, Aug. 14–18, 1961, Washington, D.C.: Government Printing Office, 1961, pp. 206–273.

Money and Credit, Their Influence on Jobs, Prices, and Growth, Report of the Commission on Money and Credit, Englewood Cliffs, N.J.: Prentice-Hall, Inc., 1961, pp. 111–113.

American Enterprise Association, *The Proposal to Increase the National Debt Ceiling*, Washington, D.C.: Jan. 31, 1962.

"Dillon Won't Ask Repeal of $4\frac{1}{2}\%$ Interest Ceiling on New Treasurys Now," *Wall Street Journal*, Feb. 8, 1963.

Henry Gemmill, "Raising the Roof, Administration Braces for Real Battle over Increasing Federal Debt Ceiling," *Wall Street Journal*, Feb. 27, 1963.

"Proposal to Increase the National Debt Ceiling," *Legislative Analysis*, H.R. 6009-Representative Mills, 88th Congress, 1st Session, Report no. 5, Washington D.C.: The American Enterprise Institute, May 9, 1963.

DEBT SPACING AND CONSOLIDATION

J. M. Culbertson, "A Positive Debt Management Program," *Review of Economics and Statistics*, vol. 41, no. 2, part I, May, 1959, pp. 89–98.

George T. Conklin, *Employment, Growth, and Price Levels, Hearings before the Joint Economic Committee*, 86th Congress, 1st Session, July 24, 27, 28, 29, 30, 1959, Washington, D.C.: Government Printing Office, 1959, part 6A, p. 1344.

"Changes in the Structure of the Federal Debt," *Federal Reserve Bulletin*, March, 1963, pp. 301–310.

Tilford C. Gaines, *Techniques of Treasury Debt Management*, New York: Graduate School of Business, Columbia University, and The Free Press of Glencoe, 1962, pp. 276–296.

DISCOUNT POLICY

Robert Wallace, "The Use of the Progressive Discount Rate by the Federal Reserve System," *Journal of Political Economy*, vol. 64, no. 1, February, 1956, pp. 59–68.

"Advances to Member Banks," *Federal Reserve Bank of Minneapolis Monthly Review,* vol. 12, no. 21, Sept. 30, 1956.

Edward C. Simmons, "A Note on the Revival of Federal Reserve Discount Policy," *Journal of Finance,* vol. 11, no. 4, December, 1956, pp. 413–421.

"Discount Policy: 1914–1939," *Federal Reserve Bank of Minneapolis Monthly Review,* May, 1957.

Charls E. Walker, "Discount Policy in Light of Recent Experience," *Journal of Finance,* vol. 12, no. 2, May, 1957, pp. 223–237.

"A Brief Review of the Past 17 Years of Discount Experience at the Federal Reserve Bank of Minneapolis," *Federal Reserve Bank of Minneapolis Monthly Review,* vol. 13, no. 7, July 31, 1957.

"Functioning of the Discount Mechanism," *Forty-fourth Annual Report of the Board of Governors of the Federal Reserve System Covering Operations of the Year 1957,* pp. 7–17.

Warren L. Smith, "The Discount Rate as a Credit-control Weapon," *Journal of Political Economy,* vol. 66, no. 2, April, 1958, pp. 171–177.

"Borrowing from the Federal Reserve Bank: Some Basic Principles," *Federal Reserve Bank of Philadelphia Business Review,* June, 1958.

"Discount Policy and the Discount Rate," *Federal Reserve Bank of Philadelphia Business Review,* January, 1959.

John A. Kareken, "Federal Reserve System Discount Policy: An Appraisal," *Banca Nazionale del Lavoro Quarterly Review,* no. 48, March, 1958, pp. 3–25.

"The Discount Rate and Recovery," *Federal Reserve Bank of Atlanta Monthly Review,* July, 1959.

"Borrowing from the Fed," *Federal Reserve Bank of New York Monthly Review,* September, 1959.

Arthur I. Bloomfield, "Discount Policy," in *Monetary Policy under the International Gold Standard: 1880–1914,* Federal Reserve Bank of New York, October, 1959, pp. 27–46.

"Discounting with the 'Fed,' " *Federal Reserve Bank of Minneapolis Monthly Review,* vol. 14, no. 12, Dec. 31, 1959.

Murray E. Polakoff, "Reluctance Elasticity, Least Cost, and Member Bank Borrowing: A Suggested Integration," *Journal of Finance,* vol. 15, no. 1, March, 1960, pp. 1–18.

Hobart C. Carr, "A Note on Regional Differences in Discount Rates," *Journal of Finance,* vol. 15, no. 1, March, 1960, pp. 62–68.

"The Discount Mechanism and Monetary Policy," *Federal Reserve Bank of St. Louis Monthly Review,* vol. 42, no. 9, September, 1960.

"Lender of the Last Resort," *Federal Reserve Bank of Richmond Monthly Review,* February, 1961.

Donald R. Hodgman, "Member-bank Borrowing: A Comment," *Journal of Finance,* vol. 16, no. 1, March, 1961, pp. 90–93, 98.

Murray E. Polakoff, "Member-bank Borrowing: A Rejoinder," *Journal of Finance,* vol. 16, no. 1, March, 1961, pp. 94–97.

"The Discount Mechanism in the 1961 Recovery," *Federal Reserve Bank of St. Louis Monthly Review,* vol. 43, no. 10, October, 1961.

Joseph Ascheim, *Techniques of Monetary Control,* Baltimore: The Johns Hopkins Press, 1961, pp. 83–98.

Murray E. Polakoff, "Federal Reserve Discount Policy and Its Critics," in *Banking and Monetary Studies,* Deane Carson (ed.), Homewood, Ill.; Richard D. Irwin, Inc., 1963, pp. 190–212.

"Techniques of Member Bank Borrowing at the Federal Reserve," *Federal Reserve Bank of New York Monthly Review,* April, 1964.

ECONOMICS OF THE DEBT

William Withers, *The Public Debt,* New York: The John Day Company, Inc., 1945.

Hedwig Reinhardt, "On the Incidence of the Public Debt," *Social Research,* vol. 12, no. 2, May, 1945, pp. 205–226.

Evsey D. Domar, "The 'Burden of the Debt' and the National Income," *American Economic Review,* vol. 34, no. 4, December, 1944, pp. 798–827, reprinted in Evsey D. Domar, *Essays in the Theory of Economic Growth,* Fair Lawn, N.J.: Oxford University Press, 1957, pp. 35–67.

Albert Gailord Hart, "Public Debt Management and Long Run Monetary Alternatives," in *Money, Debt and Economic Activity,* Englewood Cliffs, N.J.: Prentice-Hall, Inc., 1948, pp. 507–510.

Abba P. Lerner, "The Burden of the National Debt," in *Income, Employment and Public Policy, Essays in Honor of Alvin H. Hansen,* New York: W. W. Norton & Company, Inc., 1948, pp. 255–275.

Donald C. Miller, *Taxes, the Public Debt and Transfers of Income,* Urbana, Ill.: The University of Illinois Press, 1950.

Melvin I. White and Merton Miller, "Note on an Income Effect of Changing Interest Rates," *Public Finance,* vol. 6, no. 2, 1951, pp. 139–144.

Lawrence S. Ritter, "A Note on the Public Debt during Inflation," *Journal of Finance,* vol. 6, no. 1, March, 1951.

Jacob Cohen, "Distributional Effects of the Federal Debt," *Journal of Finance,* vol. 6, no. 3, September, 1951, pp. 261–275.

Abba P. Lerner, "The National Debt," in *Economics of Employment,* New York: McGraw-Hill Book Company, 1951, pp. 270–288.

Edward Nevin, *The Problem of the National Debt,* Cardiff: University of Wales Press, 1954.

O. H. Brownlee and Edward D. Allen, "Economics of Public Borrowing," in *Economics of Public Finance,* Englewood Cliffs, N.J.: Prentice-Hall, Inc., 1954, pp. 123–156.

Arthur James Ralph Smith, "The Growth of Public and Private Debt in the United States, 1914 to 1948," Ph.D. thesis, Harvard University, Cambridge, Mass., 1955.

Earl R. Rolph, "The Incidence of Public Debt Operations," *National Tax Journal,* vol. 9, no. 4, December, 1956, pp. 339–353.

E. R. Rolph, "Principles of Debt Management," *American Economic Review,* vol. 47, no. 3, June, 1957, pp. 302–320.

James Tobin, *Fiscal Policy Implications of the Economic Outlook and Budget Developments, Hearings before the Subcommittee on Fiscal Policy,* Joint Economic Committee, 85th Congress, 1st Session, June 3, 4, 5, 6, 7, 13, 14, 1957, Washington, D.C.: Government Printing Office, 1957, p. 67.

James M. Buchanan, "External and International Debt," *American Economic Review,* no. 6, December, 1957, pp. 995–1000.

Alvin H. Hansen, "The Public Debt," in *The American Economy,* New York: McGraw-Hill Book Company, 1957, pp. 32–33.

George Leland Bach, "The Problem of the Public Debt," in *Economics,* Englewood Cliffs, N.J.: Prentice-Hall, Inc., 1957, pp. 328–334.

James M. Buchanan, *Public Principles of Public Debt,* Homewood, Ill.: Richard D. Irwin, Inc., 1958.

James E. Meade, "Is the National Debt a Real Burden?" *Oxford Economic Papers,* new series, vol. 10, no. 2, June, 1958, pp. 163–183.

Abba P. Lerner, Review of James M. Buchanan, *Public Principles of Public Debt, Journal of Political Economy,* vol. 67, no. 2, 1959, pp. 203–206.

Alan T. Peacock, "Rehabilitation of Classical Debt Theory," *Economica,* new series, vol. 26, no. 102, May, 1959, pp. 161–166.

R. M. Friedman, "Principles of Debt Management: Comment," *American Economic Review,* vol. 49, no. 3, June, 1959, pp. 401–403.

E. R. Rolph, "Principles of Debt Management: Reply," *American Economic Review,* vol. 49, no. 3, June, 1959, pp. 404–405.

Alvin H. Hansen, "The Public Debt Reconsidered: A Review Article," *Review of Economics and Statistics,* vol. 41, no. 4, November, 1959, pp. 370–378.

Marshall A. Robinson, *The National Debt Ceiling,* Washington, D.C.: The Brookings Institution, 1959.

John Due, "The Economics of Government Borrowing," in *Government Finance,* Homewood, Ill.: Richard D. Irwin, Inc., 1959, pp. 509–535.

Richard A. Musgrave, "The Classical Theory of Public Debt" and "Compensatory Aspects of Debt Policy," in *The Theory of Public Finance,* New York: McGraw-Hill Book Company, 1959, pp. 556–616.

Warren L. Smith, "The Federal Debt in Perspective," *Debt Management in the United States,* Materials prepared in connection with the study of employment, growth, and price levels, Joint Economic Committee, 86th Congress, 2d Session, Jan. 28, 1960, Washington, D.C.: Government Printing Office, 1960, pp. 17–42.

J. E. Meade, "The Public Debt Reconsidered: A Reply," *Review of Economics and Statistics,* vol. 42, no. 3, part 1, August, 1960, pp. 325–326.

William G. Bowen, Richard J. Davis, and David H. Kopf, "The Public Debt, Corporate Income Taxes, and the Rate of Interest," *Journal of Political Economy,* vol. 68, no. 6, December, 1960, pp. 622–626.

James M. Buchanan, "The National Debt," in *Public Finance,* Homewood, Ill.: Richard D. Irwin, Inc., 1960, pp. 341–384.

William Vickrey, "The Burden of the Public Debt: Comment," *American Economic Review,* vol. 51, no. 1, March, 1961, pp. 137–139.

Tibor Scitovsky, "The Burden of the Public Debt: Comment," *American Economic Review,* vol. 51, no. 1, March, 1961, pp. 137–139.

J. R. Elliott, "Burden of the Public Debt: Comment," *American Economic Review,* vol. 51, no. 1, March, 1961, pp. 139–141.

W. G. Bowen, R. G. Davis, and D. H. Kopf, "Burden of the Public Debt: Reply," *American Economic Review,* vol. 51, no. 1, March, 1961, pp. 141–143.

David I. Fand, "The Problem of Public Debt Management," *Southwestern Social Science Quarterly,* March, 1961, pp. 393–406.

Abba P. Lerner, "The Burden of Debt," *Review of Economics and Statistics,* vol. 43, no. 2, May, 1961, pp. 139–141.

Oswald Brownlee and Alfred Conrad, "Macro-economic Theories of Income Distribution," *American Economic Review, Papers and Proceedings,* vol. 51, no. 2, May, 1961, pp. 14–85.

"Six Decades of Debt Management," *Federal Reserve Bank of Philadelphia Business Review,* May, 1961.

"Six Decades of Debt Management, Part II," *Federal Reserve Bank of Philadelphia Business Review,* July, 1961.

J. Wiseman, "The Logic of National Debt Policy," *Westminster Bank Review,* August, 1961, pp. 8–15.

Alvin L. Marty, Review of Joseph W. Conard, *An Introduction to the Theory of Interest, Journal of Political Economy,* vol. 69, no. 4, August, 1961, pp. 392–393.

Henry C. Wallich, "Making Sense of Money and Credit," *Saturday Review,* July 1, 1961, pp. 6–8, 27.

"Six Decades of Debt Management, Part III," *Federal Reserve Bank of Philadelphia Business Review,* October, 1961.

Review of Report of Commission on Money and Credit, Hearings before the Joint Economic Committee, 87th Congress, 1st Session, Aug. 14–18, 1961, Washington, D.C.: Government Printing Office, 1961.

George Champion, "Taxes and the Government Debt: A Plan for the 'Sixties,'" address before the State Bank Division, American Bankers Association Convention, San Francisco, Oct. 16, 1961.

F. Modigliani, "Long Run Implication of Alternative Fiscal Policies and the Burden of the National Debt," *Economic Journal,* vol. 71, no. 284, December, 1961, pp. 730–755.

Money and Credit: Their Influences on Jobs, Prices, and Growth, Report of the Commission on Money and Credit, Englewood Cliffs, N.J.: Prentice-Hall, Inc., 1961, pp. 94–99.

Robert H. Scott, "Debt Management for Economic Stability," Ph.D. thesis, Harvard University, Cambridge, Mass., 1961.

Robert H. Scott, "An Empirical Look at Debt Management," *Proceedings of the Business and Statistics Section of the American Statistical Association,* 1961, pp. 130–137.

H. Lawrence Miller, Jr., "Anticipated and Unanticipated Consequences of Public Debt Creation," *Economica,* vol. 29, no. 116, November, 1962, pp. 410–419.

Business Outlook 1963, Studies in Business Economics No. 80, New York: National Industrial Conference Board, Nov. 29, 1962.

Robert H. Scott, "The Case for Debt Management," *Papers of the Michigan Academy of Sciences, Arts and Letters* (1961 Meeting), vol. 47, 1962.

C. S. Shoup, "Debt Financing and Future Generations," *Economic Journal,* vol. 72, no. 288, December, 1962, pp. 887–898.

Michael E. Levy, *Cycles in Government Securities, Federal Debt and Its Ownership,* New York: National Industrial Conference Board, 1962.

Oswald Brownlee and Alfred Conrad, "Effects upon the Distribution of Income of a Tight Money Policy," in *Stabilization Policy,* Commission on Money and Credit, Englewood Cliffs, N.J.: Prentice-Hall, Inc., 1963, pp. 499–558.

Burton C. Hallowell and Kossuth M. Williamson, "Federal Debt Management, 1953–58," *Review of Economics and Statistics,* vol. 45, no. 1, February, 1963, pp. 47–54.

Robert F. Wallace, "What Everybody Wants to Know about Deficit Spending," *Montana Business Quarterly,* vol. I, no. 4, Montana State University, Summer, 1963.

O. H. Brownlee and I. O. Scott, "Utility, Liquidity, and Debt Management," *Econometrica,* vol. 31, no. 3, July, 1963, pp. 349–361.

E. J. Mishan, "How To Make a Burden of the Public Debt," *Journal of Political Economy,* vol. 71, no. 6, December, 1963, pp. 529–542.

Samuel B. Chase, Jr., "The Economics of Government Debt," *Asset Prices in Economic Analysis,* Berkeley, Calif.: The University of California Press, 1963, chap. 9, pp. 124–139.

Franco Modigliani, "How to Make a Burden of the Public Debt: A Reply to Mishan," *Journal of Political Economy,* vol. 72, no. 5, October, 1964, pp. 483–485.

James M. Buchanan, "Confessions of a Burden Monger," *Journal of Political Economy,* vol. 72, no. 5, October, 1964, pp. 486–488.

John C. Hause, "Comment on 'How to Make a Burden of the Public Debt,' " *Journal of Political Economy,* vol. 72, no. 5, October, 1964, pp. 489–490.

E. J. Mishan, "The Burden of the Public Debt: A Rejoinder," *Journal of Political Economy,* vol. 72, no. 5, October, 1964, pp. 491–495.

Paul A. Samuelson, "The Public Debt and Modern Fiscal Policy," in *Economics,* New York: McGraw-Hill Book Company, 1964, pp. 354–364.

Thomas Mayer, "Interest Minimization as a Criterion of Federal Debt Management Policy" (Unpublished ms.).

FACTORS AFFECTING MEMBER BANK RESERVES
(INCLUDING RELATED SEASONAL ASPECTS)

"Adjustment for Seasonal Variation," *Federal Reserve Bulletin,* June, 1941.

"Member Bank Reserves, Reserve Bank Credit, and Related Items," in *Banking and Monetary Statistics,* Washington, D.C.: Board of Governors of the Federal Reserve System, November, 1943, pp. 360–367.

"Sources and Uses of Member Bank Reserves, 1914–1951," *Federal Reserve Bank of New York Monthly Review,* July, 1952.

Federal Reserve Bank of New York, *Bank Reserves, Some Factors Affecting Them,* November, 1953.

"Seasonal Adjustment Factors for Demand Deposits Adjusted and Currency Outside Banks," *Federal Reserve Bulletin,* March, 1955.

"Christmas Cash," *Federal Reserve Bank of Chicago Business Conditions,* December, 1955.

Stephen L. McDonald, "Some Factors Affecting the Increased Relative Use of Currency Since 1930," *Journal of Finance,* vol. 11, no. 3, September, 1956, pp. 313–327.

Sally S. Ronk, "The Acceleration of Corporate Income Tax Payments," *Journal of Finance,* vol. 11, no. 4, December, 1956, pp. 474–481.

Doris Eisemann, "Forecasting Business Loans," *Banking,* vol. 50, July, 1957, pp. 40–43.

"Legal Authority for 'Float,'" *Investigation of the Financial Condition of the United States, Hearings before the Committee on Finance,* Senate, 85th Congress, 1st Session, Aug. 13, 14, 15, 16, 19, 1957, Washington, D.C.: Government Printing Office, 1957, part 3, pp. 1576–1578.

"Deposit Instability at Individual Banks," *Federal Reserve Bank of Kansas City Monthly Review,* September, 1957.

"Seasonal Factors Affecting Bank Reserves," *Federal Reserve Bulletin,* February, 1958.

"Seasonal Swings in Bank Data," *Federal Reserve Bank of Minneapolis Monthly Review,* vol. 13, no. 16, Apr. 30, 1958.

Robert Van Cleave, "How Much Seasonal Ease Ahead," *C. F. Childs and Company Review,* no. 304, Dec. 8, 1958.

Philip Cagan, *The Demand for Currency Relative to Total Money Supply,* New York: National Bureau of Economic Research, Occasional Paper 62, 1958.

"Revised Series for Seasonally Adjusted Money Supply," *Federal Reserve Bulletin,* February, 1960.

"The Seasonal Pattern of Interest Rates," *Federal Reserve Bank of St. Louis Monthly Review,* vol. 42, no. 11, November, 1960.

"Large 'Holiday' Reserve Needs Supplied," *Federal Reserve Bank of Chicago Business Conditions,* December, 1960.

"Government Receipts and Payments Seasonally Adjusted," *Federal Reserve Bulletin,* February, 1961.

"The Vault Cash Provision: Has It Changed the Way Banks Manage Their Reserves," *Federal Reserve Bank of Philadelphia Business Review,* September, 1961.

"Corporate Income Taxes and the Banking System," *Federal Reserve Bank of San Francisco Monthly Review,* January, 1962.

Robert Van Cleave, "Ides of March," *C. F. Childs and Company Review,* no. 379, Mar. 12, 1962.

"Seasonal Patterns of Business Activity," *Federal Reserve Bank of St. Louis Review,* vol. 44, no. 8, August, 1962.

"Seasonally Adjusted Series for Bank Credit," *Federal Reserve Bulletin,* July, 1962.

"Federal Reserve 'Float,'" *Federal Reserve Bank of St. Louis Review,* vol. 44, no. 11, November, 1962, pp. 6–8.

Edward A. Manookian, *Industrial Production 1957–59 Base,* Washington, D.C.: Board of Governors of the Federal Reserve System, n.d.

"Flow of Funds Seasonally Adjusted," *Federal Reserve Bulletin,* November, 1962.

W. C. Freund and R. A. Kavesh, *Seasonal Patterns in Business and Consumer Attitudes,* paper presented to the Annual Meeting of the American Statistical Association, September, 1962, at Minneapolis, Minnesota, New York: New York University, Graduate School of Business Administration, 1962.

The Seasonal Squeeze, Federal Reserve Bank of Philadelphia, n.d.

Open Market Operations, Federal Reserve Bank of New York, January, 1963.

Irving Auerbach, "Forecasting Float," *Federal Reserve Bank of New York Monthly Review,* vol. 45, no. 2, February, 1963, pp. 30–35.

"That Time of the Year, Seasonal Demand for Money and Bank Credit," *Federal Reserve Bank of Atlanta Monthly Review,* July, 1963.

"Corporations Speeded-up Again," *C. F. Childs and Company Review,* no. 427, Feb. 28, 1964.

Albert H. Cox, Jr., and Ralph F. Leach, "Settlement Periods of Member Banks," *Journal of Finance,* vol. 19, no. 1, March, 1964, pp. 76–93.

Peter D. Sternlight, "Reserve Settlement Periods of Member Banks: Comment," *Journal of Finance,* vol. 19, no. 1, March, 1964, pp. 94–95.

Stephen H. Axilrod and Janice Krummack, "Federal Reserve Security Transactions, 1954–63," *Federal Reserve Bulletin,* July, 1964.

FEDERAL FUNDS MARKET

John Maynard Keynes, *A Treatise on Money,* London: Macmillan & Co., Ltd., 1930, vol. 1, pp. 242–243, footnote 1.

Winfield W. Riefler, *Money Rates and Money Markets in the United States,* New York: Harper & Row, Publishers, Incorporated, 1930.

Bernice C. Turner, *The Federal Funds Market,* Englewood Cliffs, N.J.: Prentice-Hall, 1931.

Margaret G. Myers, Benjamin Haggott Beckhart, James G. Smith, and William Adams Brown, Jr., *The New York Money Market,* New York: Columbia University Press, 1931–1932, vol. 2, pp. 40–48.

M. A. Gilmartin, Jr., "Exploring Management Problems of U.S. Government Securities Portfolio," *Savings Bank Journal,* April, 1940, vol. 21, no. 2, p. 46.

William E. Bachert, *The Commercial Bank Money Position,* Graduate School of Banking thesis, Rutgers University, New Brunswick, N.J., 1950.

Hobart C. Carr, "Federal Funds," in *Money Market Essays,* New York: Federal Reserve Bank of New York, 1952, pp. 13–16.

Robert V. Roosa, "The New York Money Market and the Market for United States Government Securities," an address before the Fourth Meeting of Technicians of Central Banks of the American Continent, May 3–14, 1954.

Arthur Bailly-Blanchard, "Buying and Selling Federal Funds and 'RP's' Are New Money Mart," *American Banker,* Sept. 16, 1955.

Marcus Nadler, Sipa Heller, and Samuel S. Shipman, *The Money Market and Its Institutions,* New York: The Ronald Press Company, 1955, pp. 99–103.

Robert V. Roosa, *Federal Reserve Operations in the Money and Government Securities Markets,* New York: Federal Reserve Bank of New York, July, 1956, pp. 19–21.

J. S. G. Wilson, "America's Changing Banking Scene, III. The Money Market," *The Banker,* vol. 107, no. 377, June, 1957, pp. 398–401.

Parker B. Willis, *The Federal Funds Market,* Boston: Federal Reserve Bank of Boston, 1957.

"Money by the Day," *Federal Reserve Bank of Chicago Business Conditions,* January, 1958.

"Reserve Adjustments of City Banks," *Federal Reserve Bank of Kansas City Monthly Review,* February, 1958.

Comptroller of the Currency, *Regulation Regarding National Bank Loans Secured by Direct Obligations of the United States,* Apr. 17, 1958.

"Mabon Big Board Firm Enters the Federal Funds Business," *Business Week,* Nov. 8, 1958.

Katherine Finney, *Interbank Deposits,* New York: Columbia University Press, 1958.

The Federal Funds Market, Washington, D.C.: Board of Governors, Federal Reserve System, May, 1959.

"Market Place for Bank Reserves," *Business Week,* June 13, 1959.

Treasury–Federal Reserve Study of the Government Securities Market, Washington, D.C.: Treasury Department and Federal Reserve Board, February, 1960, part II, Table C-3, pp. 142–143.

"The Federal Funds Market," *Federal Reserve Bank of St. Louis Monthly Review,* vol. 42, no. 4, April, 1960.

Wesley Lindow, "The Federal Funds Market," *Bankers,* Sept. 15, 1960.

"Trading in Bank Reserves," *Federal Reserve Bank of Cleveland Monthly Business Review,* December, 1960.

Allan H. Meltzer and Gert von der Linde, *A Study of the Dealer Market for Federal Government Securities,* materials prepared for the Joint Economic Committee, 86th Congress, 2d Session, Washington, D.C.: Government Printing Office, 1960, pp. 25, 49–69, 71–95, 105–140, and table IV-2.

Sidney M. Robbins and Nestor E. Terleckyj, *Money Metropolis,* Cambridge, Mass.: Harvard University Press, 1960, pp. 17–21.

"Federal Funds in the Fifth District," *Federal Reserve Bank of Richmond Monthly Review,* June, 1961.

"The Role of Twelfth District Banks in the Federal Funds Market," *Federal Reserve Bank of San Francisco Monthly Review,* June, 1961.

"Bank Reserve Adjustments through Federal Funds," *Federal Reserve Bank of Boston New England Business Review,* August, 1961.

"Trading in Federal Funds," *Federal Reserve Bank of Cleveland Monthly Business Review,* October, 1961.

"Federal Funds Market in the Southwest," *Federal Reserve Bank of Dallas Business Review,* vol. 46, no. 11, November, 1961.

"Turnover of Business Loans at New York City Banks," *Federal Reserve Bank of New York Monthly Review,* January, 1962, p. 11.

Andrew F. Brimmer, "Foreign Banking Institutions in the United States Money Market," *Review of Economics and Statistics,* vol. 44, no. 1, February, 1962, pp. 76–81.

"New Series on Federal Funds," *Federal Reserve Bulletin,* August, 1964, pp. 944–974.

GOVERNMENT SECURITIES DEALERS

C. F. Childs, *Concerning U.S. Government Securities,* Chicago: Lakeside Press, 1947.

William B. Nants, "United States Government Securities Dealer Departments in Large Banks," Graduate School of Banking thesis, Rutgers University, New Brunswick, N.J., June, 1949.

Leroy M. Piser, *U.S. Government Bond Market Analysis,* New York: New York Institute of Finance, 1952.

"Federal Open Market Committee Report of *Ad Hoc* Subcommittee on the Government Securities Market, November 12, 1952," in *U.S. Monetary Policy: Recent Thinking and Experience, Hearings before the Subcommittee on Economic Stabilization of the Joint Committee on the Economic Report,* 83d Congress, 2d Session, Dec. 6, 7, 1954, Washington, D.C.: Government Printing Office, 1954, pp. 257–286.

Rudolf Smutny, "Trading in High-grade Securities," address at the Institute of Investment Banking, Wharton School of Finance and Commerce, University of Pennsylvania, Apr. 7, 1955.

Ira O. Scott, "The Regional Impact of Monetary Policy," *Quarterly Journal of Economics,* vol. 69, no. 2, May, 1955, pp. 280–282.

Rudolf Smutny, "Government Securities and the Money Market," addresses at the Life Officers Investment Seminar, June, 1955.

Marcus Nadler, Sipa Heller, and Samuel S. Shipman, *The Money Market and Its Institutions,* New York: The Ronald Press Company, 1955.

Arthur James Ralph Smith, "The Growth of Public and Private Debt in the United States, 1914–1948," Ph.D. thesis, Harvard University, Cambridge, Mass., 1955.

Rudolf Smutny, "Effects upon the Bond Market of a Restrictive Credit Policy," *Commercial and Financial Chronicle,* vol. 183, no. 5544, June 21, 1956.

Leroy M. Piser, "Treasury Securities Market in the Short and Long Term," *Commercial and Financial Chronicle,* Sept. 20, 1956.

Rudolf Smutny, "Trading Techniques and Mechanics and Characteristics of the Market," an address before the Investment Group of Hartford, Conn., Nov. 14, 1956.

Robert V. Roosa, *Federal Reserve Operations in the Money and Government Securities Markets,* Federal Reserve Bank of New York, 1956.

Robert Van Cleave, "The Government Securities Market," an address before the Nassau County Chapter of the American Institute of Banking, Feb. 26, 1957.

"Dealing in Governments: $5 Million a Phone Call," *Business Week,* July 12, 1958.

Irvin Friend, A. Wright Hoffman, Willis J. Winn, Morris Hamburg, and Stanley Schor, *The Over-the-counter Securities Market,* New York: McGraw-Hill Book Company, 1958.

Winfield W. Riefler, "Open Market Operations in Long-term Securities," *Federal Reserve Bulletin,* November, 1958.

William B. Harris, "The Mysterious Market in U.S. Securities," *Fortune,* February, 1959.

Employment, Growth and Price Levels, Hearings before the Joint Economic Committee, 86th Congress, 1st Session, Washington, D.C.: Government Printing Office, 1959, parts 6B and 6C.

"The Government Securities Market," *Federal Reserve Bulletin,* August, 1959.

Carl H. Madden, *The Money Side of the Street,* Federal Reserve Bank of New York, September, 1959.

Treasury–Federal Reserve Study of the Government Securities Market, Washington, D.C.: Treasury Department and Board of Governors, Federal Reserve System, 1959.

Allan H. Meltzer and Gert von der Linde, *A Study of the Dealer Market for Federal Securities,* materials prepared for the Joint Economic Committee, 86th Congress, 2d Session, Washington, D.C.: Government Printing Office, 1960.

Sidney M. Robbins and Nestor Terleckyj, *Money Metropolis,* Cambridge, Mass.: Harvard University Press, 1960.

William C. Freund and M. G. Lee, "United States Government Securities," in *Investment Fundamentals,* New York: Council on Banking Education, American Bankers Association, 1960, chap. 2, pp. 23–45.

Internal Revenue Code of 1954, as Amended and in Force on Jan. 3, 1961, Washington, D.C.: Government Printing Office, 1961, secs. 454 (b) and 1221 (5).

Arlen J. Large, "U.S. Bond Market Role Spotlight by Fed's Interest Rate Moves," *Wall Street Journal,* Mar. 21, 1961.

Leo M. Loll, Jr., and Julian G. Buckley, *The Over-the-counter Securities Markets,* Englewood Cliffs, N.J.: Prentice-Hall, Inc., 1961.

Tilford C. Gaines, *Techniques of Treasury Debt Management,* New York: Graduate School of Business, Columbia University, and The Free Press of Glencoe, 1962, chaps. 7, 8, pp. 250–386.

Roland I. Robinson and Morris Mendelson, "The Market for United States Treasury Obligations" (Unpublished ms.).

HISTORICAL, ECONOMIC BACKGROUND OF THE 1958 BREAK
IN THE GOVERNMENT BOND MARKET

Federal Reserve Bank of New York Monthly Review of Credit and Business Conditions, vol. 39, no. 8–12, August–December, 1957; vol. 40, no. 1–12, January–December, 1958; vol. 41, no. 1, January, 1959.

Annual Report of Board of Governors of the Federal Reserve System Covering Operations for the Year[s] 1957 and 1958.

Annual Report of the Federal Reserve Bank of New York for the Year[s] Ended Dec. 31, 1957, and 1958.

Goldsmith–Nagan Washington Service, *United States Government Securities,* no. 553, June 28, 1958.

Annual Report of the Secretary of the Treasury of the State of the Finances for the Fiscal Year[s] Ended June 30, 1958, and June 30, 1959.

"Interest Rates," *Townsend Letter for Savings and Loan Executives,* July 1, 1958.

"Federal Reserve Policy and the Financial Markets During the Past Year," *Federal Reserve Bank of St. Louis Monthly Review,* vol. 40, no. 8, August, 1958.

Joseph R. Slevin, "Speculation in U.S. Bonds," a collection of articles appearing in the *New York Herald Tribune,* Sept. 1–9, 1958.

"The Drop in Bond Prices: Some Fundamental Factors," *Federal Reserve Bank of Kansas City Monthly Review,* October, 1958.

Employment, Growth, and Price Levels, Hearings before the Joint Economic Committee, 86th Congress, 1st Session, July 24, 27, 28, 29, and 30, 1959, part 6A: "The Government's Management of Its Monetary, Fiscal, and Debt Operations," Washington, D.C.: Government Printing Office, 1959, pp. 1209–1228.

C. F. Childs and Company, *Record of Major U.S. Treasury Financing During 1957 and 1958.*

C. F. Childs and Company, *Bond Yields and Money Rates,* 1911–1959.

Treasury–Federal Reserve Study of the Government Securities Market, Washington, D.C.: Treasury Department and Board of Governors, Federal Reserve System, 1960, part 2.

"Interest Rates," *Townsend Letter for Savings and Loan Executives,* Aug. 5, 1960.

Tilford C. Gaines, *Techniques of Treasury Debt Management,* New York: Graduate School of Business, Columbia University, and The Free Press of Glencoe, 1962, chaps. 7, 8, pp. 250–386.

INDIVIDUAL PORTFOLIO POLICIES

O. K. Burrell, "Technical Aspects of Treasury Financing Savings Bonds in Personal Investment Programs," *Journal of Finance,* vol. 8, no. 2, May, 1953, pp. 212–223.

Joseph R. Slevin, "Speculation in U.S. Bonds," a collection of articles appearing in the *New York Herald Tribune,* Sept. 1–9, 1958.

Treasury–Federal Reserve Study of the Government Securities Market, Washington, D.C.: Treasury Department and Board of Governors, Federal Reserve System, July, 1959, part 1, p. 9.

Robert Van Cleave, *C. F. Childs and Company Review,* no. 322, Oct. 17, 1959.

Charls E. Walker, "Problems of Treasury Debt Management," address before the Annual Convention of the U.S. Savings and Loan League, Dallas, Texas, Nov. 11, 1959.

"Government Issues Attract Personal Savings," *Federal Reserve Bank of Chicago Business Conditions,* January, 1960.

Economics Department, Bankers Trust Company, New York, "Technical Notes," *Investment Outlook,* 1962.

INSTITUTIONAL PORTFOLIO POLICY

Herbert V. Prochnow (ed.), *American Financial Institutions,* Englewood Cliffs, N.J.: Prentice-Hall, Inc., 1951.

Charles H. Schmidt and Eleanor J. Stockwell, "The Changing Importance of Institutional Investors in the American Capital Markets," *Law and Contemporary Problems,* vol. 17, no. 1, Winter, 1952, pp. 3–25.

Charles C. Abbott, *The Federal Debt, Structure and Impact,* New York: The Twentieth Century Fund, 1953, pp. 130–163.

Raymond W. Goldsmith, *Financial Intermediaries in the American Economy since 1900,* Princeton, N.J.: Princeton University Press, 1958.

"Taxwise Investors Buy Treasurys for Capital Gain Element in Current Yields," *Journal of Taxation,* November, 1959, pp. 284–286.

Tax Revision Compendium, compendium of papers on broadening the tax base, submitted to the Committee on Ways and Means in connection with the panel discussions on the same subject, to be conducted by the Committee on Ways and Means, beginning Nov. 16, 1959, Washington, D.C.: Government Printing Office, 1959, vol. 3.

Roland I. Robinson, Erwin W. Boehmler, Frank Herbert Gane, and Loring C. Farwell, *Financial Institutions,* Homewood, Ill.: Richard D. Irwin, Inc., 1960.

William C. Freund and M. G. Lee, "Investment Trends in the Postwar Years," in *Investment Fundamentals,* New York: Council on Banking Education, American Bankers Association, 1960, chap. 8, pp. 113–136.

Tilford C. Gaines, *Techniques of Treasury Debt Management,* New York: Graduate School of Business, Columbia University, and The Free Press of Glencoe, 1962, chaps. 7 and 8, pp. 250–386.

Gilbert W. Cooke, Charles L. Prather, Frederick E. Case, Douglas H. Bellemore, *Financial Institutions, Their Role in the American Economy,* New York: Simmons-Boardman Publishing Corporation, 1962.

Michael E. Levy, *Cycles in Government, I. Federal Debt and Its Ownership,* New York: National Industrial Conference Board, 1962.

"Interest and Credit in Business Expansion," *Federal Reserve Bank of San Francisco Monthly Review,* February, 1963.

Thomas G. Gies, Thomas Mayer, and E. C. Ettin, "Portfolio Regulations and Policies of Financial Intermediaries," in *Private Financial Institutions,* Commission on Money and Credit, Englewood Cliffs, N.J.: Prentice-Hall, Inc., 1963, pp. 157–263.

Laurence L. Werboff and M. E. Rozen, "Market Shares and Competition among Financial Institutions," in *Private Financial Institutions,* Commission on Money and Credit, Englewood Cliffs, N.J.: Prentice-Hall, Inc., 1963, pp. 265–331.

E. Gordon Keith, "The Impact of Federal Taxation on the Flow of Personal Savings through Investment Intermediaries," in *Private Financial Institutions,* Commission on Money and Credit, Englewood Cliffs, N.J.: Prentice-Hall, Inc., 1963, pp. 383–460.

Paul M. Horvitz, *Monetary Policy and the Financial System,* Englewood Cliffs, N.J.: Prentice-Hall, Inc., 1963.

Comparative Regulations of Financial Institutions, Subcommittee on Domestic Finance, Committee on Banking and Currency, House of Representatives, 88th Congress, Nov. 22, 1963, Washington, D.C.: Government Printing Office, 1963.

Roland I. Robinson, *Money and Capital Markets,* New York: McGraw-Hill Book Company, 1964.

Irving Friend, "The Effects of Monetary Policies on Non-monetary Financial Institutions and Capital Markets," in *Private Capital Markets,* Englewood Cliffs, N.J.: Prentice-Hall, Inc., 1964, pp. 1–172.

"The U.S. Capital Markets," in *Capital Markets,* Bank for International Settlements, Monetary and Economic Department, Basle, January, 1964.

Roland I. Robinson and Morris Mendelson, "The Market for United States Treasury Obligations" (Unpublished ms.), chap. 4.

INSURANCE COMPANIES

"Life Insurance Companies and the Security Markets," *Federal Reserve Bank of New York Monthly Review*, vol. 34, no. 3, March, 1952.

"Life Insurance Companies and the Security Markets," *Federal Reserve Bank of New York Monthly Review*, vol. 34, no. 4, April, 1952.

Haughton Bell and Harold G. Fraine, "Legal Framework, Trends and Development in Investment Practices," *Law and Contemporary Problems*, vol. 17, no. 1, Winter, 1952, pp. 45–85.

David McCahan (ed.), *Investment of Life Insurance Funds*, Philadelphia: University of Pennsylvania Press, 1953.

Harris Loewy, "Net Cash Moneyflows through Life Insurance Companies," *Journal of Finance*, vol. 11, no. 4, December, 1956, pp. 442–462.

Andrew F. Brimmer, "Some Studies in Monetary Policy, Interest Rates and the Investment Behaviour of Life Insurance Companies," Ph.D. thesis, Harvard University, Cambridge, Mass., 1956.

William T. Harper, "What's What with the Casualty and Fire Insurance Business," *Commercial and Financial Chronicle*, vol. 187, no. 5736, Apr. 24, 1958.

"Life Insurance Companies in the Postwar Capital Markets," *Federal Reserve Bank of New York Monthly Review*, September, 1958.

Leroy S. Wehrle, *A Theory of Life Insurance Portfolio Selection*, Cowles Foundation Discussion Paper no. 60, Dec. 1, 1958.

Tax Formula For Life Insurance Companies, Hearings before the Committee on Finance, Senate, 86th Congress, 1st Session, Mar. 3, 4, 5, 17, 18, 19, 1959, Washington, D.C.: Government Printing Office, 1959.

Taxation of Income of Life Insurance Companies, Hearings before the Subcommittee on Internal Revenue Taxation, Committee on Ways and Means, House of Representatives, 85th Congress, 2d Session, Nov. 17, 18, 19, 20, Washington, D.C.: Government Printing Office, 1959.

"At Last an Insurance Tax Bill," *Business Week*, Jan. 27, 1959.

Alfred N. Guertin, "The Insurance Company Income Tax Act," *Eastern Underwriter*, Oct. 2, 1959.

John R. Herzfeld, "Income Tax Problem," *Best's Life News*, November, 1959.

Buist M. Anderson, *Concerning the Life Insurance Company Income Tax Act of 1959*, Hartford: Connecticut General Life Insurance Company, Nov. 12, 1959.

James J. O'Leary, *1959 Record of Life Insurance Investments*, New York: Life Insurance Association of America, Dec. 9, 1959.

James J. O'Leary (moderator), *The Trend of Saving through Life Insurance, a Symposium*, New York: Life Insurance Association of America, Dec. 19, 1959.

Life Insurance Company Income Tax Act of 1959, Committee on Ways and Means, House of Representatives, Report no. 34, 86th Congress, 1st Session, Washington, D.C.: Government Printing Office, 1959.

Life Insurance Company Income Tax Act of 1959, Committee on Finance, Senate, Report no. 291, 86th Congress, 1st Session, Washington, D.C.: Government Printing Office, 1959.

Allen L. Mayerson, "The Life Insurance Company Income Tax Act of 1959," *Journal of the Society of Chartered Life Underwriters*, Spring, 1960, pp. 171–186.

Kenneth M. Wright, "Gross Flows of Funds through Life Insurance Companies," *Journal of Finance*, vol. 15, no. 2, May, 1960, pp. 140–156.

Leroy S. Wehrle, "Life Insurance Investment: The Experiences of Four Companies," *Yale Economic Essays*, vol. 1, no. 1, Spring, 1961, pp. 70–136.

Internal Revenue Code of 1954, as amended and in force on Jan. 3, 1961, Washington, D.C.: Government Printing Office, 1961, sec. 801–806, 809–812, 815, 817, 831, 832.

James E. Walter, *The Investment Process as Characterized by Leading Life Insurance Companies*, Boston: Harvard University Graduate School of Business Administration, 1962.

Life Insurance Association of America, *Life Insurance Companies as Financial Institutions*, Commission on Money and Credit, Englewood Cliffs, N.J.: Prentice-Hall, Inc., 1962.

Property and Casualty Insurance Companies, Their Role as Financial Intermediaries, Commission on Money and Credit, Englewood Cliffs, N.J.: Prentice-Hall, Inc., 1962.

Harry J. Solberg, "A Method for Consumer Valuation of Life Insurance Policies by Types," *Journal of Finance*, vol. 17, no. 4, December, 1962, pp. 634–645.

"Investment Patterns of Fire and Casualty Insurance Companies," *Federal Reserve Bank of Cleveland Monthly Business Review*, May, 1963, pp. 3–4.

MUTUAL SAVINGS BANKS

John V. Lintner, *Mutual Savings Banks in the Savings and Mortgage Markets,* Boston: Harvard University Graduate School of Business Administration, 1948.

William Howard Steiner, "Mutual Savings Banks," *Law and Contemporary Problems,* vol. 17, no. 1, Winter, 1952, pp. 86–107.

Jules I. Bogen, *Economic Study of Savings Banking in New York State,* Savings Bank Association of the State of New York, 1956.

"Savings Institutions Less Liquid," *Federal Reserve Bank of Chicago Business Conditions,* January, 1957.

"Mutual Savings Banks in the Capital Markets," *Federal Reserve Bank of New York Monthly Review,* vol. 40, no. 7, July, 1958.

Carl G. Freese, "Federal Debt Management and the Savings Banking Industry," address before the 12th annual midyear meeting of the National Association of Mutual Savings Banks, New York City, Dec. 2, 1958.

Roger F. Murray, *Mutual Funds as a Service for Savings Banks,* Savings Banks Association of the State of New York, October, 1960.

Internal Revenue Code of 1954, as amended and in force on Jan. 3, 1961, Washington, D.C.: Government Printing Office, 1961, sec. 593.

"Mutual Savings Banks," Public Law 87–834, 87th Congress, H.R. 10650, Oct. 16, 1962, sec. 6, pp. 18–26.

George Hanc and Joseph W. Keena, "Savings Banking and the New Tax Law," *Savings Banking Journal,* vol. 43, no. 9, November, 1962, pp. 45–52.

National Association of Mutual Savings Banks, *Mutual Savings Banking, Basic Characteristics and Role in the National Economy,* Commission on Money and Credit, Englewood Cliffs, N.J.: Prentice-Hall, Inc., 1962.

OPEN-MARKET OPERATIONS

E. A. Goldenweiser, *American Monetary Policy,* New York: McGraw-Hill Book Company, 1951.

Federal Reserve Bank of Chicago Annual Report, 1955, p. 40.

Robert V. Roosa, *Federal Reserve Operations in the Money and Government Securities Markets,* Federal Reserve Bank of New York, July, 1956.

"The Fed Is in the Market," *Federal Reserve Bank of Philadelphia Business Review,* December, 1960.

A. C. L. Day and Sterie T. Beza, *Money and Income*, Fair Lawn, N.J.: Oxford University Press, 1960.

Federal Reserve System Purposes and Functions, Washington, D.C.: Board of Governors of the Federal Reserve System, 1961.

Robert G. Rouse, "Implementation of the Policies of the Federal Open Market Committee," *Federal Reserve Bank of New York Monthly Review*, July, 1961.

Alfred Hayes, "The Recording and Publicizing of Decisions Concerning Open Market Policy," *Federal Reserve Bank of New York Monthly Review*, July, 1961.

Robert W. Stone, "Federal Reserve Open Market Operations in 1962," *Federal Reserve Bank of New York Monthly Review*, May, 1963.

Leroy J. Grossman, An Evaluation of the Consistency of the Defensive and Dynamic Objectives of Federal Reserve Policy, Ph.D. thesis, Graduate School of Vanderbilt University, Nashville, Tenn., April, 1963.

Peter M. Keir, "The Open Market Policy Process," *Federal Reserve Bulletin*, October, 1963.

Daniel S. Ahearn, *Federal Reserve Policy Reappraised, 1951–1959*, New York: Columbia University Press, 1963.

Albert H. Cox, Jr., and Ralph F. Leach, "Settlement Periods of Member Banks," *Journal of Finance*, vol. 19, no. 1, March, 1964, pp. 76–93.

Peter D. Sternlight, "Reserve Settlement Periods of Member Banks: Comment," *Journal of Finance*, vol. 19, no. 1, March, 1964, pp. 94–95.

Stephen H. Axilrod and Janice Krummack, "Federal Reserve Security Transactions, 1954–63," *Federal Reserve Bulletin*, July, 1964.

POLICY MIX

Abba P. Lerner, *Economics of Employment*, New York: McGraw-Hill Book Company, 1951.

William Vickrey, "Stability and Inflation," in *Post Keynesian Economics*, Kenneth K. Kurihara (ed.), New Brunswick, N.J.: Rutgers University Press, 1954, pp. 89–122.

Richard A. Musgrave, "The Optimal Mix of Stabilization Policies," in *The Relationship of Prices to Economic Stability and Growth*, compendium of papers submitted by panelists appearing before the Joint Economic Committee, Mar. 31, 1958, 85th Congress, 2d Session, Washington, D.C.: Government Printing Office, 1958, pp. 597–609.

William S. Vickrey, "The Optimum Trend of Prices," *Southern Economic Journal*, vol. 25, no. 3, January, 1959, pp. 315-326.

"Time for a Change: Monetary Policy for All Americans," *Labor's Economic Review*, vol. 4, no. 8, August, 1959.

Employment, Growth, and Price Levels, Hearings before the Joint Economic Committee, 86th Congress, 1st Session, Washington, D.C. Government Printing Office, 1959, parts 9A, 9B.

Robert B. Anderson, "Financial Policies for Sustainable Growth," *Journal of Finance,* vol. 15, no. 2, May, 1960, pp. 127-139.

Herbert Stein, "The Division of Labor among Budget, Monetary, and Debt Management Policies," *Atlanta Economic Review,* August, 1961, vol. 11, no. 8, pp. 3-7, 23.

David I. Fand and Ira O. Scott, Jr., "The Recent Questioning of Monetary Policy," *Current Economic Comment,* vol. 21, no. 3, August, 1959, pp. 17-28, reprinted in Lawrence S. Ritter (ed.), *Money and Economic Activity,* Boston: Houghton Mifflin Company, 1961, pp. 223-231.

James M. Buchanan, "Easy Budgets and Tight Money," *Lloyds Bank Review,* n.s., no. 64, April, 1962, pp. 17-30.

J. M. Culbertson, "The Recent Policy Mix and Its Implications," read at the American Statistical Association, Cleveland, Sept. 6, 1963.

PRIVATE PENSION FUNDS

George Garvy, "The Effects of Private Pension Plans on Personal Savings," *Review of Economics and Statistics,* vol. 32, no. 3, August, 1950, pp. 223-226.

R. Duane Saunders, "Government Securities in the Corporate Pension Trust Picture," in *Proceedings of the Business and Economics Section, American Statistical Association,* 1954, pp. 159-165.

Dan M. McGill (ed.), *Pensions: Problems and Trends,* Homewood, Ill.: Richard D. Irwin, Inc., 1955.

Paul L. Howell, "A Re-examination of Pension Fund Investment Policies," *Journal of Finance,* vol. 13, no. 2, May, 1958, pp. 261-274.

Paul L. Howell, "Common Stocks and Pension Funds Investing," *Harvard Business Review,* vol. 36, no. 6, November-December, 1958, pp. 92-106.

"Private Pension Funds," *Business Week,* Jan. 31, 1959.

Robert Tilove, *Pension Funds and Economic Freedom,* New York: Fund for the Republic, April, 1959.

Victor L. Andrews, "Pension Funds and the Securities Markets," *Harvard Business Review,* vol. 37, no. 6, November–December, 1959, pp. 90–102.

Paul P. Harbrecht, *Pension Funds and Economic Power,* New York: The Twentieth Century Fund, 1959.

Adolf A. Berle, Jr., *Power without Poverty,* New York: Harcourt, Brace & World, 1959.

Internal Revenue Code of 1954, as amended and in force on Jan. 3, 1961, Washington, D.C.: Government Printing Office, 1961, pp. 182–186.

"Pension Funds: A New Financial Giant," *Federal Reserve Bank of Richmond Monthly Review,* July, 1960.

"Pension Funds Stick to Stocks," *Business Week,* May 13, 1961.

Victor L. Andrews, "The Supply of Loanable Funds from Non-insured, Corporate, State, and City-administered Employee Pension Trusts," *Journal of Finance,* vol. 16, May, 1961, pp. 328–350.

Eugene Miller, "Trends in Private Pension Funds," *Journal of Finance,* vol. 16, no. 2, May, 1961, pp. 313–327.

Victor L. Andrews, "Noninsured Corporate and State and Local Government Retirement Funds in the Financial Structure," in *Private Capital Markets,* Commission on Money and Credit, Englewood Cliffs, N.J.: Prentice-Hall, Inc., 1964, pp. 381–531.

Roger F. Murray, *The Impact of Public and Private Pension Systems on Saving and Investment,* to be published by the National Bureau of Economic Research, New York.

RISK STRUCTURE OF ASSET YIELDS

Abba P. Lerner, *Economics of Control,* New York: The Macmillan Company, 1946, pp. 253–255.

Bonnar Brown, "Common-stock Price Ratios and Long-term Interest Rates," *Journal of Business,* vol. 21, no. 3, July, 1948, pp. 180–182.

"New Moves to Ease Money," *First National City Monthly Letter, Business and Economic Conditions,* May, 1958.

Wesley Lindow, "The Outlook for the Money Market," *Journal of Finance,* vol. 13, no. 2, May, 1958, pp. 311–317.

Warren L. Smith, "Monetary Policy and the Structure of Markets," in *The Relationship of Prices to Economic Stability and Growth,* Joint Economic

Committee, 85th Congress, 2d Session, March 31, 1958, Washington, D.C.: Government Printing Office, 1958, pp. 493–511.

Roger F. Murray, "Are Stock Prices Too High?" *Trusts and Estates,* November, 1958.

Townsend Letter for Savings and Loan Executives, Jan. 30, 1959.

Saunders Cameron, Ltd., *Tight Money Can Make Second Grade Bonds Reflect a Risk Factor,* Toronto, Canada, Sept. 8, 1959.

"Interest Rates and Credit," *Federal Reserve Bank of St. Louis Monthly Review,* vol. 41, no. 9, September, 1959.

"Growth vs. Income," *Economist,* Nov. 7, 1959, p. 553.

Alan Greenspan, "Stock Prices and Capital Evaluation," in *Proceedings of the Business and Economic Statistics Section, American Statistical Association,* 1959, pp. 2–26.

"Capital Market," *Townsend Letter for Savings and Loan Executives,* Jan. 14, 1960.

"General Business," *Townsend Letter for Savings and Loan Executives,* Feb. 4, 1960.

"Analysis of the Reverse Gap," *Midland Bank Review,* May, 1960, pp. 3–7.

"The Reverse Yield Gap," *Federal Reserve Bank of Chicago Business Conditions,* January, 1961.

Salomon Brothers and Hutzler, *Short Term Money Rates from 1945 to March 22, 1961,* New York, 1961.

"Interest Rates," *Townsend Letter for Savings and Loan Executives,* June 1, 1961.

James B. Ludtke, "Financial Markets," in *The American Financial System,* Boston: Allyn and Bacon, Inc., 1961, pp. 565–593.

"The Prime Rate," *Federal Reserve Bank of New York Monthly Review,* vol. 44, no. 4, April, 1962.

"The Prime Rate II," *Federal Reserve Bank of New York Monthly Review,* vol. 44, no. 5, May, 1962.

O. H. Brownlee and I. O. Scott, "Utility, Liquidity, and Debt Management," *Econometrica,* 1963.

B. G. Malkiel, "Equity Yields and Structure of Share Prices," *American Economic Review,* vol. 53, no. 3, December, 1963, pp. 1058–1077.

Roger F. Murray, "Money Market, Quality and Liquidity at a Discount," *Financial Analysts Journal,* July–August, 1964.

ROLE OF THE GOVERNMENT SECURITIES PORTFOLIO
IN TRANSMITTING THE EFFECTS OF MONETARY POLICY

Robert V. Roosa, "Interest Rates and the Central Bank," in *Money, Trade, and Economic Growth, in Honor of John Henry Williams,* New York: The Macmillan Company, 1951, pp. 270–295.

Warren L. Smith, "On the Effectiveness of Monetary Policy," *American Economic Review,* vol. 46, no. 4, September, 1956, pp. 588–606.

"Interest Rates and Credit Availability at Commercial Banks," *Federal Reserve Bank of Kansas City Monthly Review,* February, 1957.

John H. Kareken, "Lenders' Preferences, Credit Rationing, and the Effectiveness of Monetary Policy," *Review of Economics and Statistics,* vol. 39, no. 3, August, 1957, pp. 292–302.

John H. Kareken, "Post-accord Monetary Developments in the United States," *Banca Nazionale Del Lavoro Quarterly Review,* no. 42, September, 1957, pp. 322–351.

Ira O. Scott, Jr., "The Availability Doctrine: Development and Implications," *Canadian Journal of Economics and Political Sciences,* vol. 23, no. 4, November, 1957, pp. 532–539.

Ira O. Scott, "The Availability Doctrine: Theoretical Underpinnings," *Review of Economic Studies,* vol. 25, no. 1, pp. 41–48.

Robert V. Roosa, "Interest Rates, Wage Rates and Uncertainty," *Federal Reserve Bank of Cleveland Monthly Review,* December, 1959.

Jack Guttentag, "Credit Availability, Interest Rates, and Monetary Policy," *Southern Economic Journal,* vol. 26, no. 3, January, 1960.

Assar R. Lindbeck, *The "New" Theory of Credit Control in the United States,* University of Stockholm, Stockholm Economic Studies, Pamphlet Series 1, 2d ed., 1962.

SAVINGS AND LOAN ASSOCIATIONS

F. Newell Childs, "Your Government Holdings," *National Savings and Loan Journal,* March, 1955, pp. 6–7.

"Savings and Loan Associations in the Mortgage Market," *Federal Reserve Bank of New York Monthly Review,* vol. 38, no. 7, July, 1956.

Gordon W. McKinley, "The Federal Home Loan Bank System and the Control of Credit," *Journal of Finance,* vol. 12, no. 3, September, 1957.

American Bankers Association, *Savings and Loan Associations,* New York, February, 1958.

Savings Association League of New York State, *A Program to Revitalize the Federal Home Loan Bank System,* New York, May 23, 1958.

"The Rise of Savings and Loan Associations," *Federal Reserve Bank of Richmond Monthly Review,* September, 1958.

"The Federal Home Loan Bank System," *Federal Reserve Bank of New York Monthly Review,* vol. 40, no. 12, December, 1958.

Charles F. Haywood, "A Comment on the Federal Home Bank System and the Control of Credit," *Journal of Finance,* vol. 13, no. 4, December, 1958, pp. 542–544.

Gordon W. McKinley, "A Comment on the Federal Home Loan Bank System and the Control of Credit: Reply," *Journal of Finance,* vol. 13, no. 4, December, 1958, pp. 545–546.

Lawrence V. Conway, *Savings and Loan Principles,* Chicago: American Savings and Loan Institute Press, 1958.

United States Savings and Loan League, *The Next Decade and Its Opportunities for the Savings and Loan Business,* Chicago, 1959.

"Required Liquidity Reserves," *Townsend Letter for Savings and Loan Executives,* Apr. 18, 1960.

Charles M. Torrance, "Gross Flows of Funds through Savings and Loan Associations," *Journal of Finance,* vol. 15, no. 2, May, 1960, pp. 157–169.

"Government Bonds," *Townsend Letter for Savings and Loan Executives,* July 7, 1960.

Internal Revenue Code of 1954, as amended and in force on Jan. 3, 1961, Washington, D.C.: Government Printing Office, 1961, sec. 593.

Edward S. Shaw, *Savings and Loan Market Structure and Market Performance,* a study of California state-licensed savings and loan associations, California Savings and Loans Commissioner, 1962.

Leon T. Kendall, *The Savings and Loan Business,* United States Savings and Loan League, Englewood Cliffs, N.J.: Prentice-Hall, Inc., 1962.

"Tax Planning," in *Savings and Loan Fact Book,* Chicago: United States Savings and Loan League, 1963, pp. 98–99.

SAVINGS BONDS

United States Savings Bonds, Series F and Series G, Treasury Department Circular no. 654, Sept. 12, 1950.

United States Savings Bonds, Series J and Series K, Treasury Department Circular no. 906, Apr. 29, 1952.

Helen J. Cooke, "Cash Borrowing of the United States Treasury: Nonmarketable Issues," in *The Treasury and the Money Market*, Federal Reserve Bank of New York, May, 1954, pp. 16–23.

United States Savings Bonds, Series E, Treasury Department Circular no. 653, 5th revision, Sept. 23, 1959.

United States Savings Bonds, Series H, Treasury Department Circular no. 905, 2d revision, Sept. 23, 1959.

"20th Anniversary, U.S. Savings Bonds Program, 1941–1961," *Federal Reserve Bank of Dallas Business Review*, vol. 46, no. 2, February, 1961.

United States Savings Bonds, Series E, first amendment to Treasury Department Circular no. 653, 5th revision, Mar. 21, 1961.

"Twentieth Anniversary of Savings Bonds," *Federal Reserve Bank of Chicago Business Conditions*, May, 1961.

"Savings Bonds Anniversary," *Federal Reserve Bank of Kansas City Monthly Review*, May, 1961.

"20th Birthday for 'E' Bonds," *Federal Reserve Bank of Minneapolis Monthly Review*, May, 1961.

"The Role of Savings Bonds in Government Finance," *Federal Reserve Bank of New York Monthly Review*, vol. 43, no. 6, June, 1961.

United States Savings Bonds, Series H, first amendment to Treasury Department Circular no. 905, 2d revision, Aug. 2, 1961.

George Hanc, *The United States Savings Bonds Program in the Postwar Period*, New York: National Bureau of Economic Research, 1962.

STATE AND LOCAL INVESTMENT FUNDS

Colin D. Campbell, "Investment in United States Government Securities by State and Local Government," *National Tax Journal*, vol. 10, no. 1, March, 1957, pp. 78–87.

Adolf E. Grunewald, *Investment Policies of Public Pension Funds: Present and Prospective*, Chicago: Municipal Finance Officers Association of the United States and Canada, Special Bulletin 1957c, June 1, 1957.

"State and Local Governments Retirement Systems," *Federal Reserve Bank of Boston New England Business Review*, December, 1959.

Joseph Bower, "Investment in United States Government Securities by State Governments," *National Tax Journal*, vol. 13, no. 2, June, 1960, pp. 127–140.

Roland Robinson, *Postwar Market for State and Local Government Securities*, Princeton, N.J.: Princeton University Press, 1960, pp. 158–201.

"Liquidity of State and Local Governments," *Federal Reserve Bank of Cleveland Monthly Business Review,* November, 1963, pp. 14–19.

TERM STRUCTURE OF INTEREST RATES

Frederick R. Macaulay, *The Movements of Interest Rates, Bond Yields and Stock Prices in the United States since 1856,* New York: National Bureau of Economic Research, 1938.

J. R. Hicks, *Value and Capital,* Fair Lawn, N.J.: Oxford University Press, 1939, pp. 141–152.

Frederick A. Lutz, "The Structure of Interest Rates," *Quarterly Journal of Economics,* vol. 55, no. 1, November, 1940, pp. 36–63; reprinted in William Fellner and Bernard F. Haley (eds.), *Readings in the Theory of Income Distribution,* New York: McGraw-Hill Book Company, 1946, pp. 499–529.

Joan Robinson, *The Rate of Interest,* New York: The Macmillan Company, 1952.

Michael Kalecki, "The Rate of Interest," in *Theory of Economic Dynamics,* London: George Allen & Unwin, Ltd., 1954, pp. 73–88.

William J. Korsviks and Tom M. Plank, "The Pattern of Interest Rates," *Burroughs Clearing House,* vol. 40, no. 4, April, 1956.

J. M. Culbertson, "The Term Structure of Interest Rates," *Quarterly Journal of Economics,* vol. 71, no. 4, November, 1957, pp. 485–517.

Sidney Weintraub, "The Long and the Short of It: Making Sense of Interest Rate Patterns," *Business Scope,* vol. 1, no. 15, Nov. 30, 1957.

"The New Look in U.S. Securities," *Federal Reserve Bank of Atlanta Monthly Review,* December, 1957.

Robert Van Cleave, "Observations on the Yield Curve," *C. F. Childs and Company Review,* no. 288, March, 1958.

David Durand, "A Quarterly Series of Corporate Basic Yields, 1952–1957, and Some Attendant Reservations," *Journal of Finance,* vol. 13, no. 3, September, 1958, pp. 348–356.

L. S. Wehrle, "Culbertson on Interest Structure: Comment," *Quarterly Journal of Economics,* vol. 72, no. 4, November, 1958, pp. 601–606.

J. M. Culbertson, "Culbertson on Interest Structure: Reply," *Quarterly Journal of Economics,* vol. 72, no. 4, November, 1958, pp. 607–613.

Dudley G. Luckett, "Professor Lutz and the Structure of Interest Rates," *Quarterly Journal of Economics,* vol. 72, no. 1, February, 1959, pp. 131–144.

Harry C. Sauvain, "Changing Interest Rates and Investment Portfolio," *Journal of Finance*, vol. 14, no. 2, May, 1959, pp. 230–244.

"Short-term Interest Rates in a Speculative Boom Period," *Townsend Letter for Savings and Loan Executives*, Aug. 27, 1959.

"Changing Yield Curve," *Federal Reserve Bank of St. Louis Monthly Review*, vol. 41, no. 8, August, 1959.

"Interest Rates," *Townsend Letter for Savings and Loan Executives*, Sept. 10, 1959.

Richard Goode and Eugene A. Birnham, "The Relation between Long-term and Short-term Interest Rates in the United States," *International Monetary Fund Staff Papers*, October, 1959, pp. 224–243.

Joseph Conard, "The Term Structure of Interest Rates," in *An Introduction to the Theory of Interest*, Berkeley, Calif.: University of California Press, 1959, pp. 287–368.

"Taxes and the Term Structure of Yields," *Federal Reserve Bank of Kansas City Monthly Review*, December, 1960.

A. C. L. Day and Sterie T. Beza, "Interest Rates on Long-term and Short-term Securities," in *Money and Income*, Fair Lawn, N.J.: Oxford University Press, 1960, pp. 112–122.

Warren L. Smith, "The Maturity Structure of Interest Rates," *Debt Management in the United States*, materials prepared in connection with the study of employment, growth, and price levels, Joint Economic Committee, 86th Congress, 2d Session, Jan. 28, 1960, Washington, D.C.: Government Printing Office, 1960, pp. 81–88.

"A Closer Look at Interest-rate Relationships," *Morgan Guaranty Survey*, April, 1961.

David I. Fand, "Interest Rates Since 1953: A Statistical Analysis," paper read before the Econometric Society, Stillwater, Okla., Sept. 1, 1961.

Douglas A. Hayes, "Federal Government Securities and Yield Curves," in *Investments: Analysis and Management*, New York: The Macmillan Company, 1961, pp. 495–510.

David Meiselman, *The Term Structure of Interest Rates*, Ford Foundation, Doctoral Dissertation Series, 1961 Award Winner, Englewood Cliffs, N.J.: Prentice-Hall, Inc., 1962.

Burton G. Malkiel, "Expectations, Bond Prices, and the Term Structure of Interest Rates," *Quarterly Journal of Economics*, vol. 76, no. 2, May, 1962, pp. 197–218.

Reuben A. Kessel, "The Cyclical Behavior of the Term Structure of Interest Rates," paper read before the Econometric Society, Pittsburgh, Penna., Dec. 27, 1962.

John H. Wood, "An Econometric Model of the Term Structure of Interest Rates," paper read before the Econometric Society, Pittsburgh, Penna., Dec. 27, 1962.

W. T. Newlyn, "The Structure of Interest Rates," in *Theory of Money,* Fair Lawn, N.J.: Oxford University Press, 1962, chap. 9., pp. 110–118.

Peggy Heim, "Communications: the Use of Monetary Policy: Comment," *Southern Economic Journal,* vol. 29, no. 4, April, 1963.

John H. Wood, "Expectations, Errors, and the Term Structure of Interest Rates," *Journal of Political Economy,* vol. 71, no. 2, April, 1963, pp. 160–171.

Graeme S. Dorrance, "The Term Structure of Interest Rates," *International Monetary Fund Staff Papers,* July, 1963, pp. 275–298.

Robert Haney Scott, "A 'Liquidity' Factor Contributing to Those Downward Sloping Yield Curves: 1900–1916," *Review of Economics and Statistics,* vol. 45, no. 3, August, 1963, pp. 328–329.

Arthur M. Okun, "Monetary Policy, Debt Management, and Interest Rates: A Quantitative Appraisal," in *Stabilization Policies,* Commission on Money and Credit, Englewood Cliffs, N.J.: Prentice-Hall, Inc., 1963, pp. 331–380.

Burton G. Malkiel, "The Term Structure of the Interest Rates," *American Economic Review, Papers and Proceedings,* vol. 54, no. 3, May, 1964, pp. 532–543.

John H. Wood, "The Expectations Hypothesis, the Yield Curve, and Monetary Policy," *Quarterly Journal of Economics,* vol. 78, no. 3, August, 1964, pp. 457–470.

TREASURY BILLS

Helen J. Cooke, "Marketing of Treasury Bills," in *The Treasury and the Money Market,* Federal Reserve Bank of New York, May, 1954, pp. 33–39.

"The Bill Market; Its Nature and Structure," *Federal Reserve Bank of Philadelphia Business Review,* September, 1955.

"Treasury Bill Financing," *First National City Bank Monthly Letter, Business and Economic Conditions,* December, 1958.

"The New Issues and the Market," *C. F. Childs and Company Review,* no. 309, Mar. 23, 1959.

"New Techniques in Debt Management," *Federal Reserve Bank of Chicago Business Conditions*, April, 1959.

"Bills, Bills, Bills," *Federal Reserve Bank of Richmond Monthly Review*, May, 1960.

"Treasury Bills," *Federal Reserve Bank of St. Louis Monthly Review*, vol. 42, no. 7, July, 1960.

Salomon Brothers and Hutzler, *Short-term Investments*, New York, 1960.

"The Auction of Treasury Bills in the Twelfth District," *Federal Reserve Bank of San Francisco Monthly Review*, January, 1961.

"Treasury Lumps New Bill Issues," *New York Times*, June, 3, 1961.

Tax Basis for Purchase of Strips of Treasury Bills, Federal Reserve Bank of New York, Circular No. 5045, June 6, 1961.

United States Government Securities, Goldsmith–Nagan Washington Service, Bulletin no. 632, June 10, 1961.

Andrew F. Brimmer, "Price Determination in the United States Treasury Bills Market," *Review of Economics and Statistics*, vol. 44, no. 2, May, 1962, pp. 178–183.

"Floating Debt: An Instrument of Financial Policy," in *Money Market Instruments*, Federal Reserve Bank of Cleveland, July, 1962, pp. 10–16.

Milton Friedman, "Price Determination in the United States Treasury Bill Market: A Comment," *Review of Economics and Statistics*, vol. 14, no. 3, August, 1963, pp. 318–320.

Michael Rieber, "The Primary Market for United States Treasury Bills," Ph.D. thesis, Massachusetts Institute of Technology, Cambridge, Mass., 1963.

"Treasury Bills," *Federal Reserve Bank of Richmond Monthly Review*, March, 1964, pp. 8–10.

TREASURY TAX AND LOAN ACCOUNTS

Esther Rogoff Taus, *Central Banking Functions of the United States Treasury 1789–1941*, New York: Columbia University Press, 1943.

"The Treasury's Cash Balances," *Federal Reserve Bank of New York Monthly Review*, vol. 33, no. 7, July, 1951.

"The Treasury and the Money Market," *Federal Reserve Bank of New York Monthly Review*, vol. 34, no. 8, November, 1952.

Monetary Policy and the Management of the Public Debt, Their Role in Achieving Price Stability and High Level Employment, replies to questions and other material for the use of the Subcommittee on General Credit Control and Debt Management, Joint Committee on the Economic Report, 82d Congress, 2d Session, Washington, D.C.: Government Printing Office, 1952, part 1, pp. 43–46.

Lawrence S. Ritter, "Monetary Aspects of Treasury Operations," in *Money and Economic Activity, A Selection of Readings,* Boston: Houghton Mifflin Company, 1952, chap. 12, pp. 283–317.

"Why the Federal Government Keeps Funds in Commercial Banks," memorandum submitted by Secretary of the Treasury G. M. Humphrey, in *United States Monetary Policy: Recent Thinking and Experience, Hearings before the Subcommittee on Economic Stabilization of the Joint Committee on the Economic Report,* 83d Congress, 2d Session, Dec. 6, 7, 1954, Washington, D.C.: Government Printing Office, 1954, pp. 184–199.

Helen J. Cooke, "Managing the Treasury's Cash Balances," in *The Treasury and the Money Market,* Federal Reserve Bank of New York, May, 1954, pp. 7–11.

The Treasury and the Money Market, Federal Reserve Bank of New York, May, 1954.

H. C. Carr, "The Treasury and the Money Market," in *The Treasury and the Money Market,* Federal Reserve Bank of New York, May, 1954, pp. 1–6.

Helen J. Cooke and Kathleen N. Straus, "Treasury Tax and Loan Accounts at Commercial Banks," in *The Treasury and the Money Market,* Federal Reserve Bank of New York, May, 1954, pp. 12–15.

"Bank Must Repay a Treasury Call," *New York Times,* May 13, 1955.

C. Edgar Johnson and James J. Saxon, "Treasury-Bank Teamwork on Tax and Loan Accounts," *Banking,* September, 1955.

"A Note on Group 'C' Banks," in *The Treasury and the Money Market,* Federal Reserve Bank of New York, May, 1956, pp. v–vi.

R. Duane Saunders, "The Development of the Flow of Institutional Savings in the Analysis of Treasury Borrowing Problems," *Journal of Finance,* vol. 11, no. 2, May, 1956, pp. 277–287.

"The Treasury's Deposit Balances and the Banking System," *Federal Reserve Bank of New York Monthly Review,* vol. 40, no. 4, April, 1958.

Regulations Governing the Deposit with Federal Reserve Banks and Depositary Banks of Employer and Employee Taxes under the Internal Revenue Code of 1954; Employer and Employee Taxes under the Railroad Retirement Tax Act; and Certain Federal Excise Taxes; Treasury Department Circular no. 848, 2d revision, May 2, 1958.

Samuel M. Cohn, "Problems in Estimating Federal Government Expenditures," *Journal of American Statistical Association,* vol. 54, December, 1959, pp. 717–729.

Employment, Growth, and Price Levels, Hearings before the Joint Economic Committee, 86th Congress, 1st Session, Washington D.C.: Government Printing Office, 1960, part 10, p. 3325.

Report on Treasury Tax and Loan Accounts, Services Rendered by Banks for the Federal Government, and Other Related Matters, Treasury Department Fiscal Service, June 15, 1960.

"Federal Budgets and Fiscal Policy," *Federal Reserve Bank of Minneapolis Monthly Review,* September, 1962, pp. 2–6.

Treasury Comment Concerning a Report of the Comptroller General of the United States to the Congress of the United States, Dated May 1962, Relating to a Study Made by the Treasury of Tax and Loan Accounts, Services Rendered by Banks for the Federal Government, and Other Related Matters, Treasury Department, Fiscal Service, Nov. 7, 1962.

"*Further Comment on Desirability of Establishing More Equitable Arrangement between the Federal Government and Commercial Banks Maintaining Treasury Department Tax and Loan Accounts,*" Report to the Congress of the United States, by the Comptroller General of the United States, December, 1963.

Irving Auerbach, "United States Treasury Cash Balances and the Control of Member Bank Reserves," in *Fiscal and Debt Management Policies,* Commission on Money and Credit, Englewood Cliffs, N.J.: Prentice-Hall, Inc., 1963, pp. 311–398.

TRUST FUNDS

Raymond W. Goldsmith and Eli Shapiro, "An Estimate of Bank-administered Personal Trust Funds," *Journal of Finance,* vol. 14, no. 1, March, 1959, pp. 11–17.

Joseph H. Wolfe, "Report of National Survey of Personal Trust Accounts," *Trust Bulletin,* September, 1959, pp. 2–7.

"Assets in Personal Trust Accounts Top $62 Billion in 1960," *Trusts and Estates,* vol. 100, no. 10, pp. 852, 964.

Board of Governors of the Federal Reserve System, *Trust Powers of National Banks,* Regulation F, as amended effective May 18, 1961.

"Developments at Southwestern Trust Departments in 1961," *Federal Reserve Bank of Dallas Business Review,* vol. 47, no. 7, July, 1962.

Stanley Silverberg, "Bank Trust Investments: Their Size and Significance," *National Banking Review,* vol. 1, no. 4, June, 1964, pp. 577–598.

Geoffrey P. E. Clarkson, "Trust Investment: A Study in Decision-making" (Unpublished ms.).

UNITED STATES INVESTMENT ACCOUNTS

W. N. Peach, "Treasury Investment Funds and Open-market Operations," *Journal of Finance,* vol. 6, no. 1, March, 1951, pp. 46–53.

"Marketable Issues of the United States Treasury," *Federal Reserve Bank of New York Monthly Review,* March, 1953.

"Federal Investment Funds in the Money Market," *Federal Reserve Bank of Kansas City Monthly Review,* November, 1956.

"Growth in Treasury Trust Accounts Slows Down," *Federal Reserve Bank of Chicago Business Conditions,* December, 1957.

Ira O. Scott, Jr., "The Implications of the Changing Ownership of Federal Securities," *Proceedings of the Business and Economic Statistics Section, American Statistical Association,* 1957, pp. 154–158.

Deane Carson, "Treasury Open Market Operations," *Review of Economics and Statistics,* vol. 41, no. 4, November, 1959, pp. 438–442.

Warren Smith, "The Economic Significance of Trust Funds," in *Debt Management in the United States,* Study Paper No. 19, materials prepared in connection with the study of employment, growth, and price levels, Joint Economic Committee, 86th Congress, 2d Session, Jan. 28, 1960, Washington, D.C.: Government Printing Office, 1960, pp. 40–42.

Investment of Insurance Funds, Hearings before the Committee on Veterans' Affairs, House of Representatives, 86th Congress, 2d Session, Feb. 2, 1960, Washington, D.C.: Government Printing Office, 1960.

Answer of the Secretary of the Treasury to questions regarding government trust accounts, in *Employment, Growth, and Price Levels, Hearings before the Joint Economic Committee,* 86th Congress, 2d Session, Washington, D.C.: Government Printing Office, 1960, pp. 3320–3322.

INDEX

15-20

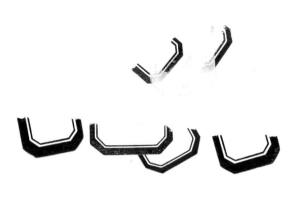